Women, Gender, and World Politics

PERSPECTIVES, POLICIES, AND PROSPECTS

Edited by
Peter R. Beckman
&
Francine D'Amico

BERGIN & GARVEY
Westport, Connecticut • London

Library of Congress Cataloging-in-Publication Data

Women, gender, and world politics : perspectives, policies, and
    prospects / edited by Peter R. Beckman and Francine D'Amico.
        p.   cm.
    Includes bibliographical references and index.
    ISBN 0-89789-305-0 (alk. paper). — ISBN 0-89789-306-9 (pbk : alk.
paper)
    1. Feminist theory.   2. World politics.   3. International
relations.   I. Beckman, Peter R. II. D'Amico, Francine.
HQ1190.W685   1994
305.42—dc20   94–15857

British Library Cataloguing in Publication Data is available.

Library of Congress Catalog Card Number: 94–15857
ISBN: 0-89789-305-0
        0-89789-306-9 (pbk.)

First published in 1994

Bergin & Garvey, 88 Post Road West, Westport, CT 06881
An imprint of Greenwood Publishing Group, Inc.

Printed in the United States of America

The paper used in this book complies with the
Permanent Paper Standard issued by the National
Information Standards Organization (Z39.48-1984).

10 9 8 7 6 5 4 3 2

For Douglas, Jamie, and Patrick—FJD
For Toby—PRB

Contents

Part II. Policies

Part III. Prospects

Preface

In this book, we explore a relatively new question in the study of world politics: What is the connection between gender and world politics? We do so by considering a range of viewpoints, some traditional, some new. Although many of the contributors employ a variety of Feminist perspectives, this is not exclusively a Feminist treatment of the question. Rather, we and the contributors to this volume brought our own training and experience to two basic questions: Does gender matter in world politics? How might students of world politics go about answering this question?

Some of us suspect that gender is quite important, so much so that a failure to consider it renders our understanding of world politics incomplete, incorrect, or undesirable. Others of us may be more skeptical, not certain that gender is important or as critical as other factors might be. Although we cannot encompass all the diverse literature that has emerged on women, gender, and world politics, we can provide informed commentary on three key areas: (1) the effect of gender and a gender awareness on our thinking about world politics; (2) the ways in which world politics has had a specific effect on women; and (3) how a gender consciousness might change the agenda of world politics and create a different future.

In a companion volume to this text, *Women in World Politics,* we examine the questions, Where are the women? How have women, from those in top leadership positions to women in revolutionary movements, shaped world politics?

We see the book you are now reading as an important complement to traditional textbooks on world politics. Its structure parallels the traditional texts, but it adds a critique of the tradition and suggests a new way to think about world politics. It makes women and women's experiences the focus, broadening and deepening our perspective on world politics. We hope that this will be a clear, useful introduction for those unfamiliar with the field. In spite of the different voices in this text, it reflects with some fidelity the energy and insight of those who have attempted to develop a new perspective on world politics.

Why should we look at gender? Women have always been involved in world politics, although their participation has often been obscured. Some have been leaders of nations; some have gone to war; some have served as diplomats. Many have made it possible for men to lead, to wage war, and to conduct their nation's business abroad. Women have been the victims and beneficiaries of wars, trade agreements, and alliances. Indeed, as Cynthia Enloe suggests, we need to expand our notion of "world politics" so that we may see women's ongoing connection to world politics—from making it possible to sustain military bases overseas to a government's ability to acquire foreign exchange. At the very least we should know what world politics has meant for half the human species. And we should ask why women's role in world politics and the effect of world politics on women have been obscured.

Second, we can predict with some certainty that women will become increasingly involved in all aspects of world politics. 1992 was called "the year of the woman" in U.S. politics. The continuing global movement for sex equality has reduced legal barriers to formal political participation and has encouraged more women to seek political and governmental positions. The growth in the number and activity of nongovernmental organizations has expanded the paths to participation for women. Increasing political participation by women suggests that the concerns that women articulate— be they about equity, human rights, world peace, or whatever—will have a more prominent place in the international political arena. In addition, the end of the cold war may create a political context that permits greater participation by women and a greater attention to their concerns, as policies predicated on the East-West confrontation decay.

Third, by thinking of gender, we may be better able to respond to the normative question, What *should* world politics be about? Does a greater attention to gender allow us to envision and shape a more peaceful world? Would it encourage us to change the tendencies in our various cultures to devalue women? Can a gender consciousness provide us with different values, which in turn would lead us to make different choices as citizens?

Fourth, by thinking of gender, we have the possibility of making important advances in our theoretical understanding of world politics—not just of future world politics, but of the past as well. Even if gender or the ideas raised by a gender consciousness do not ultimately provide a new conceptual or normative means of addressing world politics, at least the questioning of our existing beliefs and theories may reveal some of the hidden assumptions that merit greater thought.

This project began in the mid-1970s, in an exchange between a teacher and a student in an introductory world politics course. The student wanted to know what role women played in world politics and why there was no discussion of gender in the textbook. The perplexed teacher, after tossing out the names of several women policy makers, allowed that it was a good question. A dialogue began and developed as the student went on to become a teacher in the same field. A decade later, the two of us found ourselves in conversation, regretting the fact that while some academics had begun to work with this "good question," there were no textbooks for introductory world politics courses that addressed the issue of gender. We said that it was a project that really had to be done, and was something we might try to do—after completing all the other projects in which we were immersed.

In 1989, over the coffee and cake at the wedding of a mutual friend, we talked again about the need for such a book. Our idea to "do something" translated itself into an outline for a book and dozens of calls and letters to individuals asking if they might be willing to contribute a chapter. And we discussed the questions and ideas that began to emerge with the students in our classes. This anthology, then, is the product of an ongoing student-teacher dialogue, and we invite you to participate in the discussion.

That more than a dozen diverse contributors were willing to consider these questions is a tribute to their interest and patience and to the importance of the questions themselves. We are grateful for the opportunity to work with and learn from them. In addition, we want to thank several anonymous reviewers, as well as Zillah Eisenstein and Judith Reppy for their thoughtful criticism, and, most particularly, Sophy Craze and Lynn Flint at Bergin & Garvey for their support and encouragement. Others who helped make this book possible include the library reference staffs at our colleges, particularly Debra Lamb-Deans at Ithaca College; Donna Freedline at Ithaca College; and Hobart and William Smith Colleges and the Ithaca College Office of the Provost, which provided financial support. And for our students, our patient families, and our many friends and colleagues who along the way expressed interest and offered support and suggestions, we are thankful.

We hope that the readers of this book will be provoked by our efforts. As we suggest in the last chapter, the future began when you picked up this book.

WOMEN, GENDER,
AND
WORLD POLITICS

Introduction

Francine D'Amico and Peter R. Beckman

The study of world politics has traditionally focused on the relations between states. In this view of the world, women seem almost invisible, since few have been leaders of states. There are the exceptions, of course, from historical rulers such as Catherine the Great of Russia or Elizabeth I of England to contemporary national leaders such as Margaret Thatcher or Corazon Aquino. Such women, however, are often regarded as unusual in a world of power, high stakes, threats, and war. Such an environment is said to be a man's world, and these women are doing "a man's job." They are the visible exceptions that prove the "rule" that world politics is ultimately a male endeavor.

To the extent that political leaders, scholars, and citizens see the world in this way, they—and we—may have a woefully incomplete understanding of world politics. The experience of half the human race is ignored or interpreted to fit within this traditional view. We set out here to discover the relationship of women to world politics. To do that, we have organized this text around three related questions:

1. How do we think about world politics? Traditional *perspectives* on world politics say little or nothing about women. Is that because decisions about world politics "have pretty much been stag affairs"?[1] Or have those perspectives simply overlooked women, perhaps because men have devised the theories from their own experience? Whatever the reason, women will remain invisible until we know how to look for them. But when we start looking for women, we find something else— *gender*—and that concept enables us to reformulate the question: How does gender help us think about world politics?

2. How do new perspectives help us understand how the *policies* pursued by states and international organizations have affected women? Have women been affected in ways different from men?

3. What are the *prospects* for the future? Having (re)discovered the connection between women and world politics and assessed the relation, we need to ask what
tomorrow might—or should—bring.

There is another important question: How have women been *participants*
in world politics? We cover that question in a companion volume, *Women
in World Politics.*[2]

WORLD POLITICS

In order to answer these questions about perspectives, policies, and prospects, we need to develop a set of concepts and review some of the basic
questions about women and their relationship to the political world. At
times, however, the very concepts we use can hinder our understanding.
Consider the definition that we used for world politics at the beginning of
this chapter: the relations between states. A "state" (or "nation") is an intan-
gible thing, a mental construct that allows us to talk in a shorthand way
about what *humans* with particular capabilities, positions, and interests do.
That is, an official from the United States might talk with an official from
Israel, or the individuals organized in the armed forces of the United States
and other nations might use force to expel individuals in the Iraqi army
from Kuwait. Our shorthand versions might be "The United States promises aid to Israel" or "The United States and its coalition allies defeated
Iraq in the Gulf War." This shorthand obscures the fact that *males* have
typically done the interacting. It also masks the possibility that women,
too, have been involved.

The definition of world politics as "the relations between states" also
reflects a tradition of seeing the state as the only entity in world politics
worthy of consideration. From this traditional perspective, participants in
world politics are "soldiers and states*men*," and textbooks written from this
perspective focus on *Man, the State, and War* and *Politics among Nations.*[3] If
there are few women making and implementing foreign policy, then focusing on women seems unimportant for an understanding of world politics.
On the other hand, if we expand our vision about who or what participates
in world politics, we increase the number of places where women might be
found. Three types of entities immediately suggest themselves in addition
to the state: international organizations such as the United Nations and the
European Community, transnational organizations such as IBM and General
Motors, and nongovernmental international organizations such as the International Red Cross and Amnesty International.

There is another tradition imbedded in thinking of world politics as the
relations between states: a focus on what some call "high politics," or issues
such as war and peace, national security, and prestige, which seem bound
up with the state. That perspective, while important, does not encourage

us to think about other ways in which humans interact across national borders that may be more connected with their day-to-day concerns, such as employment, pollution, and a sense of belonging to a particular cultural community. State leaders and international organizations as well as citizens' groups and nongovernmental organizations are paying increasing attention to these issues, as the Earth Summit in Rio de Janeiro, Brazil, in June 1992 or the various conferences on AIDS testify. When we think of world politics as including these issues of "low politics" as well, we expand our scope of inquiry to include economic and environmental issues and the relations between governments and their citizens (human rights). Women may now be increasingly visible in world politics, as they are active on and affected by these issues.

SEX AND GENDER

But are "women" what we are looking for? Once again, the very concepts that we use may confuse us. In common parlance, the terms "woman" and "man" often refer to one's biological *sex*. As you will see, we suggest a different meaning for these two terms. Perhaps it is better to use the terms "female" and "male" when we refer to this biological difference, which is primarily expressed in physical characteristics (notably genitalia), in the different roles that each sex has in the physical process of reproduction, and in the different levels of certain chemicals within the body.

Does one's biological sex express itself in politics, leading to distinctive attitudes, values, and behaviors of females as compared to males? Some argue that it does. Perhaps, as Sara Ruddick suggests, the reproductive/nursing functions of females lead them to be more caring of others than males are.[4] Or, as Doreen Kimura has argued, "The bulk of the evidence suggests . . . that the effects of sex hormones on brain organization" lead to differences in the way in which males and females solve intellectual problems.[5] Or perhaps those hormones have continuing influences: Melvin Konner has hypothesized that different amounts of testosterone in the two sexes account for greater aggressiveness in males.[6] The biological thesis thus claims that there are certain *essential, natural* characteristics of males and females that at least pressure them to think and behave in different ways. From this perspective, biological sex seems the crucial feature for us to consider when considering females and world politics.

There is, however, another viewpoint, one that distinguishes between sex and *gender*. Gender refers to characteristics linked to a particular sex by one's culture. For instance, some claim that aggressiveness and a desire to dominate are—at least in Western societies—*masculine* gender traits and that men are expected to exhibit them. Women are expected to show different, *feminine,* traits. But instead of these traits being linked to a particular sex because of biology, the gender perspective argues that most, if not all, gender characteristics are *cultural* creations, passed on to new members of a society through a process called socialization. If a culture assigns a particular characteristic such as aggressiveness to a particular sex, the practices of child rearing and language generally mold most individuals in that culture to accept and enact those characteristics. Sandra Harding calls gender "a systematic social construction of masculinity and femininity that is little, if at all, constrained by biology."[7] Thus, we need a concept such as gender to stand apart from biological sex to describe what it means to be a "man" or a "woman" in a particular society.

GENDER AS DIFFERENCE

We need not think that *either* "nature" (biology) *or* "nurture" (culture) creates those differences. *Both* are likely to be involved, but in different degrees and different ways. For our discussion, we will call the differences between men and women gender differences, principally because we suspect that culture is more prevalent in this matter. Thus, when we think of *gender-as-difference,* we concentrate on the differences between men and women, or on the characteristics said to be masculine or feminine, such as aggressiveness.

We still need to ask if there really *are* meaningful gender differences. Many people believe so. For instance, in a recent poll of U.S. citizens, 58 percent said that men and women were basically different regarding "personalities, interests, and abilities."[8]

There are persistent cultural stereotypes or generalizations about specific gender characteristics. In Western culture we often find these paired characteristics that are said to describe gender differences. Notice that they are framed as opposing but related characteristics. Men are said to be rational. Women are of an opposite characteristic: not rational—that is, emotional.

Masculine	*Feminine*
rational	emotional
resolute	flexible/fickle
competitive	cooperative
assertive	compliant
domination oriented	relationship oriented
calculating	instinctive
restrained	expressive
physical	verbal
aggressive	passive
detached	caring

Let us suppose for the minute that most men—either because of biology or socialization—display the masculine characteristics listed above. We can hypothesize that those characteristics may shape world politics in particular ways. For instance, men—as leaders, elites, and citizens—may tend to look on the actions of other states as attempts to gain an advantage. The world from this perspective appears to be a *zero-sum* world, where the gains of other states come at the expense of one's own state. In such a circumstance, one attempts to impose solutions on other states favorable to one's interests through a calculated mixture of threats and promises. Other states, led by men, pursue the same strategy. In this world, it presumably pays to be tough and unyielding, making world politics a never-ending cycle of conflict with little cooperation.

Conversely, if we replace those masculine characteristics with the stereotypic feminine ones, world politics of a quite different nature might emerge. Other states' actions might not seem as challenging; indeed, more often they would appear to be supportive of the interests of one's own state. Perhaps international issues would be defined as problems to be solved through a creative, flexible discussion, rather than as power contests in which winners impose solutions on losers. World politics would be a *positive-sum* game, where everyone wins.

And—continuing our hypothesis linking gender characteristics to a particular sex—if we wanted to *create* a particular world politics, we might ask, Should women replace men in positions of power? Should we resocialize men to have feminine characteristics? The concept of gender allows us to think about change in creative ways. And it encourages us to ask if there *should be* gender differences. The social construction of these opposing characteristics denies the *commonality* of what it means to be human: Each of us can be both rational *and* emotional, competitive *and* cooperative.

We have said all this on the assumption that meaningful gender differences exist. But do public beliefs and stereotypes reflect reality? After all, even in the poll cited above, 40 percent felt that gender differences did not exist. Moreover, our own experiences can contradict claims about gender differences. All of us, for instance, know men who are not aggressive and women who are. The scholarly evidence about gender differences is mixed. It casts doubt on claims of systematic gender differences, although aggressiveness seems to be more common with men.[9]

Some men are not aggressive, and some are very aggressive. Perhaps the conscientious objector and General George S. Patton, Jr., might symbolize the extremes. Most men probably fall somewhere in between. The same can be said of women. Why is there this variation within each sex? If biology determined certain characteristics, we would expect a clear distinction between men and women, with relatively little variation within one sex. Culture, on the other hand, can overlay the biological pressures to think or act in particular ways with different messages about attitudes and behavior appropriate for women and men.

Culture, in fact, may provide *similarly sexed* individuals with *different* messages. For instance, upper-class males may manifest less overt aggressiveness because their class position has instilled in them the belief that one essentially gets what one wants from life. Males from the working class may be socialized to believe that getting is a matter of pushing (and upper-class males may have been socialized to expect pushy behavior from the lower-class males). Class, race, ethnic background, and the like may lead to diversity in how members of a particular sex think and act. To say that aggressiveness, for example, is a characteristic of males may be accurate in the main, but it may obscure important variations among individuals. We therefore need to be careful in our statements linking men or women to world politics.

Similarly, an attempt to generalize about gender and world politics runs the risk of seriously misunderstanding gender differences when we *compare societies*. Women in a particular society may act differently from men in that society, but they may also act differently from women in other cultures. Indeed, women in one culture may be expected to exhibit behaviors associated with men in a different culture.[10] To the degree that cultures differ on gender characteristics that are relevant to world politics, generalizations about women and world politics will be limited—and seriously incomplete—unless we are aware of the differences.

Thus, there are real limitations for the concept of gender as difference and its usefulness for us in making generalizations. Perhaps at best we might be able to say that gender differences do have consequences for world politics but that the consequences will differ according to the culture and the specific individuals whom we are considering. On the other hand, we do not want to miss generalizations that may be applicable for many societies and to world politics as a whole.

GENDER AS POWER

There is, however, another way to think about gender. The *gender-as-power* viewpoint claims that gender really speaks about a *relationship* between humans, a relationship that is based on power. This viewpoint begins by noting that the characteristics associated with a particular sex were not handed out by chance as in a lottery. Rather, this argument goes, societies found it useful to allocate certain values or characteristics to men and others to women. Historically, the allocation established and reinforced the dominant position of men, creating the condition known as patriarchy: men's control over women. If men are taught to be dominant in a relationship, and women to be subordinate, the inequality perpetuates itself. If "masculine" characteristics are prized, and "feminine" characteristics less valued, the existing power distribution is sustained.

The conception of gender-as-power allows us to take a further step: to suggest that our whole way of *thinking* and *talking* about humans is based on power. The very terms "women" and "men" are a reflection of that power.[11] To label individuals as "women" (or "men") is to exercise power, for the label creates for human beings a set of expectations about who they are, who they are not, and what range of choice is available to them.

Gender-as-power argues that women and men are made, not born. They are created by those labels—labels that open some doors and close others. Labeling creates a fictitious being ("you are 'a woman,' " "you are 'a man' "), but it is a harmful fiction for two reasons. The label denies the commonness that makes us all humans and perpetuates inequalities because the humans carrying one label have more rights or privileges than those carrying the other label.

To think of gender as power may give us new insights into world politics. For instance, consider the term "politics." It brings to mind elections, votes by legislators, and diplomatic negotiations. But what about violence in the home or rape? Typically, we say that those actions are not about politics but fall in another sphere, the private or personal sphere. The political or "public" sphere of elections, voting, and diplomacy has traditionally been associated with men, while women have been associated with the private, personal realm of the home. This gendered division of the political from the nonpolitical has meant that issues in the "private" domain such as wife beating or rape did not appear for a long time as political issues because they seemed unsuitable for public consideration. They were, after all, "private matters."

Thus, the way in which culture defined gender made certain things politically invisible, and women became invisible as political beings as well. Women "naturally" did not belong in world politics, the most public of the political realms. "Tis no less unbecoming [in] a Woman to levy Forces, to conduct an Army, to give a Signal to the Battle," declared a late sixteenth-century Briton, "than it is for a Man to tease Wool, to handle the Distaff, to Spin or Card, and to perform the other Services of the Weaker Sex."[12] Many people today share similar sentiments.

With a *gender consciousness,* however, we can see women as political participants beyond the Margaret Thatchers of the world. Women struggling against wife beating, rape, and *suttee* (the cremation of the wife on the husband's funeral pyre) are engaged in politics. Indeed, breaking free of the traditional definition of politics allows us to see anyone who tries to effect a change in her or his life as a political actor. Politics, therefore, is shaped by all individuals who strive to put those "personal" issues on the political agenda. And as individual efforts coalesce and develop connections across borders in the attempt to change lives, these personal struggles become part of world politics itself.

Gender-as-power does suggest a generalization that might be true across different cultures and time periods: Women and women's values, orientations, and behavior are generally devalued by society. This devaluation is a result of unequal power: Men have power over women.

This generalization about gender as an expression of men's power over women has provided Feminist scholars of world politics with a different way to think about their subject. Cynthia Enloe, for instance, begins with the Feminist point that the creation of public and private spheres is an expression of men's political power in domestic politics. She then suggests that we apply this insight to world politics. Once we do this, we have a

radical new imagining of what it takes for governments to ally with each other, compete with and wage war against each other. . . . Governments depend upon certain kinds of allegedly private relationships in order to conduct their foreign affairs. Governments need more than secrecy and intelligence agencies; they need wives who are willing to provide their diplomatic husbands with unpaid services so these men can develop trusting relationships with other diplomatic husbands. They need not only military hardware, but a steady supply of women's sexual services to convince their soldiers that they are manly. To operate in the international arena, governments seek other governments' recognition of their sovereignty; but they also depend on ideas about masculinized dignity and feminized sacrifice to sustain that sense of autonomous nationhood.[13]

In Enloe's view, gender—which she thinks of as power that defines masculine and feminine and that structures the relationships between men and women—underpins world politics.

Our discussion of the concepts of sex, gender, gender-as-difference, and gender-as-power has provided us with clues about how we might rediscover women in world politics. We can look for sex: What women have been involved in world politics? We can look for gender differences: In crises do female policy makers behave differently from their male counterparts? We can look for gender relationships: Do women support their nations in war in ways that maintain their subordination to men? There are many questions, many paths to follow. How shall we proceed?

CONNECTING WOMEN, GENDER, AND WORLD POLITICS

Cynthia Enloe's prescription for the student of world politics is clear and compelling: "It is always worth asking, 'Where are the women?' "[14] Clearly, one could treat women as *actors* in world politics, and this theme is explored extensively in our companion volume, *Women in World Politics*. In the book you are now reading, we look at women as actors, too, but principally from the perspective of theories of world politics. That is, we begin our inquiry with a principal concern with this general relationship: gender → world politics. Does gender have an effect on world politics, and in what ways?

In Part I, we turn to the *perspectives* that scholars have fashioned in order to describe and explain world politics. In their search for women, Peter R. Beckman, Karen A. Feste, and Francine D'Amico ask what role sex or gender plays in four traditional theories of world politics: Realist theory, Behavioralism, Pluralism, and Critical Theories. We will not be divulging too big a secret to tell you that these traditional theories do not seem to be aware of sex or gender as important considerations. The contributors then ask what might happen if sex or gender were introduced into each theory.

J. Ann Tickner and Sandra Whitworth critically assess traditional theory from a Feminist perspective, for Feminism is the only perspective that has made gender a central feature for understanding the world. Indeed, the Feminist perspective suggests that because traditional theories are too much a part of a Western intellectual tradition that equates men and men's experience with the human experience, they should not be retained. Tickner and Whitworth use Feminist theory as a powerful means of broadening our understanding of world politics. Tickner recasts Realist theory while Whitworth examines several varieties of Feminist theory to see how each might envision world politics. Part I closes with Hamideh Sedghi's examination of Third World Feminist perspectives on world politics. She suggests that these perspectives are a needed balance to the tendency of equating Western experience with human experience.

Thinking of women or gender as a shaper of world politics is an important step, but this needs to be complemented with a exploration of women as *targets* of world politics as well. How do women experience world politics? Is the experience different from that of men? For example, beginning in the 1960s the U.S. Agency for International Development promoted population limitation as a strategy for economic development but emphasized controlling *women's* reproductive capabilities through government-run campaigns to manipulate women's behavior.[15] Women in the Third World experienced U.S. foreign policy quite differently from the way in which men did.

Thinking of women as objects of world politics can be a helpful corrective to assuming that men's experiences are equivalent to human experience. Equally important, if world politics has a differential effect on men and women, what women *as actors* may want to make of world politics may depend heavily on how they have been *affected* by world politics. As world politics feeds back into the lives of women and men, it may create quite different incentives to respond.

Part II discusses how three types of *policies* have affected women. Jean Bethke Elshtain and Rebecca Grant examine the effect of security policy:

war and the cold war. Margaret E. Galey describes the United Nations' specific attention to "women's issues" and its effect on women. Nüket Kardam and Geeta Chowdhry explore how strategies for economic development and the operation of the international political economy affect women.

Part III begins with the assumption that we might want to create something different in the patterns of world politics. For a time, the end of the cold war encouraged the presumption that "things would take care of themselves." For many, the major issue of the day, the superpower conflict, had been favorably resolved—or, at least, so it seemed to many citizens of the United States. Old problems—like war, starvation, and rival territorial claims—soon resurfaced, however, and continuing problems such as trade and environmental concerns received new impetus. The question of restructuring world politics remains as real and as relevant as ever. Now, however, our perspective is enlarged to ask: How does an understanding of gender provide us with different visions about the future and with different strategies for change?

The contributors to Part III assess the *prospects* for alternative futures and the different paths that we would need to take to realize those futures. Birgit Brock-Utne suggests that adult education incorporating a Feminist perspective is crucial if we hope to realize a peaceful world. Ralph Pettman reviews the various perspectives that we have discussed in this book, discussing what each offers as a means of creating desirable futures. And Anne Sisson Runyan presents the fictional utopias created by feminist novelists as ways of expanding our thinking about imaginable futures for men and women and world politics.

Finally, the two of us come back at the end of the book, not so much to provide a conclusion—even though custom gives that name to the last chapter—but to suggest a beginning. With this introduction to gender and world politics, what steps should *you* now take?

NOTES

1. Jack Hexter, book review of Mary Beard's *Woman as Force in History, New York Times Book Review,* March 17, 1946, 5; quoted in Berenice A. Carroll, "Mary Beard's *Woman as Force in History,*" in Berenice A. Carroll, ed., *Liberating Women's History* (Urbana: University of Illinois Press, 1976), 34.

2. Francine D'Amico and Peter Beckman, eds., *Women in World Politics* (Westport, CT: Bergin & Garvey, 1995).

3. Kenneth Waltz, *Man, the State, and War* (New York: Columbia University Press, 1959), and Hans Morgenthau, *Politics among Nations: The Struggle for Power and Peace,* various editions (New York: Knopf).

4. Sara Ruddick, *Maternal Thinking* (Boston: Beacon, 1989).

5. Doreen Kimura, "Sex-Differences in the Brain," *Scientific American* 267 (September 1992): 119.

6. Melvin Konner, "The Aggressors," *New York Times Magazine,* August 14, 1988, 33–34.

7. Sandra Harding, "Introduction," in Sandra Harding, ed., *Feminism and Methodology* (Milton Keynes, England: Open University Press, 1987), 6; quoted by Rebecca Grant and Kathleen Newland, "Introduction," in Rebecca Grant and Kathleen Newland, eds., *Gender and International Relations* (Bloomington: Indiana University Press, 1991): 5.

8. Gallup survey conducted in December 1989; results reported in *The Gallup Poll Monthly* 293 (February 1990), 29. Forty-five percent of those polled felt that biology was the main reason for the difference, 40 percent said upbringing (culture), and 13 percent volunteered that both contributed equally.

9. See Carol Tavris and Carole Wade, *The Longest War: Sex Differences in Perspective* (San Diego: Harcourt Brace Jovanovich, 1984), 38–78.

10. The pioneering study is Margaret Mead, *Sex and Temperament in Three Primitive Societies* (New York: Morrow, 1963).

11. Elizabeth Weed, *Coming to Terms: Feminism, Theory, Politics* (New York: Routledge, 1989), and Denise Riley, *"Am I That Name?": Feminism and the Category of "Women" in History* (Minneapolis: University of Minnesota Press, 1988).

12. George Buchanan, quoted in Antonia Fraser, *The Warrior Queens* (New York: Knopf, 1989), 326.

13. Cynthia Enloe, *Bananas, Beaches, & Bases: Making Feminist Sense of International Politics* (Berkeley: University of California Press, 1990), 196–97.

14. Ibid., 133.

15. Jane S. Jaquette and Kathleen A. Staudt, "Politics, Population, and Gender: A Feminist Analysis of US Population Policy in the Third World," in Kathleen B. Jones and Anna G. Jonasdottir, eds., *The Political Interest of Gender* (London: Sage, 1988), 215.

Part I

PERSPECTIVES

❖ 1 ❖

Realism, Women, and World Politics

Peter R. Beckman

Theories provide us with systematic ways to think about world politics. They take the diverse participants and policies of world politics and suggest patterns that make sense of what otherwise might appear to be a chaotic world. Theories, such as "democracies rarely wage war against other democracies," provide us with descriptions of patterns of world politics. They provide explanations of world politics, such as "economic interests push a state toward aggressive international behavior," and they provide predictions, such as "a great power (like the United States) expands its sphere of influence and then goes into a period of decline."

Each theory is built upon a set of assumptions about who and what is important to observe and think about if we want to understand world politics. In this and the next several chapters, we examine the assumptions and conclusions of four prominent theories of world politics: Realism, Behavioralism, Pluralism, and Critical Theory. We pose three questions for each of these theories:

1. How does the theory deal with women? How does it address the question of gender?
2. What critique can we make of the theory with a consciousness about gender?
3. Can we develop more gender-conscious theories that provide a better understanding of world politics than existing theories do?

One general answer to these questions might be to see women or gender as an "overlooked" factor, and what we need to do is to make women or gender an explicit part of the theory. For instance, we might ask what difference it would make for the theory if women rather than men were the key decision makers. This response has been called the "add-women-and-stir" perspective.[1]

Thinking of gender may also lead us to question the usefulness or desirability of the existing theories of world politics. These theories purport to tell us how *humans* shape world politics; but perhaps all that they tell us is how *males* shape world politics, or what the consequences of world politics are for *males*. Thus, they may only be *partial* descriptions or explanations of what happens in world politics. Furthermore, traditional theories may overemphasize why world politics is as it *is*, rather than ask if there are alternative visions about what world politics *can be* and *should be*. An explicit consideration of gender may help us with theory's *normative* role: to provide alternative visions and choices. It is true that traditional theories contain normative assumptions (typically that whatever exists is the most reasonable way of organizing human life). It is also true that some long-standing theories such as Critical Theory offer an alternative vision of world politics. But these normative assumptions or assertions may be shaped by *male* perceptions and values and may not present a fully *human* view of alternatives. They may reinforce the power that some humans wield at the expense of others. What happens to these theories when we find an alternative to the gendered way in which we look at the world?

This chapter begins our exploration of theory and gender by describing *Realism*. Realism is the dominant theoretical tradition in the study of world politics, reaching back to Thucydides' description of the Peloponnesian War in the fifth century B.C. and having a recent reworking in *Neo-Realism* (or *Structural Realism* as it is sometimes called).[2] In the United States, Realism came to academic prominence after World War II, principally through the work of Professor Hans Morgenthau.[3] The descriptions and explanations offered by the theory have survived a series of challenges from other theories, such as Pluralism and Marxism, which are discussed in Chapter 4.

Every general theory, such as Realism, has a large number of advocates who create a number of variations of the theory. In a short essay such as this, I can only refer to the general tenets of Realist theory, pausing occasionally to suggest some important difference between the traditional Realist theory exemplified by Morgenthau and the Neo-Realist (Structural Realist) variant exemplified by Kenneth Waltz.[4]

STATES AND POWER

Realists concentrate on the nation-state or on the leaders of nation-states. They emphasize power and the crucial role that it plays in world politics. For a traditional Realist such as Morgenthau, international politics, like all politics, is a struggle for power. Whatever the ulti-mate aims of international politics, power is always the immediate aim. Statesmen and peoples may ultimately seek freedom, security, prosperity, or power itself. They may define their goals in terms of a religious, philosophic, economic, or social ideal. . . . But whenever they strive to realize their goal by means of international politics, they do so by striving for power.[5]

Since all states seek to assemble power as a means to accomplish their goals, the Realist argues, those states behave in similar ways, producing patterns in world politics, thus making a theory of world politics possible. "We assume," said Morgenthau, "that statesmen think and act in terms of interest defined as power," and as they do so, there is an "astounding conti-nuity in foreign policy which makes American, British, or Russian foreign policy appear as an intelligible, rational continuum, by and large consistent within itself, regardless of the different motives, preferences, and intellec-tual and moral qualities of successive statesmen."[6]

In its Neo-Realist version, security is the central concern of states, and power is intimately involved. Kenneth Waltz points out that too little power can invite attack by others. Sufficient power can deter such an attack. But too much power in the hands of one state can lead other states to increase their own power or to form a coalition to oppose the powerful state, thus leaving the once-powerful state in a more threatened circum-stance.[7] Both too little and too much power can endanger security.

Moreover, for the Neo-Realist, the threat to security is not usefully dis-cussed as a relation between just two states—the way in which a Realist might treat the cold war between the United States and the Soviet Union. Rather, the Neo-Realist examines the *general* distribution of power among *all* states, for it is that overall distribution of power that creates particular threats to the security of the states and thereby encourages systematic pat-terns of response.

Figure 1.1 helps illustrate this point. The size of the circles represents the power of each state. Traditional Realists often describe the components of power as a variety of ingredients, including military capabilities, the strength of the economy, available resources, characteristics of the popula-tion, and political stability. For them, power is "man's control over the minds and actions of other men."[8] In this view, State A must seek power

Figure 1.1
A Hypothetical Distribution of Power

over B to advance its interests, whatever they may be. For the same reason, State B must seek power over A. This continual struggle for power shapes world politics.

The Neo-Realist, on the other hand, examines the overall distribution of power (with the emphasis on military capabilities) to determine how states with varying amounts of power can protect themselves and promote their interests. The Neo-Realist is more interested in asking about the behavior of the international system as a whole rather than the behavior of a particular nation. Does the particular distribution of power in Figure 1.1, with one powerful state and six weaker states, produce common patterns of behavior every time that particular distribution of power occurs? Will war, for example, be a common feature of the system depicted in Figure 1.1; will alliances be common as well?

To get a sense of what the general argument has to offer as a way of understanding world politics, imagine yourself the leader of State C. What do you find yourself thinking? Realism argues that the weakness of your state, compared to others, is glaringly apparent, and overrides all other possible factors that might determine the behavior of your state, such as your personality or the opinions of your citizens. You expect other states to attempt to advance their interests at your expense. More powerful states may attempt to force you to give up something of great value, such as your territory, your resources, or your right to govern yourself. Such threats cause weak states to behave in particular ways—for instance, by seeking protection through an alliance (as Belgium has done) or by becoming a heavily armed neutral (as Sweden has done).

Even if you are the leader of a powerful state—for instance, State D— the fears and hopes generated by power are still the crucial determinant of action. In 1961, for example, the United States was arguably the most powerful nation in the world (like State D), yet the new president, John F. Kennedy, saw a menacing world surrounding the United States:

No man entering upon this office . . . could fail to be staggered upon learning . . . the harsh enormity of the trials through which we must pass in the next four years. Each day the crises multiply. Each day the solutions grow more difficult. Each day we draw nearer the hour of maximum danger, as weapons spread and hostile forces grow stronger.[9]

ANARCHY, SELF-HELP, AND CONFLICT

Traditional Realists and Neo-Realists begin with the premise that world politics is made by states responding to power. They argue that this responsiveness to power is the result of living in an *anarchic* world—that is, a world without a global government. *Within* most nations, citizens usually do not expect that power differences between them will lead to grievous harm at the hands of fellow citizens. The government acts to secure our individual rights in spite of the power disparities among us. In the international system, on the other hand, there is no government that performs this protective function. Therefore, states rely on *self-help* for both protection and the promotion of their interests.

There are three general means of self-help. The first is to increase power by internal efforts, such as expanding the nation's army or moving from an agrarian to an industrial economy. The second means of self-help is to expand the state's territory or political control and thereby secure the resources of other nations or peoples. This is a policy of conquest, imperialism, or spheres of influence. The third mechanism is to form an alliance with other states, adding their power to one's own.

States are thus involved in a continual "power race," even if it is only to prevent others from dominating them. By its very nature, the power race, even if pursued by states that fundamentally accept the status quo, is likely to increase conflict between states. The acquisition of foreign territory and resources by conquest or intimidation is likely to be resisted by others or to set off a race for colonial empires or spheres of influence. Even apparently benign internal self-help measures can pose a threat to others, especially if they allow a state to modernize or expand its military forces. Similarly, alliance formation can appear threatening, especially to the state with no allies. Hence, the power race, necessary to provide security, also jeopardizes that security, creating what Realists call "the security dilemma."

In addition, as the relative power of states change, new opportunities and threats emerge. For instance, if the power of a state increases much faster than that of the other states, it may be tempted to exploit the growing power disparity by pressing new demands on the other states, as Iraq did in 1990 in its dispute with Kuwait, thereby increasing conflict. Other states may be tempted to halt or reverse the rising state's power growth, perhaps through direct attack, by encouraging the breakup of the rising state, by encouraging rebellion against the government, or by organizing an economic boycott to disrupt its economy—all of which were used by the coalition arrayed against Iraq after it had seized Kuwait.

BALANCE OF POWER

From a Realist perspective is world politics essentially a continual war of all against all? No, because the very power that creates the threat also encourages behavior that helps manage the threat. In Realist theory, world politics is based on *calculations* of (1) power, (2) a state's interests, and (3) the costs and benefits of various actions. States behave purposefully in light of that calculation. Calculation often dictates *caution.*

States will behave cautiously when they are uncertain about success in a direct clash of power. Not only might they lose the contest, but even if they win, the costs of winning may make the winner vulnerable to the enhanced power of others. Because relative power is difficult for states to determine with precision, that uncertainty can reinforce caution.

Moreover, Realist theory points to another recurring feature of world politics that strongly reinforces caution: *the balance of power.* Realists argue that the balance of power operates to impose limitations on state behavior. Indeed, the power race itself is an attempt to ensure that power remains balanced. Typically, however, alliance formation is the principal means of balancing. Alliances form in opposition to a state or a coalition of states that threatens to amass overbearing power. At times, one state may even elect to play a specialized role, serving as a "balancer" that throws its weight to the side that is weaker. Some Realists argue that the balance of power is the closest that the study of world politics has come to developing a "law" of international political behavior.

A balance limits states' behavior because states cannot be sure that the aggressive promotion of their interests will bring success. This is clearest where war is a possibility. War between *balanced* forces is likely to be an unproductive stalemate. Would-be aggressors are deterred from initiating war. They must look to negotiation and compromise for the satisfaction of their interests. Thus, in an ironic way, while anarchy makes conflict a recurring feature of world politics, it also constrains the raw use of power and tempers ambitions. Indeed, the theory suggests that states are forced to be prudent, accepting the adage that "politics is the art of the possible."[10] Politics is for limited ends, and self-limitation may at times be necessary.

While the pressure to balance power may be inherent in an anarchical system, some Neo-Realists argue that balancing may be more successful

Figure 1.2
Two Different Structures of Power

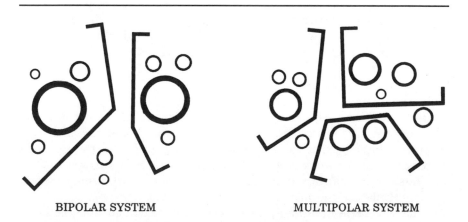

BIPOLAR SYSTEM   MULTIPOLAR SYSTEM

] - Current Alliance

depending upon how power is distributed. This distribution of power is called the "structure" of the system—giving us Structural Realism. Consider the two distributions of power in Figure 1.2. In which system will balancing work better? To this crucial question there are conflicting answers. For instance, John Mearsheimer suggests that a bipolar system makes alliance formation easier because there are only two poles around which alliances are likely to form. That makes it easier to achieve a balance and to calculate the distribution of power.[11] In the multipolar world, there may be more alliances, more shifting of nations between alliances, and a greater ambiguity about power. War, in this view, becomes more likely in a multipolar system. Others have said that in a bipolar system, all conflicts tend to become confrontations between the two rival alliances, greatly increasing the likelihood of war. While there is disagreement about which system is the most stabilizing, Structural Realists assume that the distribution of power is significant for explaining world politics.

GENDER

Now that I have sketched Realist theory, we can ask if gender makes a difference. One of the traditions of the Realist approach is a concern with the ingredients of power—those capabilities that make some states more powerful than others. The size and quality of the population (its literacy, nationalism, and the like) and the effectiveness of the government have received attention, but gender issues have not. Cynthia Enloe's analysis of world politics does suggest that women may undergird many of these components of power.[12] The ability of wives of diplomats to create conditions that make informal negotiations between diplomats possible or the role of prostitution in supporting a state's military power and its alliance networks are just two examples. Ignoring the role of women in the creation of power, especially in the nonobvious ways that Enloe suggests, may limit our understanding of how power in world politics is created and maintained.

The components of power, however, are not the core of Realist theory. How states respond to power—whatever its source—is at the core. The Realists' focus on the state would appear to make gender irrelevant. A Neo-Realist like Kenneth Waltz argues that a theory based on the distribution of power can "tell us about the forces the units [states] are subject to. From [those forces], we can infer some things about the expected behavior and fate of the units: namely, how they will have to compete with and adjust to one another if they are to survive and flourish." Such theories "explain why different units behave similarly and, despite their variations, produce outcomes that fall within expected ranges."[13] While Waltz may never have given a thought to women or gender as theoretically important, his theory would rule gender out as a powerful explanatory factor. Gender, like other characteristics of individuals, is not a force that states are subjected to.

When Realists write about *leaders* of states, they, like most International Relations theorists, speak of men, as in Morgenthau's constant references to "statesmen." Morgenthau did, however, mention four female leaders, but he saw them behaving as male leaders had done. Maria Theresa of Austria and Catherine II of Russia—along with Frederick the Great of Prussia, Louis XIV of France, and Peter the Great of Russia—were "the moving forces" of an imperialism that sought to establish local preponderances of power. Elizabeth I of England, like her father, Henry VIII, played the traditional role of the balancer. And Queen Victoria, "like all of us," wanted a fixed set of policies to deal with other nations, not wanting to acknowledge "the dynamic, ever changing character of the power relations between nations."[14]

On the surface, therefore, Realist theory has no difficulty with women or gender. It says that gender—like the other characteristics of leaders—is essentially *irrelevant* to world politics. In an anarchic world, states led by females will be subject to the same forces as the current predominantly male-led states.

"Ah," we might say, "perhaps the forces operating on leaders will be the same, *but will the responses be similar?*" Waltz admits that Neo-Realist theory "cannot tell us just how, and how effectively, the units of the system will respond to those pressures and possibilities,"[15] although he would still expect the realities of power to make the responses similar. Other Realists, such as Stephen Krasner, admit that "Realism can offer its most precise explanations when states have few options because they are narrowly constrained by the international distribution of power."[16] However, when the international system is less constraining—as it may be for a very powerful state in a system of weaker states—then "the values embodied in its domestic political order" or "the interests of particular bureaucracies or the unconscious psychological drives of specific leaders might be equally compelling" explanations for state behavior.[17] Would gender be one of those possible explanations? Could gender be important *even when the power distribution provides few alternatives?*

TRANSLATING MECHANISMS

To explore these questions, we need to consider the "translating mechanism" that converts the pressures exerted by power into a state's responses. That is, every theory contains—either as assertions or assumptions—a set of claims about *how* one element of the theory (like power) brings about a response (like warfare). The translating mechanism usually consists of humans, be they single persons such as a prime minister or many individuals organized into a bureaucracy such as the U.S. Department of State. In Realist theory, humans link power to actions in world politics by perceiving power, making rational calculations about that power, their security, and their interests, and then acting to achieve their goals in light of that power.

In some cases, the process might be quick and invariable. Consider what happens when your body is exposed to a sudden, loud noise nearby. You jump—the result of the biological translating mechanism in your body that is responding to the noise. You may not jump exactly as I jump, but almost everyone's behavior falls within the predictable range of which Waltz spoke. This kind of translating mechanism seems closest to the Neo-Realist argument. Humans in different states more or less automatically translate the pressures of power in similar ways.

But how is it that humans in different societies come to respond in similar ways? That we all jump is probably a result of genetic evolution, since this reflex increased chances for survival. Waltz does not argue that genetic endowment has molded humans in different societies to respond to power in similar ways. Rather, he points to two processes:[18] *socialization processes*—"Nobody tells all of the teenagers in a given school or town to dress alike, but most of them do"[19]—and *competition,* which "spurs the actors to accommodate their ways to the socially most acceptable and successful practices." There is, to be sure, some variation. "Some do better than others, whether through intelligence, skill, hard work, or dumb luck. . . . [However,] either their competitors emulate them or they fall by the wayside."[20] In the anarchy of world politics, socialization and competition may lead the human translating mechanism in various states over time to behave in similar ways regarding power.

How might gender be important to this translating mechanism? I would suggest that humans in the translating mechanism *bring* with them *personal* sets of values—values created through *domestic* socialization processes. I would hypothesize that individuals or groups in different states will respond in similar ways to the pressures of power in an anarchic world *if* these personal sets of values are congruent with the demands that power places on those humans. If a state, for instance, must attempt to increase its power (because that is what other states expect and because it is effective in promoting security), then *personal* values should not reject power considerations. Without the congruence, individuals may be pulled in different directions, leading to quite different responses.

Realism thus appears to assume that the translating mechanism is well fitted to respond to the pressures of power in an anarchic world. Do male cultures meet this requirement? A contentious issue is, of course, what men's (or women's) values "really" are. Let us assume for the moment that the gender stereotypes attributed to either sex have some validity, if only because this is the way in which culture has attempted to link attributes to sex. John Williams and Deborah Best report on such stereotypes held by members of a relatively elite group (college students) in twenty-five diverse nation-states. Across almost all the societies studied, men were said to be (among other things) dominant, forceful, aggressive, autocratic, enterprising, logical, and unemotional.[21] These values would provide a hospitable translating mechanism for power politics. Perhaps unknown to its proponents, Realist theory may have been—and may still be—a reasonably good and long-lived theory precisely because it *did* incorporate gender in a meaningful way.

What happens, however, if the domestic or personal culture of the state is ill fitting and unsupportive of the Realist vision of world politics? Let us assume for the moment that women in various nations have characteristics different from men. Are women in fact ill fitted for the requirements of a Realist world? According to the Williams and Best study, women were said to be sentimental, submissive, affectionate, dreamy, sensitive, dependent, emotional, fearful, and softhearted—values seemingly out of place in a Realist world.[22] As women become a more important part of the translating mechanism, will the relevance of Realist theory decline because the values in the translating mechanism become inhospitable to the requirements of Realism?

Not necessarily. Realists might argue that humans—not just males—are essentially malleable. Women with their ill-fitting culture will be remolded as they enter leadership positions, becoming "iron women." Remolding occurs in part because women enter a world now dominated by men and are therefore forced to respond like men, but more importantly because of the pressures of dealing with an anarchic world. Those pressures create "iron *people*." The quick entry of many women into leadership positions might overwhelm this remolding process; but given the usually slow process of movement through the political ranks, where advancement is often a function of adopting the dominant values, women will adopt those "masculine" values by the time they come to meaningful positions. Gender thus remains irrelevant for an understanding of world politics even if women's culture itself is ill fitting.

On the other hand, if most women are ill fitted to the demands of an anarchical world of power and remain so while in leadership positions, Realists might argue that the theory still describes the pressures of power accurately and predicts the consequences of inappropriate responses. For instance, suppose women reject the need for maintaining a balance of power. Without that balance, Realist theory suggests that the security of states is threatened and war made more probable. In this interpretation, women become a threat to international stability and peace.

Realists' concern for dangerously inappropriate behavior is not new. Indeed, much of traditional Realist theory reads like an exhortation about how political leaders *should* behave. Woodrow Wilson and British Prime Minister Neville Chamberlain are often cited as examples of leaders who misunderstood the requirements of power and brought on major tragedies in world politics. For some Realists, Wilson and Chamberlain represented two undesirable tendencies: utopianism and liberalism. A utopian thinks in terms of what should be rather than what is, and the Realist "knows" that, at bottom, world politics revolves around power and that the attempt to abolish power is futile. Utopians argue that power considerations should be removed from world politics, and they often behave as if power were no longer operative. In Realist eyes, the liberal has three dangerously mistaken beliefs: that public opinion can restrain the ambitions of states, that a harmony of economic interests between the states can keep the peace, and that international institutions such as the United Nations can keep power under control.[23]

If such perspectives are characteristic of most women (as well as a few men), if women are plentiful in leadership positions, and if the socialization process fails to remold women's values, Realist theory might predict the kinds of damaging consequences that might occur as world politics plays itself out. Visions of a peaceful world led by women—a topic that Anne Sisson Runyan explores in chapter 14—would probably seem irrelevant to many Realists because those visions ignore the effect that power in an anarchic world has on people's behavior. Indeed, the Realist agenda might be to devise ways to keep women (and men) who have such threatening values from leadership positions. Gender now becomes an important factor—threatening but potentially controllable.

This "women-as-threat" image in Realist theory may be balanced, however, by the other side of the Realist equation—the side that usually receives less attention. Realists suggest that states need to have the ability to accept the stalemate that a balance creates and, thus, *accept the necessity to negotiate* solutions to issues. In this part of the equation, the characteristics associated with women may be what facilitate those essential activities. Indeed, from this perspective, *men* are a threat to peace and stability because their culture is less supportive of these activities. The recognition of gender in Realist theory may help explain, even in Realist terms, why things sometimes "turn out badly" when men govern.

GENDER, POWER, AND WORLD POLITICS

To this point we have explored how Realist theory might respond to the question, Is gender likely to have a significant impact on world politics? Realist theory's concentration on power seems to make gender irrelevant. On the other hand, to the degree that Realist theory acknowledges that under some conditions (as in a unipolar world) other factors might be important, gender would seem to be worth considering. In fact, to the degree that Realist theorists explicitly build humans into the analysis, they might wish to think more carefully about gender. For instance, some Realists like Morgenthau appear to make humans central by claiming that there is an innate, *human* drive to acquire and wield power. We now need to ask if this is a heavily gendered assumption, true for some humans, but not humans as a species. If women are either biologically or culturally less interested in acquiring and wielding power, then gender may make a fundamental difference in world politics, and Realist theory needs to rethink this fundamental premise.

It may also be that women, like men, do have interests in power, *but that the kinds of power that the two genders emphasize may be quite different.*[24] Men may emphasize power as domination: the *power over* others and their actions. Women may emphasize the *power to* bring about certain conditions, especially through a cooperative process. "Power over" clearly fits Realist theory, especially as power races and balancing actions. A "power to" approach may be less supportive of those activities. With its interest in *outcomes,* a "power to" orientation may consciously choose *not* to use one's capabilities in order to bring about a collective decision.[25] More generally, a "power over" orientation may produce balancing, while "power to" may promote negotiated outcomes in a balanced situation.

Because Realist theory speaks to recurrent features of world politics such as "power over," anarchy, and conflict, it is likely to continue to be an attractive means of understanding world politics. It is not clear if gender in fact makes a difference, and Realist theory predicts that individuals will be socialized to meet the requirements of "power over." Realism's strength as a theory may be tested as more women enter policy-making positions, and such a test is likely over the next two decades.

But our ability to detect the effect of gender will be made more difficult by the momentous change occurring in the world. The collapse of the power of the Soviet Union into fifteen separate republics and the slow emergence of a united Europe have changed the distribution of power in dramatic ways. Realist theory suggests that the behaviors of states will change when the distribution of power changes. Since it is likely to take some time for states to adapt themselves to these new conditions, it may be quite difficult to determine if that adaptation is induced by the change in the system or by the entry of women in positions of power—or both.

The theory does say, however, that there is an irreducible core of behaviors, such as states' attempting to increase their power and to balance the power of others—all with the goal of meeting the states' security needs. This core will not change as long as anarchy prevails. To the extent that states appear to undertake those tasks, Realist theorists may see no reason to think of gender as a relevant concern.

NOTES

I would like to thank Francine D'Amico and Iva E. Deutchman for their helpful comments on this chapter.

1. The metaphor is Charlotte Bunch's; see Elizabeth Kamarck Minnich, *Transforming Knowledge* (Philadelphia: Temple University Press, 1990), 27–29.

2. Thucydides, *The Peloponnesian War,* trans. R. Cawley (New York: Modern Library College Editions, 1981). For a review of Realism, see James Dougherty and Robert Pfaltzgraff, Jr., *Contending Theories of International Relations,* 2d ed. (New York: Harper & Row, 1981), 84–180, and Robert Keohane, "Realism, Neorealism, and the Study of World Politics" and "Theory of World Politics: Structural Realism and Beyond," in R. Keohane, ed., *Neorealism and Its Critics* (New York: Columbia University Press, 1986), 7–24, 158–203.

3. See the various editions of Hans Morgenthau, *Politics among Nations* (New York: Knopf); Morgenthau citations are from the 3d ed., 1964.

4. Kenneth Waltz, *Theory of International Politics* (New York: Random House, 1979). For Waltz's contrasting of Realism with Neo-Realism, see "Realist Thought and Neorealist Theory," in Robert L. Rothstein, ed., *The Evolution of Theory in International Relations* (Columbia, SC: University of South Carolina Press, 1991), 21–37.

5. Morgenthau, *Politics among Nations,* 27.

6. Ibid., 5, 6.

7. Waltz, "Realist Thought," 36.

8. Morgenthau, *Politics among Nations,* 28.

9. John Kennedy, 1961 State of the Union, *Public Papers of the Presidents: John F. Kennedy* (Washington, DC: Government Printing Office, 1962), 22–23.

10. R. N. Berki, *On Political Realism* (London: Dent, 1981), 19.

11. John Mearsheimer, "Back to the Future: Instability in Europe after the Cold War," *International Security* 15 (Summer 1990): 5–56; reprinted in Sean M. Lynn-Jones, ed., *The Cold War and After: Prospects for Peace* (Cambridge, MA: MIT Press, 1991), 150.

12. Cynthia Enloe, *Bananas, Beaches, & Bases: Making Feminist Sense of International Politics* (Berkeley: University of California Press, 1990).

13. Waltz, *Theory,* 72.

14. Morgenthau, *Politics among Nations,* 57, 196, 157.

15. Waltz, *Theory,* 71

16. Stephen D. Krasner, "Realism, Imperialism, and Democracy," *Political Theory* 20 (February 1992): 40.

17. Ibid., 41.

18. Waltz, *Theory,* 74.

19. Ibid., 75.

20. Ibid., 77.

21. John E. Williams and Deborah L. Best, *Measuring Sex Stereotypes: A Thirty-Nation Study* (Beverly Hills, CA: Sage, 1982), 76.

22. Ibid., 77.

23. E. H. Carr, *The Twenty Years' Crisis, 1919–1939,* 2d ed. (London: Macmillan, 1954), 22–64.

24. Iva E. Deutchman, "Feminist Theory and the Politics of Empowerment," *Women and Politics* 11:2 (1991): 1–18.

25. Ibid., 4.

❖ 2 ❖

A Feminist Critique of Political Realism

J. Ann Tickner

The previous chapter outlined the central ideas of political Realism, the dominant approach to the discipline of international relations in the United States. We learned that Realism focuses on power politics and interstate conflict. Given that Realists see the international arena as a dangerous environment devoid of a government that could enforce impartial rules of behavior upon aggressive states, the central concern of Realism has been with national security. Since foreign policy practitioners are frequently trained in the Realist approach, Realist thinking has influenced the way in which both our leaders and the general public view international relations.

For Realists, security is linked to the military security of the nation-state. Given their pessimistic assumptions about the likely behavior of states in an "anarchic" international environment, most Realists doubt that states can ever achieve perfect security. In an imperfect world, where many states have national security interests that go well beyond self-preservation and where there is no international government to curb their ambitions, Realists tell us that war could break out at any time because there is nothing to prevent it. Therefore, they advise, states must rely on their own capabilities to achieve security: The accumulation of power and military strength is necessary to assure states' survival. Moreover, Realists warn us that moral behavior is usually ineffective and possibly self-defeating in this dangerous world: A "realistic" understanding of the amoral and instrumental behavior, characteristic of international politics, is necessary if states are not to fall prey to others' ambitions.

Given this preoccupation with national security, it follows that Realists are primarily concerned with conflict and its causes; indeed, much of their analysis focuses on understanding the causes of war. In order to explain the causes of international wars, Realists look at three levels of analysis: the individual, the state, and the international system. Through an examination of these three levels of analysis, Realists seek to discover whether wars are caused by aggressive individuals, power-seeking states, or an anarchic international environment devoid of any mechanism to prevent aggressive behavior. While structural Realists, such as Kenneth Waltz, see the international system of anarchy as the primary cause of conflict, traditional Realists, such as Hans Morgenthau, focus on individuals and, most importantly, on states. Morgenthau tells us that all states try to maximize their power in order to protect themselves against the aggressions of others. States are populated by power-seeking individuals who project their aggressions onto the international system where this type of behavior is rewarded as the patriotic duty of defending one's country; while it has been men to whom this duty has been assigned, women are supportive of such policies too.

Although Realists rarely talk about women or gender, they would probably claim that gender is irrelevant for understanding international politics and the causes of war. In this chapter we will challenge this assertion by examining each of the three levels of analysis described by Realists. If we look more closely at the individual, the state, and the international system, we will find that each is described in terms that we associate with masculinity and is based on the behavior and experiences of men. Indeed, characteristics associated with "manliness," such as toughness, courage, power, independence, and even physical strength, have throughout history been those most valued in the conduct of international politics. We will see that Realists have projected these masculine characteristics onto the behavior of states whose success in achieving security is described in a framework of power capabilities and their capacity for self-help and autonomy.

"POLITICAL MAN"

In his well-known book *Politics among Nations,* Realist scholar Hans Morgenthau claims that individuals are engaged in a struggle for power whenever they come into contact with each other. While Morgenthau is primarily concerned with explaining the international behavior of states, he claims that the tendency to dominate exists in all facets of human life—the family, the polity, and the international system.[1] Since women rarely occupy positions of power in any of these arenas, we can assume that, when Morgenthau talks about the tendency to dominate, he is basing his description of human behavior primarily on that of men. For purposes of explaining individuals' political behavior as well as the foreign policy of states, Morgenthau constructs an abstraction called "political man," an individual whose political behavior is motivated by instrumentally rational, self-serving behavior lacking in moral restraints. Given that Morgenthau believes that states who act morally or altruistically are doomed to failure because of the immoral behavior of others, this power-seeking behavior of political man, which is projected onto the behavior of states in the international system, is not only permissible but prudent.

Political man embodies characteristics such as toughness, rationality, autonomy, and power. While real men exhibit many other characteristics, we associate these particular ones with a stereotypical masculinity. Characteristics such as weakness, emotion, interdependence, and idealism which have been labeled "feminine" in our culture have no place in the realm of international politics and, according to Realists, would be a liability. Morgenthau's political man is quite compatible with a militarized version of citizenship that has a long history in Western writings about international politics and that can be traced all the way back to the ancient Greeks. For the Greeks, the most honored way to achieve recognition as a citizen was through heroic performance and sacrifice in war. The Greek city-state was a community of warriors. Women and slaves who worked in the economy or the household were not included as citizens because, it was thought, they would pollute the higher realm of politics.[2]

When we think about international politics today, our understanding of what it means to be a good citizen or a successful policy maker still remains bound up with the ancient Greeks' depiction of the citizen-warrior. The most noble sacrifice that a citizen can make is giving his life for his country, a sacrifice that is denied to women since they are not allowed to serve in combat in most armed forces. The relation between soldiering, masculinity, and citizenship—an important part of the Western historical tradition in international politics—remains very strong in most societies today. It is a tradition upon which Morgenthau was drawing, although perhaps unconsciously, when he constructed political man.

Just as the Greeks gave special respect to citizens who had proved themselves in war, to be a war veteran is still a mark of respect in many countries, an honor that has usually been denied to virtually all women as well as to certain men. In the United States, military service helps to gain votes for political offices, even those not exclusively concerned with foreign policy: Ex-generals are looked upon favorably as presidential candidates, and many American presidents have run on their war record. When women run for political office they are at a disadvantage because they are often perceived as not tough enough to stand up to foreign aggressors. To be a first-class citizen, therefore, one must be a warrior and a protector. It is an important qualification for the politics of national security, for it is to such men that the state entrusts its most vital interests.

When Realists write about foreign policy making and national security, they generally ignore these gendered images of citizen warriors and male protectors. Many Realists use abstract and depersonalized language that ignores individual behavior altogether. Yet even when Realists ignore the individual and focus on the behavior of states in the international system they are constructing a worldview that is shaped out of these gendered identities. The notion of "manhood," discussed above, which is crucial for describing and legitimizing the national security interests of the state, is an image that Realists frequently draw upon when they analyze the behavior of the state itself.

THE MASCULINE STATE

When structural Realists, such as Kenneth Waltz, discuss the international behavior of states, they portray the states as unitary actors whose internal characteristics are irrelevant for understanding their international behavior. All states, whatever their political and economic systems, are assumed to be maximizing their security by increasing their power capabilities or by engaging in power-balancing activities to protect themselves against others' aggressive acts. This "unitary actor model," sometimes referred to as the "billiard-ball model," denotes the similarity of states' international behavior given an anarchic international system. Investigating the gendered behavior of their policy makers—or, indeed, any of their internal characteristics—is not considered necessary for helping us to understand states' foreign policies. Indeed, Realists would deny that gender plays any role in understanding the behavior of nation-states. However, if we look at some of the metaphors that Realists use to describe the international behavior of states, frequently we find that they draw upon activities that we generally associate with men, such as stag hunts or "games nations play."[3]

To describe the likely security-seeking behavior of states in an anarchic international environment, Kenneth Waltz uses the metaphor of a stag hunt, invented by the eighteenth-century political philosopher Jean-Jacques Rousseau. Five hungry men agree to trap a stag; but when a hare runs by, one man grabs it, thereby letting the stag escape: By defecting from the common goal, this hunter sacrifices the long-term cooperative interests of the group, his own included, for his immediate short-term interest.[4] For Realists, the metaphor of the stag hunt illustrates the problematic nature of cooperation under anarchy, whereby it is assumed that each state must rely on its own capabilities to protect its interests. Since other states' intentions may create problems in an environment that lacks impartial enforceable rules, each state must depend on itself for its own security even if cooperation would further the collective interests of all.

This metaphor of the stag hunt—which emphasizes individualism, autonomy, and self-help rather than behavior that is more interdependent and cooperative—draws on behavior that we associate with masculinity. Since the beginning of the state system in the seventeenth century, the foreign policy behavior of states has frequently been described by using these masculine gendered images. For example, as states have evolved over the last 300 years, success in war has been important not only for their survival but also for gaining the support of their citizens: Nationalist movements have used gendered imagery that exhorts masculine heroes to fight for the independence and defense of the "mother country." Our identity as citizens depends on telling stories about and celebrating wars of independence or national liberation and other great victories in battle. National anthems are frequently war songs, just as holidays are celebrated with military parades and uniforms that recall great feats in past conflicts. These collective historical memories are very important for the way in which we define ourselves as citizens as well as the way in which states command support for their foreign policies. Rarely, however, do these national songs or memories include experiences of women or female heroes. The metaphors and images upon which Realist theories are based are drawn, therefore, from a worldview in which women are, for the most part, absent.

While the functions of states today extend well beyond the provision of national security, national security issues, particularly in time of international crises or war, offer a sense of shared political purpose that is lacking in most other areas of public policy. In the name of national security citizens are willing to make sacrifices often unquestioningly. Military budgets are the least likely area of public spending to be contested by politicians and by the public whose support for military spending is gained by linking such spending to patriotism. When we think about the state acting in matters of national security, we are entering a policy world almost exclusively inhabited by men. Men make national security policy both inside and outside the military establishment. In spite of growing numbers of women in the U.S. military—which at present has the largest percentage of women of any military establishment—it remains a male institution in terms of its leadership and culture. Similarly, planning strategies for present and future security threats is conducted by civilian national-security specialists, most of whom are men. Strategic planning is done in secret far removed from public debate in a language that—with its emphasis on strength, power, and rationality—parallels an idealized image of masculinity.[5] Frequently the rationale for fighting wars is presented in gendered terms, such as the necessity of standing up to aggression rather than being pushed around or appearing to be a sissy or a wimp. Support for war is often garnered through an appeal to masculinity. Indeed, war is a time when masculine and feminine characteristics are most polarized. It is an event in which men are portrayed as the protectors, and women and children as the protected. Little has been written about women's roles in wars, but generally women are seen as victims rather than as actors. This gendered way of thinking about war and national security grows out of the way in which we are taught to think about the international system.

THE INTERNATIONAL SYSTEM: THE WAR OF EVERYMAN AGAINST EVERYMAN

When Realists describe the international system as an "anarchy," the metaphor that they often use is the depiction of the state of nature by the seventeenth-century English philosopher Thomas Hobbes. Hobbes used the metaphor of "a state of nature" to describe what he imagined life was like before the establishment of governments.[6] Hobbes thought that without a government to make and enforce laws, humans would engage in a competitive struggle for power and survival that would result in what he called "a war of every man against every man." In such a world, even when actual fighting was not taking place, people would live in constant fear of death and would not be able to engage in everyday activities such as business or industry.

Although Hobbes was not writing about international relations, Realists have used his description of men's behavior in the state of nature to describe relations between states in an anarchic international system. However, as a model of human behavior, Hobbes' depiction of men in the state of nature is partial at best; it could be argued that such behavior could only be applicable to adult males, for if life was to go on for more than one generation women must have been involved in activities such as child bearing and child rearing rather than in warfare. These kinds of activities require an environment that can provide for the survival of infants and behavior that is interactive and nurturing.

Even though they would probably claim that gender is not relevant for the development of their theories, Realists have given us a three-tiered picture of a world in which survival in a violence-prone international system requires war-capable states peopled by heroic masculine warrior-citizens. These gendered depictions of political man, the state, and the international system generate a way of thinking about international relations that focuses on conflict and war and tends to exclude other ways of thinking about security. If we were to acknowledge that this worldview has been constructed out of a partial view of human nature that is based on gender stereotypes and experiences more typical of men than of women, we could begin to think about constructing alternative perspectives on international relations that could offer equally plausible prescriptions for the achievement of national security.

AN ALTERNATIVE TO REALISM: A FEMINIST PERSPECTIVE ON INTERNATIONAL RELATIONS

We have described political Realism as a masculine perspective on international relations. We have observed that Realists believe that characteristics typically associated with masculinity, such as power, independence, rationality, and autonomy, are those that are most desirable if states are to be successful in international politics. We have also identified some characteristics typically associated with femininity, such as emotion, relatedness, interdependence, and idealism. If we are to construct an alternative feminist perspective on international relations, should we base it on these feminine characteristics when they have so often been considered a liability for a "realistic" foreign policy? Scholars who write about women are very reluctant to engage in this type of gender stereotyping because it has often been used to devalue women and reinforce the inequality between the sexes. Therefore, before constructing a Feminist perspective on international relations, we need to acknowledge that gender stereotypes, which do not necessarily fit all men and women, have been used not only to devalue women but also to devalue certain types of behavior in international relations. We also need to consider how characteristics associated with femininity could be revalued and be seen as equally plausible and legitimate for helping us to think about international relations as those associated with masculinity. Since, as we have seen, Realism's views on international relations are based on masculine models of human behavior, we can assume that a Feminist perspective on international relations would grow out of quite different assumptions about the individual, the state, and the international system.

Since Feminists believe that militarism, racism, and sexism are interconnected, we must begin by questioning the assumption made by Realists that the behavior of individuals and the domestic policies of states can be separated from states' behavior in the international system. Our Feminist perspective should also question whether the levels of analysis that Realists employ are a useful way to think about national security and the causes of international conflict. Traditional views of national security, which grow out of Realist thinking, present us with images of (mostly) male military protectors defending civilians against dangerous threats from outside the state; however, the National Organization for Women has estimated that 80 to 90 percent of casualties caused by conflict since World War II have been civilians, the majority of which have been women and children.[7] In societies that are highly militarized, women are particularly vulnerable to rape, and evidence suggests that domestic violence is higher in military families or in families that include men with prior military service. This kind of evidence points toward a different boundary between anarchy and order from the one used by Realists when they describe a dangerous world outside the state. Domestic violence also occurs outside the public political space protected by the rule of law, in the private space of the family where, in many cases, no legal protection exists.

This line that demarcates public and private separates state-regulated violence (the rule of right for which there are legally sanctioned punishments) and family violence (the rule of might for which, in many societies, no such legal sanctions exist). The rule of might and the rule of right are descriptions that have also been used in international relations to distinguish the international sphere of anarchy from the domestic sphere of government. By drawing our attention to the frequently forgotten realm of family violence that is also often beyond the reach of law, a Feminist perspective allows us to consider the interrelation of conflict and violence across levels of analysis. Feminist perspectives on international relations would assume that violence, whether it be in the international, national, or family realm, is interconnected. Family violence must be seen in the context of wider power relations; it is produced within an unequally gendered society in which male power dominates at all levels. Therefore, a Feminist perspective on national security must include not only an analysis of international conflict and war, but also an analysis of all types of violence including violence produced by these unequal gender relations of domination and subordination. The achievement of this more comprehensive vision of national security requires both a rethinking of the way in which citizenship, or political man, has traditionally been defined as well as a provision of alternative models for describing the behavior of states in the international system.

CITIZENSHIP REDEFINED

The prevailing belief that women and children are protected by males contributes to the legitimation of a militarized version of citizenship that, as we have seen, results in unequal gender relations that can precipitate violence against women. If women were to have equal access to the military, in leadership and combat positions, we would have a society in which all adult citizens would be equally likely to experience violence and to be responsible for its exercise. If everyone—women and men alike—were protectors, there would be less emphasis on the manliness of war, and new questions about its morality could be raised.[8] An equal role for women in the military would lend itself to a new concept of citizen-defender rather than warrior-patriot. Citizen-defenders would change our image of combat and could be consistent with a defensive strategy in war that, if followed by all states, would result in less aggressive international behavior.

Besides advocating women's equal role as protectors, a Feminist perspective on international relations should also raise the possibility of different models of citizenship that would depend less on military values and more on an equal recognition of women's contributions to society. In their roles as mothers and caregivers women are making contributions to society that could be useful for thinking about nonviolent resolution of conflict. Tasks that are oriented toward the preservation of life and the growth of children require techniques that contribute to the peaceful settlement of disputes, a mode of operation that could be useful for a politics of peace.[9] While holding down jobs, millions of women also care for children, the aged, and the sick outside the economy. When more resources go to the military, additional burdens are placed on these women as public-sector resources for social services shrink. While certain women are able, through access to the military, to give service to their country, many more are serving in these traditional caregiving roles. A Feminist challenge to the traditional definition of patriotism should, therefore, question the meaning of service to one's country. In contrast to a citizenship that rests on the assumption that it is more glorious to die than to live for one's country, a more constructive view of citizenship could grow out of the courage to sustain life. These alternative models of citizenship and the behavior of individuals can help us to think about different models for states' behavior in the international system.

A FEMINIST PERSPECTIVE ON STATES' SECURITY-SEEKING BEHAVIOR

We have outlined Realists' use of Hobbes' state of nature as a metaphor for states' security-seeking behavior in the international system. Let us now consider an alternative story that could equally plausibly be applied to the behavior of individuals in the state of nature. It is a true story, not a myth, about a state of nature in early nineteenth-century America. Among those present in the first winter encampment of the 1804–1806 Lewis and Clark expedition into the Northwest territories was Sacajawea, a member of the Shoshone Native American tribe. Sacajawea had joined the expedition as the wife of a French interpreter; her presence was proving invaluable to the security of the expedition's members whose task it was to explore uncharted territory and establish contact with the Native Americans to inform them of claims to these territories by the United States. Although unanticipated by its leaders, the presence of a woman served to assure the native inhabitants that the expedition was peaceful since the Native Americans assumed that war parties would not include women: The expedition was safer, therefore, because it was not armed and not composed entirely of men.

This story shows how the introduction of women can change the way in which humans are assumed to behave in the state of nature. Just as Sacajawea's presence changed the Native Americans' expectations about the behavior of intruders into their territory, the introduction of women into our state-of-nature myths could change the way in which we think about the behavior of states in the international system. The use of the Hobbesian analogy in international relations is based on a partial view of human nature that is stereotypically masculine; a more inclusive perspective would see human nature as both conflictual and cooperative, containing elements of social reproduction and interdependence as well as domination and separation. Generalizing from this more comprehensive view of human nature, a Feminist perspective on international relations would assume that the potential for international community also exists and that an atomistic, conflictual view of the international system is only a partial representation of reality. Similarly, a Feminist perspective would assume that Rousseau's metaphor of the stag hunt is also based on a partial model of human behavior.

Neither Hobbes' state of nature nor Rousseau's stag hunt emphasizes the existence of interdependence or the likelihood of successful cooperation in international relations. Yet states frequently exhibit aspects of cooperative behavior when they engage in diplomatic negotiations. However, diplomacy works best when there is trust and confidence between negotiators. Interestingly, many agreements between states are negotiated in an informal setting in the residences of ambassadors where the presence of diplomatic wives creates an atmosphere in which trust can best be cultivated.[10] Women, although they usually occupy positions that are unremunerated and undervalued, remain vital to the process of creating and maintaining trust between men in a hostile world.

We have seen that Realism puts a great deal of emphasis on autonomy and independence as desirable goals for states' international behavior. In international relations autonomy is associated with national sovereignty and is, therefore, very important for achieving national security. But this preoccupation with autonomy tends to blind us to the realities of interdependence in the present world situation.[11] As we know, the international system is highly interdependent as individuals, corporations, money, and goods move across international boundaries in ways that require coordination and cooperation. Since a Feminist perspective assumes that interdependence is as much a human characteristic as autonomy, it allows us to question the desirability of autonomy. Striving for attachment is also a part of human nature that, while it has been suppressed by the policies and practices of the nation-state system, should be reclaimed and revalued if we are to survive in our highly interdependent world.

A Feminist perspective on international relations can also offer us a different definition of power. Hans Morgenthau defined power as the control of men's minds and actions; this sense of control over or domination is the way in which power is usually defined in international relations. Power as domination has been associated with masculinity since the exercise of power has generally been a masculine activity. When women write about power, they stress energy, capacity, and potential.[12] According to this definition, power can be seen as mutually enabling or as collective action to achieve a desired goal. This definition has some similarities with strategies of small states operating from a position of weakness in the international system. It also fits the process of building the European Community, an organization that has successfully integrated the economies of states in Western Europe. Building community is an activity in which states also engage although it is one that tends to get obscured when power is seen solely as domination.

Thinking about power in a different way helps us to think constructively about the potential for cooperation as well as conflict in international relations. While this is an aspect of international relations that is generally downplayed by Realism, it is one that is becoming increasingly important if we are to begin to solve collective problems such as poverty and the pollution of the natural environment.

This Feminist critique has demonstrated that political Realism bases its analysis of the behavior of states in the international system on a partial view of reality that is constructed out of the experiences of men and characteristics that we associate with masculinity. We have seen that a Feminist perspective can offer us some models of international relations that are different from Realism's statist, power-oriented representations. By speaking out of experiences more typical of women, this Feminist perspective opens up new possibilities for thinking about international relations in ways that have previously been ignored. While the alternative models of citizenship and states' international behavior described in this chapter are not a complete representation of reality either, they begin to revalue ways of behaving that have too often been dismissed as impractical and idealistic, often by associating them with women. Legitimizing states' behavior by applauding characteristics associated with a stereotypical masculinity that is not necessarily representative of the way in which many men behave is not the best way to achieve security in our highly interdependent world. But working toward the broader, more inclusive vision of international relations outlined in this chapter requires that we work simultaneously toward achieving equality between women and men. Only when gender relations of domination and subordination no longer exist can we envisage a world that is truly secure for us all.

NOTES

This chapter draws heavily on J. Ann Tickner, "Hans Morgenthau's Principles of Political Realism: A Feminist Reformulation," *Millennium* 17:3 (Winter 1988): 429–40, and J. Ann Tickner, *Gender in International Relations: Feminist Perspectives on Achieving Global Security* (New York: Columbia University Press, 1992).

    1. Hans J. Morgenthau, *Politics among Nations: The Struggle for Power and Peace,* 5th ed. (New York: Knopf, 1973), 34.

    2. Wendy Brown, *Manhood and Politics: A Feminist Reading in Political Theory* (Totowa, NJ: Rowman & Littlefield, 1988), 43–59.

    3. *Games Nations Play* is the title of a popular international relations textbook by John Spanier.

    4. Kenneth Waltz, *Man, the State, and War* (New York: Columbia University Press, 1959), 167. This description of structural Realism also draws on Kenneth Waltz, *Theory of International Politics* (New York: Random House, 1979).

    5. Carol Cohn, "Sex and Death in the Rational World of Defense Intellectuals," *Signs: Journal of Women in Culture and Society* 12:4 (1987): 687–718.

6. Thomas Hobbes, *Leviathan,* Part 1, Chapter 13.

7. National Organization for Women, "Resolution on Women in Combat," July 16, 1990.

8. Judith Stiehm, ed., *Women and Men's Wars* (Oxford: Pergamon, 1983), 367.

9. Sara Ruddick, "The Rationality of Care," in Jean Bethke Elshtain and Sheila Tobias, eds., *Women, Militarism, and War* (Savage, MD: Rowman & Littlefield, 1990), chap. 12.

10. Cynthia Enloe, *Bananas, Beaches, & Bases: Making Feminist Sense of International Politics* (Berkeley: University of California Press, 1990), chap. 5.

11. Betty A. Reardon, *Sexism and the War System* (New York: Teachers College Press, 1985).

12. Nancy C. M. Hartsock, *Money, Sex, and Power: Toward a Feminist Historical Materialism* (Boston: Northeastern University Press, 1985), 210.

❖ 3 ❖

Behavioral Theories: The Science of International Politics and Women

Karen A. Feste

As an approach to the study of international relations, quantitative Behavioralist theories of politics are of recent origin; these were popularized in the 1960s and, interestingly, are dated concurrently with the beginning of the women's movement in consciousness raising. *The Behavioral Persuasion in Politics* by Heinz Eulau and *The Feminine Mystique* by Betty Friedan were both published in 1963.[1] Each perspective represented a freshness in analyzing and understanding social relations at the time, each advocated a different look at the way in which the world worked or what people believed about its functioning, and each pressed for consideration of an alternative view. But this is where the commonality ends. The timing, antiestablishment message, and sheer newness that these movements once shared might have led to an expectation that quantitative Behavioralist thinkers would examine ideas of international politics that incorporated aspects of women's role in war or peace. Or perhaps they would show a willingness to build on principles of feminism with their efforts at theory construction and data analysis. At the very least, they would add the gender variable to the list of indicators and concepts used in research. However, "women" as a variable has not appeared in either the theories or data studies produced by the Behavioralists.

There are several reasons for this. Understanding the principles of the Behavioral approach is a necessary step before accounting for this lack of attention to the role of women in the world and their effects on global politics. Accordingly, this chapter will address several specific questions: What is the scientific approach to the study of international relations and how does Behavioralism differ from other forms of theorizing? What would we expect to learn about women and international politics from a

Behavioralist perspective? Where might the gender factor be important in Behavioralist theories and how could it be incorporated?

THE SCIENTIFIC APPROACH

A Behavioralist is a theorist of international politics who employs the quantitative approach or scientific method. Behavioral theories of international politics apply principles of the scientific method to understand how the world operates in political, economic, diplomatic, and military relations. Rather than emphasize moral prescriptions or policy recommendations to evaluate U.S. foreign policy or debate whether war is ever justified, this approach looks at existing conditions and operating behaviors to explain events. The ultimate criterion for discovering knowledge lies beyond common sense ("what everybody knows"), beyond plausibility ("it seems reasonable"), and beyond individual values ("this is what should be done").

The essence of the scientific method is based on testing generalizations by performing a thorough examination of observable instances that would support or refute the particular claim. Thus, scientific inquiry seeks to explore, describe, explain, and predict events in the world through properly gathered and widely supported empirical evidence. Such evidence is obtained in many different ways: by experimentation, by systematic observation, by interviews or surveys, by psychological tests, by careful examination of documents. This dependence on empirical evidence distinguishes the sciences from other forms of knowledge acquisition. The scientific method always treats correspondence with the real world as the final test of any proposition: All generalizations must be subjected to a test, where the words and phrases contained in them are defined by observable phenomena. Mental states of human reasoning—motivations, for example—are relevant only if they can be represented accurately by observable phenomena. What we see, not what we feel or believe, is the last word, the decisive feature in knowing.

Moreover, a Behavioralist is skeptical. No explanation is absolute, no finding final; all knowledge is regarded as tentative, and advancing our understanding is a continuous, unfolding process. This tentativeness and the importance of measurement and testing mean, however, that very little international-politics theory actually exists. Demanding scientific standards have minimized the significance of traditional speculation; anecdotal and intuitive procedures of gathering facts are inadequate for the kind of data needed for a science of international politics.

A variety of procedures do exist, however, to transform international-politics data into scientifically appropriate material. These include content analysis, game theory, and operational definitions of war. Content analysis is a technique for measuring the quantity and meaning of messages communicated between states. It led to the confirmation that cross-cultural differences may result in misunderstandings and that frequently spoken harsh words convey hostility. Game theory is a set of mathematical rules for analyzing rational behavior in conflict situations that has found that individually determined cost-benefit strategies always prevail. Operational definitions of war offer observable criteria to determine the meaning and application of the concept of "war" in the expectation that battle fatality figures and volume of armaments committed to the conflict convey more information than legal declarations of war.

Behavioralism and Women

Behavioralism, with its emphasis on variables, searches for patterns to highlight differences and also to discover similarities. Due to its focus on *human activity,* the variables or factors leading to friction or harmony, whether in the context of inter*national* or inter*personal* relations, are often the same. International problems as well as social problems arise because communication across different cultures is difficult. The notion of "psychological distance," for example, has been used to account for the way in which men and women interpret the world around them. Deborah Tannen's point of "different words, different worlds" captures this principle to explain gender-based difficulties in conversations.[2] It is interesting to note that one of the very earliest Behavioral studies on international politics identifies precisely the "psychological-distance" factor in trying to understand levels of friendly or hostile relations between states in the international community. Frank Klingberg analyzed cross-national differences in predicting the outbreak of World War II, hypothesizing that greater distances between pairs of countries (measured by amounts of hostility determined by experts' ratings) would be more likely to produce conflict.[3]

In spite of these commonalities, no cross-fertilization of thinking or theorizing between interpersonal and international relations has occurred on the gender question. Quantitative, Behavioral theories of world politics have not examined male-female differences. Why? Perhaps it is because scientists have operated under an assumption that the environment of international politics is *gender-blind,* meaning that behavior is reflected and determined by position (a decision-making role in a given country, for example) not by sex. Thus, any woman who rises to the top will conform to the dominant operating model of power and influence and begin to think and act like a man. Or have scientists made a deliberate assumption of *gender-exclusion?* Since men rule the world of international politics, a fact derived from strict observation, then women must be unimportant to this environment; they are disregarded because they do not matter.

As changes occur throughout the world—specifically, the recognition of the addition of women to the work force of world politics—it is reasonable to challenge the validity of these claims and operating norms. In the following discussion of specific types of Behavioral theories and quantitative approaches, I will argue that some hypotheses of international politics are most likely *gender-tied* truths rather than generalizations about human nature, and I will suggest how a *gender-inclusion* research strategy might alter our existing knowledge about international politics.

Some of the important issues raised by feminist groups pertaining to international politics do not find a voice in the work of practitioners of Behavioralism. Questions are excluded that imply a certain value preference, for example, in promoting how things ought to be. How much better would the world be if national defense ministers throughout the world were women? What are the possibilities for global peace with an all-female army? Should more women be encouraged to become active in promoting Third World disarmament?

The Behavioral school is not immune from such topics, but owing to its emphasis on empirical information and strict rules of evidence for scientifically drawn conclusions, coupled with the male bias in its implicit assumptions, these issues have not been addressed. Simply *asserting* that men restrict women from professional advancement or *assuming* that women are inherently more peace-minded is not a proper scientific argument. Behavioralists demand full, observable documentation with comprehensive evidence to support their claims. The issues above could be transformed to correspond to a scientific mode of analysis in the following way: How many cases exist of female defense ministers and, as a group, how do their actions compare with those of men in the same position? What differences may be noted between the behavior of male and female soldiers? What are the effects of single versus mixed-gender military units? What are the observable effects of women's peace groups on national security policy? Overall, the Behavioralist seeks to discover what observable factors are connected together, that is, what correlations explain the existing situation.

INTERNATIONAL CONFLICT AND WOMEN

Most Behavioral studies focus on international conflict, specifically the causes of war. Quantitatively oriented scholars have suggested, on the basis of their interpretation of data, that a homogeneous world would be more peaceful, that militant ideology might be a cause of war, and that the personality of political leaders probably contributes to the outbreak of conflict. All of these conclusions give force to the "psychological-distance" thesis, but remain tentative, since it has not been determined how much and what kind of supporting evidence is required to form an acceptable generalization.

War does not appear to be an accidental, randomly appearing event, according to scientific analysis, but is to a large extent governed by factors concerning power: how certain dimensions of power capabilities are distributed across states, such as industrial strength, military-weapons arsenals, or population, and how they help shape political leaders' perceptions about the power status of individual nations. On the basis of scientific evidence, Behavioralists have concluded that the great powers are more often involved in conflict than small, weak states, and that a national policy of sharply increased defense expenditures is a signal of power enhancement and often symbolizes a preparation for war. Power has figured as an important explanatory concept in quantitative approaches to international politics, which is consistent with the traditionally dominant framework of *Realism*. Has gender been brought into the picture by the Behavioralists? Where does the sex variable fit? A few examples of major contributions in the quantitative study of international conflict are described here to examine these issues.

The Correlates of War (COW) project[4] is devoted to discovering the trends and fluctuations in the frequency, magnitude, severity, and intensity of wars between nation-states in the nineteenth and twentieth centuries. J. David Singer and Melvin Small sought to determine the causes of war by searching for patterns that describe when and where wars occur, who participates, the number of casualties, and the gains and losses for the winners and losers. They turned to Realism for guidance in selecting indicators to provide measurable, observable information: Their data consist of national-capability measures, including population figures, size of armed forces, iron and steel production, and memberships in alliances. Singer and Small are Realists who use the scientific method to try to substantiate hypotheses regarding the centrality of power. Consequently, the analysis tends to favor power-politics principles in drawing interpretations of trends. On the basis of these data, researchers have discovered that big powers have participated in more wars, that major powers undergoing rapid growth in capabilities are more likely to fight with other major powers, and that international disputes between large countries tend to escalate to war if there has been an arms race between them (disputes without arms races did not). These results are based on a data set of 118 international wars between 1816 and 1980.

The project focused on the nation-state, not on individual personalities. Because the researchers assumed that gender made no difference, no references to women were included. It would, however, be possible to divide their data into countries ruled by men versus those ruled by women and conduct an analysis of war participation and its consequences under the gender variable. There were several prominent female leaders during this period: Queen Victoria and Prime Minister Margaret Thatcher in England, Queen Beatrix of the Netherlands, Queen Margarete of Denmark, Golda Meir in Israel, and Indira Gandhi in India. Benazir Bhutto of Pakistan and

Gro Harlem Bruntland of Norway were both prime ministers during the 1980s. Further back in history, Catherine of Russia, Elizabeth I of England, and Christina of Sweden, to name a few prominent, aristocratic rulers in important European countries, also would provide data for analyzing the war participation-gender correlation. Questions about differences in war engagement and alliance memberships could be drawn between women-led and men-led states. Of course, factors other than gender do seem to account for national behaviors in foreign policy, but such a breakdown would yield additional information about war occurrences and about leadership; whether there are differences or not would be vital to know if the goal is to understand gender effects on international war.

Further quantitative investigations of Realist theory have been conducted by Bruce Bueno de Mesquita in *The War Trap.*[5] He asked whether leaders of big countries behaved differently from small ones in their decisions to go to war. And he wondered if decision-making patterns varied across cultures or if political leaders used the same calculations to implement policy. To address these questions, the COW data were used in testing a general theory of foreign-conflict initiation and escalation, based on a cost-benefit perspective. He concluded that leaders will commit their states to go to war if they feel they have a chance to win. The probability of victory, Bueno de Mesquita asserts, is calculated from the relative power differentials between a state and its enemy. Political leaders are assumed to be rational creatures who will seize an opportunity to acquire more power (although some are more risk-acceptant while others are risk-adverse). Following an expected utility-theory calculus, the decision to initiate war is ultimately a function of perceived relative strength. If a leader concludes its own state outpaces its enemy in power measures, there will be a greater willingness to start a conflict, since it is quite likely that victory will result. The theory of Realism dominates the behavioral framework both in selection of indicators (national-capability measures are used) and in making an argument for participation and expected victory:

The key leader would not, therefore, start a war or continue to fight in a war if he perceived the net expected result to be less than that of remaining at peace or surrendering to the adversary. Of course, this does not mean that he must expect his nation always to win its wars. Rather, he must expect it to win or at least not to lose more than the leader believed would be lost without the war.[6]

This illustrates the male perspective described by Tannen, who states that men engage the world in a hierarchical social order in which people try to achieve and maintain the upper hand and to protect themselves from being put down or pushed around. Life is a contest, a struggle to preserve independence and avoid failure. For women, life is a community, a struggle to preserve intimacy and avoid isolation. According to Tannen, women's hierarchies are of friendship rather than of power and accomplishment.[7]

Using data on all wars from 1816 to 1974, Bueno de Mesquita found that of 251 conflicts between a pair of countries the initiator had positive expected utility much of the time, while the opponent did not; this was true in both the nineteenth and twentieth centuries. The situation was the same in Europe, the Middle East, Asia, and the Western hemisphere—no cultural differences were noted.

Some of the psychological underpinnings associated with male behavior and motivations seem to be documented in the evidence provided by Bueno de Mesquita. Machiavellian principles rule supreme here, and the danger is that these are treated as generalizations of international politics, when they actually may reflect mind-sets of male leaders. Where might women fit into this picture? Differences between nations' experience in war might be noted if comparisons between men and women leaders were made or if connections were drawn between war initiation strategy and leader gender. Of course, the small number of cases in the female group would render statistical assessments rather limited, but at least some tabular data could be offered for evidence.

A second type of Behavioral-oriented understanding of international politics has turned away from Realism as the central organizing concept and followed a strategy of collecting a large number of attributes of states, and domestic conditions within them, to understand why some states come into conflict with others. A pioneering study was conducted by Lewis Fry Richardson and published as *Statistics of Deadly Quarrels* in 1960.[8] One of his conceptions was that all deadly quarrels arise from measurable conditions and relations between people. Richardson treated various actions, scattered in time and place, as expressions of the quarrel phenomenon. International wars, city riots, and single murders, though differing in political, social, legal, and ethical aspects, are all manifestations of aggressiveness. His initial premise might have led to an appreciation of gender differences in discovering, for example, that in deadly domestic quarrels women lose their lives more often than men, and his list of variables could have reflected this factor in broader levels of conflict. However, his subsequent collection of data, while extremely rich in detail, ignores the woman variable altogether. In order to manage the scope of his research, he excluded all situations where fewer than 300 people had died. This systematically eliminated crimes of domestic violence and reduced dramatically the possibility of observing gender variation in conflict participation.

Richardson believed that the ostensible cause of quarrels derives from social relations of many types. Some relations might be important in preventing conflict, others could be their cause. He asserted that trade between countries would encourage peaceful conditions but that fear developing out of hostile relations might cause war or encourage submission and that leaders who felt insecure might be more willing to initiate conflict, while confident leaders would behave more cautiously. He created three categories for evaluating the effects of social relations on conflict potential: situations making for amity, for ambivalence, and for enmity. Comparing pairs of actors, he found that amity was a result of intermarriage, similar bodily characteristics, similar dress customs, common level of wealth or poverty, and common government, which tended to prevent civil and local wars. The absence of these things increased the likelihood of conflict. Enjoyment of fighting, exceptional nationalistic pride, and personal resentments were some of the items that encouraged conflict.[9]

Among the facts discovered from his study of conflicts, including both civil uprisings and international global wars occurring between 1820 and 1949, are that world population increases seem not to have been accompanied by a proportionate increase in the frequency or severity of war, as would have been expected if belligerency had been constant. He thus concludes that "*man*kind has become less warlike since 1820."[10] Expected pacifying influences such as similarity of language, however, seem to have had little influence on the occurrence of wars, nor has common religion made for peace. Most wars are localized affairs, he discovered, and sharing frontiers with many other states increases a country's probability of war participation. Some of these data support the interpretation that social contact breeds cooperation, while others lend support to the counterproposition, namely, that social contact breeds contempt.[11]

The most notable feature of the Richardson approach is the sensitivity to social differences in people and it is rather surprising that he missed the gender variable. He might easily have incorporated matriarchal-run societies versus patriarchal ones, or differing national attitudes of social status and rights for each sex. He could have looked at women participants in the social world and provided more information about subgroups in his warring-factions data. But his approach was on the right track.

The Dimensions of Nations (DON)[12] project is another example of a large data-collection exercise to delineate the major differences between nations on their attributes and foreign-conflict behavior. After compiling an original list of about 600 variables, Rudolph Rummel chose a core set of 230 indicators that he hoped would encompass a wide array of social phenomena, including the domestic and international characteristics of eighty-two nations. The data are grouped under twenty-seven categories. These categories ranged from "arts and culture" to "colonialism," from "trade" to "conflict behavior." Each of these categories contains a series of indicators. The category "agriculture," for instance, included an indicator of the percentage of workers in agriculture. What is truly remarkable, however, is that of more than 200 variables only two are related to gender! These are grouped under "values": the percentage of students who were females and the percentage of workers who were females.

Rummel's particular attribute approach in quantitative international politics does not have an overt framework of Realism behind it, but many of the factors support a power-politics orientation, at least covertly. Although not exclusively focused at the state level nor devoted exclusively to war, but interested in broadly defined conflict, nation-state concepts and war do in fact become important in the analysis. It would be far easier to fill in the women participants in the social community and their relationship to conflict in studies like these, though, than in the COW project, since the preoccupation with indicators and looser reliance on a specific theory for guidance allows for greater flexibility in the attempts to explain international conflict. As one example, subdividing indicators into separate male/female statistical scores, such as the percentage of women who are agricultural workers, would yield valuable information on the relation between country attributes and foreign conflict behavior.

The final group of studies considered in this assessment are those devoted to decision making, that is, theories that seek to understand foreign policies of states through the perspective of national leaders. This approach delineates the orientation, perceptions, images, and world-views of political leaders by extracting data from their writings and speeches, which form the "observable" information for data analysis and evidence gathering. Such research looks mostly at times of crisis and attempts to understand how different decision makers behave and what attributes of their personality and perception emerge in crises. A major project, focused on the outbreak of World War I in 1914[13] was undertaken with these ideas in mind. The memos, diaries, telegrams, reports, and other documents prepared by the leading foreign policy makers in England, Russia, Austria-Hungary, Germany, and France were subjected to content analysis as a way to extract themes and perceptions of enemies, allies, and the probability of war. Among the main discoveries from the analysis was that as World War I became more imminent, perceptions of hostility that these countries held toward one another became more intense. Information received in a foreign office was interpreted more negatively. This proposition about perceptions of hostility has become a general principle of international relations, even though all of the decision makers were men. By behavioral principles, however, tested hypotheses emerge from the existing picture (all policy makers were men), not from a hypothetical world. The analysis and conclusions were entirely appropriate following scientific methodology.

More recently, a study explored leadership performance in crisis.[14] Some of the central figures from the cold war were subjects in the analysis—U.S. presidents and leaders of the former USSR—who were compared with important nineteenth-century European politicians. All of them were men. The conclusion, that a leader's ability to deal with complexity and see a myriad of forces and options in policy making when facing threats, seemed to be a function of prolonged career success. This would be an ideal situation for testing gender differences; specifically, do women or men in similar positions manage complexity to the same degree and in the same way? How would this be related to their inherited abilities or learned behavior? Sadly, although the authors call for further research on the complexity-in-crisis problem, they fail to take notice of the gender factor and how it might be incorporated into their main theory design. It would be an easy step.

EXCLUDING THE GENDER VARIABLE

From this brief overview, it is clear that women have not figured at all in quantitative Behavioral international politics research. Gender has been ignored in variable lists and hypothesis selection and in theoretical explanations of conflict and peace. There are several reasons for this. First, the essence of science is to report what *is*, not what ought to be. The dearth of women in high-level foreign policy positions means that gender pales as a meaningful variable. Second, the overwhelming dominance of the nation-state in most international politics theories has led to a focus on state-level variables rather than descriptions of conditions and differences within societies. The state has been seen as a unified actor historically, usually pursuing a common goal such as power. Third, the emphasis falls on quantifiable evidence, in line with scientific norms. Alternative visions of preferred situations of international politics are not imagined in a standard scientific study. Fourth, the categories of concepts and key variables are derived almost always from conventional terms and ideas of traditional analysis such as Realism. Innovative thinking plays a secondary role and gender variables would be part of that revised perspective. Lastly, self-defined feminists are not Behavioralists so there has been no revolutionary or ideological zeal to define this component in the field. Mostly, the Behavioralists have assumed that meaningful gender differences do not exist at the level of leadership.

Who participates in war? How do state leaders behave at times of crisis? What kind of leader personality makes for what kind of world? All of these questions have been addressed, using men only, because there have generally been only men in positions that seem to matter for world politics. The number of instances of women in such roles is too limited for complete, methodologically appropriate comparisons for drawing statistically significant conclusions.

Thus, if war is a man's game and Behavioral theories of international politics are largely linked to war, then we have propositions about male play parading as facts of world politics. Sam Keen, in *Faces of the Enemy,* writes that, with few exceptions, women have never organized or taken part in systematic violence. They have seldom been warriors; there has been no matriarchal society in which women organized mass violence against other societies. The male, by contrast, has been conditioned to protect and defend his tribe or nation against all enemies. Society molds men into warriors who perceive the world as hostile and territorial.[15] This breeds a belief in power politics in international relations and explains the dominance of Realism theory.

This conclusion seems so obvious and simple, why was it not recognized before? For one thing, gender bias has never been analyzed in Behavioral theories. Perhaps this is because there are very few women scholars who specialize in this approach to international politics. Those who do have tried to fit in, to teach courses and write books just like everybody else. They have chosen to emphasize the dominant, not dissident, strains in their empirical and theoretical work. They have not analyzed "women" as a variable.

Since women were excluded from the variable lists of Behavioralism, and there were other factors that did account for the differences in war or peace behavior, there appeared to be little reason for taking the gender issue seriously. So it was ignored. The main issue seemed to be, how do we quantify national capabilities (borrowing from Realism)? rather than, should we include all those easy-to-measure variables (like gender)? Behavioralists have not counted the percentage of women in foreign policy leadership posts, of women in the military, of women who negotiate international deals, of women peace activists, or of women delegates to international organization conferences. Nor have they tested for correlations between these features and consequences in politics.

Do women make different decisions than men? As women become more prominent in foreign policy circles, do state policies change? By scientific evidence criteria, we simply do not know. As the world changes and nationalism, dependency, and feminism become more important, as themes of equality, of development, and of peace assume greater significance in world politics, then sets of variables defining sex differences and consequences will become part of Behavioralist theory and theory testing. Once a gender sensitivity is introduced, many currently accepted truths of international relations may prove unsupportable.

CONCLUSION

For some reason, Behavioralism and gender-based studies never connected. This is odd, for the people who first engaged in Behavioralism were younger and came of age at a time of feminist consciousness-raising. Behavioralists' theories, however, are mainly status quo theories. Older, longstanding theory premises usually dictate what ideas the scientist is geared to examine. These all exclude the gender factor. The dominance of

Realism has meant that models of peace are few when compared to models of war. Peace, like women, appears to be part of the periphery of international relations. International politics, according to Behavioralists, consists of the collection of nation-state foreign policies—actions of governments in the global arena. This excludes most activity of women.

Betty Reardon has called for an integration of feminist scholarship with international peace research in order to abolish sexism and war—both phenomena depend on violence, she asserts. Her position is that the masculine mind tends to reject the sphere of feelings, and that the masculine scientific approach depersonalized the process of political change, obscuring it with the "objective" analysis of social science. The distortion of science, resulting in a separation of human and ethical concerns, has fractionated knowledge, fragmented experience, and reduced the significance of intuitive and imaginative capacities.[16] This has created an effect whereby the subject of women becomes secondary to the central concern of peace.

Should it be surprising that Behavioral theories of international politics have continued to ignore gender? The tradition of feminist thought comes from social commentary, radical theorizing, critical perspectives on society—all are far from the normal interests, reading patterns, or general curiosity of the scientists. Moreover, nearly everyone in Behavioral international politics is a man. Women in this particular subfield—in the best tradition of scientism—have been scientists first (accepting status quo theory, relying on old variables) and not "gender-variable" conscious simply because they are women. Basically, little thought has been given to this special perspective.

From Betty Friedan to Gloria Steinem to Germaine Greer to *Ms.* magazine to NOW, the pillars of consciousness raising did not constitute extracurricular reading for the Behavioralists. World politics analysis meant indicators, variables, statistical tests, graphs, figures, tables, numeric presentations on things that mattered, things that scientists believed defined political life in the global arena. In this, the scientists' approach constantly reinforced the idea that women and gender issues were peripheral to foreign policy understanding.

In the post–cold war world, a period of ideological reordering, new geographical boundaries, shifting alignments, and new symbols of identity, theories of international politics may also change. Today there is an awareness of the gross discrepancies between the economic conditions of women and the real privileges accorded to them. These changes are likely to contribute to the agitation for equal rights for women in public life and equal roles in economic and political activities. Such broad considerations will determine whether and how the "woman" variable enters into behavioral analysis of international politics in the future. Aside from this, the contributions that women—as women—can make to foreign affairs will be important in theory development. As issues of food, population control, physical quality of life, and informal sector employment become subjects for international conferences and negotiations, then gender will assume some role in theories of international politics.

Scientific theories have not been "people" centered, but state centered. Concepts like alliances, negotiations, war, crises are mostly derived from the Realist paradigm. Gender is an obvious variable candidate—it is unambiguous, clear for counting. But it has been excluded, maybe because there are no women in the system routinely, regularized, and well represented. Rather, women enter sporadically, and there are few cases. Women are anomalies; this makes a poor case for scientific theory testing.

If one operates on the assumption that gender *is* significant as a central variable in international politics, then most of the theory conclusions and evidence (which exclude any reference to the gender issue) can be dismissed. This is because it is *assumed* that women in similar situations *would* act differently. However, if one believes that gender is *not* significant, then the current conclusions may be accepted as true. Both positions remain valid until empirical evidence relating to the gender variable is carefully collected and analyzed.

Since this factor has been ignored until now, scientific study has a way to go to catch up with changes in thinking and in conceptualizations of world politics—including definitions and attributes of "national capabilities." Fortunately, the developed ideas in normative theory and Feminism have generated an array of interesting propositions and speculations that could be subjected to scientific testing. Behavioralist research on women and international politics has many possibilities. Do women make a difference? Only systematically drawn evidence will permit us to discover the truth.

NOTES

1. Betty Friedan, *The Feminine Mystique* (New York: Norton, 1963), and Heinz Eulau, *The Behavioral Persuasion in Politics* (New York: Random House, 1963).

2. Deborah Tannen, *You Just Don't Understand: Men and Women in Conversation* (New York: Ballantine, 1990), 23–48.

3. Frank Klingberg, "Studies in Measurement of the Relations among Sovereign States," *Psychometrika* 6:6 (December 1941): 335–52.

4. J. David Singer and Melvin Small, *The Wages of War, 1816–1965: A Statistical Handbook* (New York: Wiley, 1972). See also, J. David Singer and Paul F. Diehl, eds., *Measuring the Correlates of War* (Ann Arbor: University of Michigan Press, 1990).

5. Bruce Bueno de Mcsquita, *The War Trap* (New Haven: Yale University Press, 1981).

6. Ibid., 29.

7. Tannen, *You Just Don't Understand,* 23.

8. Lewis Fry Richardson, *Statistics of Deadly Quarrels* (Chicago: Quadrangle Books, 1960). See also, David Wilkinson, *Deadly Quarrels: Lewis F. Richardson and the Statistical Study of War* (Berkeley: University of California Press, 1980).

9. Richardson, *Statistics,* 19–27.

10. Ibid., 167.

11. Ibid., x–xiii.

12. Rudolph Rummel, *The Dimensions of Nations* (Beverly Hills, CA: Sage, 1972).

13. Known as the Stanford Studies in International Conflict and Integration, the principal investigator was Robert North. A bibliography of publications can be found in Francis W. Hoole and Dina A. Zinnes, *Quantitative International Politics: An Appraisal* (New York: Praeger, 1976), 514–19. Two women, Nazli Choucri and Dina Zinnes, both widely respected scholars in this field, were associated with this project.

14. Michael D. Wallace and Peter Suedfeld, "Leadership Performance in Crisis: The Longevity-Complexity Link," *International Studies Quarterly* 32:4 (December 1988): 439–51.

15. Sam Keen, *Faces of the Enemy: Reflections of the Hostile Imaginations* (New York: Harper & Row, 1986).

16. Betty Reardon, *Sexism and the War System* (New York: Teachers College Press, 1985), 76, 79.

❖ 4 ❖

Pluralist and Critical Perspectives

Francine D'Amico

So far in this book, we have examined the Realist perspective, a Feminist critique of that perspective, and Behavioral approaches to the study of world politics. Before Feminist theorists like J. Ann Tickner criticized the Realist vision of international relations as incomplete and inaccurate, Pluralist theorists and Critical theorists offered alternatives to Realism. Both promised to provide a more inclusive explanation of the range of activities that constitute world politics than Realist theory offers, yet neither has systematically incorporated women or gender into these "inclusive" perspectives. In this chapter, I sketch Pluralist and Critical perspectives, pointing out how each challenges the Realist perspective. I consider why each has neglected the experiences and voices of women and the concept of gender in attempting to explain world politics, and then I suggest how these perspectives might include a discussion of the roles of women and address the concept of gender.[1]

THINKING ABOUT THEORY

In simplest terms, a *theory* is an explanation. All theories try to describe or explain something by simplifying the complex. In doing so, the theorist is selective: What is important to describe and explain? What isn't? Theorists of world politics differ in how much they simplify and in what they select in building their theories. How does the theorist decide what to simplify, what to select? Why do many theorists not select women or gender?

How, for instance, did Realist theorists make their choices? They did so by drawing on their particular experiences and concerns. Others accepted and popularized the Realist perspective because it fit their experiences and concerns as well. A *perspective* is a point of view about what "counts" and what doesn't in trying to come up with an explanation or *theory* of world politics.

Realist theorists typically expound this vision of world politics during a time of international conflict or tension. For example, let's examine the work of Hans Morgenthau and Kenneth Waltz, who are recognized as two main proponents of this perspective. Morgenthau published *Politics among Nations* in 1948, just after World War II and as the cold war between the United States and the USSR was beginning. Waltz published *Man {sic}, the State, and War* in 1959, during a tense period of the cold war, following the stalemated settlement of the Korean conflict and as the confrontation between the West and the Chinese and Vietnamese in Asia grew.[2]

Who does the theorizing? Realist theorists are predominantly men—and, generally, men from the educated elite in "First World" or economically developed societies.[3] They may well see the world from a particular perspective, one in which power defined as domination is central. Realist theorists like Morgenthau and Waltz are typically well educated, white, male citizens of the United States, one of the most powerful states in that world of power. These authors are thus at the top of intersecting race, gender, and international hierarchies, as are many of the academics, diplomats, and politicians in their audience.[4] From their vantage point, we get the "view from the top of the world," as it were.

Of course, not all scholars who promote or accept this theoretical perspective share these same characteristics. Nor is Realist theory uniform; there are many variants. But in the main, theory reflects the perceptions and circumstances of its creators. People who are not similarly situated and privileged are likely to see quite a different world.

Pluralist and Critical theorists see the world differently from Realists. Do their alternative visions of world politics include women or gender? Or do they also merit J. Ann Tickner's observation that "too often women's voices have been silenced by traditional theory that draws on politically powerful men's understandings as a source for comprehending and managing state behavior"?[5] I turn now to those two perspectives. Table 4.1 provides a comparative summary of the central assumptions and features of the different perspectives on world politics that we are discussing.[6]

THE PLURALIST PERSPECTIVE

The first critique of the Realist perspective that I will examine is the Pluralist view. This perspective is called "Pluralist" because it sees many types of entities instead of one single type of actor in world politics. Where Realists see *states* as the central and only significant actors on the world stage, Pluralists argue that, while states are important, many other actors

Table 4.1
Perspectives on World Politics

	Realist	Pluralist	Critical	Feminist
Actors	States	States, IOs, MNCs regimes	Classes, Social Mvmts	People
System	Anarchy	Community	Hierarchy	Multiple Hierarchies or Patriarchy
Character	Independence	Interdependence	Dependence	Multiple Relations
Problem solving	Military Power	Negotiation Law Military Power	Consciousness Organization	
Focus	Conflict	Conflict/ Cooperation	Context/ History	
Issues	"High" war/security	"High/Low" war/security human welfare environment	Political Identity Epistemology Ontology Axiology	

engage in and affect world politics. In addition to states, Pluralists urge us to examine *suprastate* actors such as international organizations (IOs) where states are members, like the United Nations. Some Pluralists also recommend that we study *nonstate* actors, such as multinational corporations (MNCs) like IBM, and transnational or nongovernmental organizations (NGOs) like Amnesty International. They assert that these organizations and institutions are part of a complex "web" of international relations. So if all the world's a stage, as Shakespeare wrote, states may have the starring roles, but there is a whole supporting cast to consider, say the Pluralists.[7]

Just as there are a variety of Realist theories, Pluralists offer a range of theories as well. Some share the Realists' concern with the power that states have, while others envision the emergence of a world government. What Pluralists have in common is a core belief in a "multicentric" world politics where more than states count. Secondly, they challenge the Realist assumption that we can think of the state as a unified actor, making policy according to a rational decision-making process. Pluralists encourage us to consider how policy decisions are made and who is doing the decision making, what leaders' perceptions and misperceptions are, and how these shape not only leaders' policies but world politics as well.[8]

But perhaps the clearest disagreement with Realist theory comes in the behaviors that Pluralists think we need to focus on. As Peter Beckman pointed out in chapter 1, Realists see *conflict* (including war) as the defining characteristic of world politics. Realists argue that conflict is a consequence of an anarchichal international system; there is no government above independent states. Wait a minute, says the Pluralist. What about the many examples of cooperative behavior among states? How do you explain the longstanding friendship between nations like the United States and Britain, or the United States and Australia? And there were certainly many other things happening in the 1940s and 1950s when, for example, Morgenthau and Waltz were developing their explanations of world politics. A Pluralist might note the founding in those years of international organizations like the United Nations (1945) and the European Community (1957), the beginning of a revolution in global communications, and the expansion of multinational corporations. But Realist theorists focused on conflictual interstate relations, especially war. From the Realist perspective, this is what "counts" when we want to describe and explain what's going on in the world. Realist theory, say its Pluralist critics, misses much of world politics with this narrow focus on conflict.

Pluralists see and seek to explain instances of both *conflict* and *cooperation*. For example, Pluralists might point to the signing of the North American Free Trade Agreement (NAFTA) by Canada, the United States, and Mexico, as evidence that regional integration and cooperation are also crucial in world politics. During the long years of the cold war, even the rival superpowers conducted high-level diplomatic negotiations in a conscious effort to avoid war. Indeed, one Pluralist analyst of world politics has observed that most behaviors in world politics are cooperative, but that conflict, like disaster on the evening news, gets the headlines.[9] Conflict remains important to the Pluralist; indeed, conflict avoidance, management, and resolution are the focus of much of the activity of states and of international organizations like the United Nations. But war is not the whole drama of world politics, say the Pluralists.

Where Realist theorists see *anarchy* as the central characteristic of an international system of *independent* states, some Pluralists see a system of *interdependent* states. "Interdependence" means a situation in which two or more states are mutually or reciprocally dependent upon one another. The dependence is shared but not always symmetrical or equal. What happens in one state—particularly regarding economy or ecology—has costly effects in other states. For example, the explosion of the Chernobyl nuclear power plant in the Soviet Union in April 1986 and the continuing acid rain in Canada caused by sulfur dioxide emissions of U.S. industries illustrate this mutual dependence. These costly effects may be more or less immediate, which is expressed by the term "sensitivity," and more or less costly, which is described by the term "vulnerability."[10]

Pluralists thus see in world politics more than just the Realists' concern for the "high politics" of war, security, and military power. Pluralists also see the issues of so-called low politics, such as the economy, the environment, and human welfare. For example, Pluralists see recent international conferences such as the "Earth Summit" in Rio de Janeiro, Brazil, in June 1992, and the Human Rights conference in Vienna, Austria, in June 1993, as evidence that the *agenda* of world politics includes important issues that the Realists neglect.

The most optimistic Pluralists—among them, individuals envisioning a world government—even go so far as to describe the world system as a *community*. These Pluralists herald international organizations of which states are members, such as the UN, as institutions in which the common interests of the members can be served. For example, these Pluralists argue that cooperative management of the "global commons"—our shared resources of air and water—is in everyone's interest, so that national interests coincide with the collective good much of the time.[11] Those common interests are discovered through discussion in meetings of international organizations like the UN General Assembly.

In looking for cooperation, Pluralists seek to discover the mechanisms of cooperation and the peaceful settlement of conflicts. Negotiation, the creation of international law and its application by the International Court of Justice (the "World Court"), and the collective problem solving undertaken by the UN Security Council become important for Pluralists. Pluralists argue that as interdependence grows, military power is still important, but less so, because there are many situations in which the use of force would accomplish nothing or would not be considered.[12] For example, it is difficult to imagine the United States threatening or using force against Canada or Israel to achieve a policy goal. Even among rivals such as the superpowers, the importance of military power changed, as both became mutually dependent upon the other for survival in a nuclear world.

Pluralists have suggested that world politics has created rules of state behavior. When a set of rules emerges regarding a particular issue, Pluralists say that a *regime* has emerged. Regimes are "networks of rules, norms, [institutions,] and procedures that regularize behavior and control its effects." They are the "rules of the game"[13] of world politics. Many of these rules are commonly agreed upon and understood; some rules are explicitly agreed to in writing in formal treaties.

One example of a regime is the international free-trade regime, where rules of the game are set in bilateral negotiations between two states, as in recent meetings between U.S. and Japanese government officials, and in multilateral negotiations among many states, as in the recently concluded "Uruguay round" of the General Agreement on Tariffs and Trade (GATT).

Another example is the nuclear weapons nonproliferation regime, which has produced the Nonproliferation Treaty (NPT) and has established the International Atomic Energy Agency (IAEA) to inspect and evaluate state compliance with the terms of the treaty.

Some Pluralists assert that the central rule in international relations is that states respect the territorial integrity and political sovereignty of other states. Violators of this rule are labeled "aggressors" and may be punished by the community in a number of ways, ranging from severance of diplomatic ties to economic sanctions to military enforcement action, as in the Iraq-Kuwait war. *Most* members of the international community obey the rules *most* of the time—including this fundamental rule—argue the Pluralists, because it is in their interest to do so. Thus, suggests the Pluralist, states can avoid the Realist vision of "each against all" of power politics and achieve meaningful *collective security.* That is, the community of nations can work together to prevent or to end aggression against any one of their number: "All for one and one for all." Members of the UN who expelled Iraqi forces from Kuwait is an example.

How did this challenge to Realist theory emerge? When is Pluralist theory produced? As I pointed out above, cooperative actions such as the creation of the European Economic Community can occur at the same time as deepening cold war conflicts. But I would suggest that Pluralist visions emerge and find receptive audiences when there are two kinds of interrelated conditions: when there is a relaxation of tension (a situation of détente) and when there has been a debilitating conflict (such as a world war) that calls into question the utility of war and the ability of states to survive.

For example, on January 8, 1918, Woodrow Wilson offered a positive vision of world politics in presenting his "Fourteen Points" for peace. The centerpiece of his proposal was the establishment of an international organization, called the League of Nations, to pursue the common good and to provide collective security. Thus, the lesson that Wilson saw in the context of the bloody conflict of World War I was not the Realist conclusion that "might makes right" or that war is inevitable, but rather that nations must work together to avoid war's recurrence.

Some sixty years later, Robert Keohane and Joseph Nye wrote their influential *Power and Interdependence,* pointing out how increasing interdependence among states reduced the usefulness of military power and increased the role that international organizations, institutions, and regimes played in world politics. The context of the time supported this Pluralist vision: the end of the Vietnam war, détente between the United States and the USSR, and *rapprochement* between the United States and the People's Republic of China. Questions about how to manage a regionally and perhaps globally integrated economy and evidence of cross-national environmental damage and danger in the 1970s also supported the analysis offered by Pluralists. Now, in the 1990s, some believe that the end of the cold war and the rise of trading blocs like NAFTA support Pluralist interpretations of world politics.

Who does the theorizing? Like the Realist theorists discussed earlier, Pluralist theorists are predominantly men from the educated elite in the developed nations of the First World. Here we still have the "view from the top" of intersecting power hierarchies. Again, this is not to claim that all who support this perspective are similarly situated, but rather to point out that many of the key authors of this explanation of world politics write from a vantage point of relative privilege that shapes their vision of the world.

Pluralists share with Realists a concern with states as important actors and conflict as a part of world politics. Pluralists, however, also see—and hope for—cooperation and compromise between actors, or they see beyond conflict to other types of transnational activities already occurring, such as the exchange of people, products, and ideas that occurs with international migration, trade, and communications media. Thus, their vision of world politics is more optimistic or positive and more expansive than, though not fundamentally different from, that of the Realists.

What might Pluralist theory look like if we begin to ask "Where are the women?" and to analyze gender? In the Pluralist vision, the state's "national interest" and the "interest of the international community" frequently converge. State leaders are not simply power maximizers, as Realists assert, though some may have this goal. Leaders of different states may have different preferences and goals and may make different kinds of decisions in similar circumstances. Thus, from the Pluralist perspective, who the state leaders are does matter, because Pluralists do not assume that "the state" is a "unitary rational actor" as the Realists do. Considering how women leaders may behave similarly to or differently from men leaders would be a useful inquiry from this perspective.

In adding international organizations and institutions to the list of actors in world politics, Pluralists also create more places to look for women's political participation and their particular effect as women. For example, women are about a third of the personnel at the United Nations and are active in many transnational nongovernmental organizations.[14] And expanding the agenda of world politics to include issues relating to so-called low politics, such as the environment and human rights, also reveals more of the ways in which women participate in world politics because of their activism on these issues.[15]

Some Pluralist theorists such as Robert Keohane have acknowledged that inclusion of *women* may be important if we want to create a good explanation of world politics.[16] Writing in 1989, Keohane defined gender as "the institutionalisation of sex differences," which is the first definition of gender that we looked at in the introduction.[17] He thus focuses on *gender-as-difference,* which permits a discussion of a "feminine perspective." Keohane seems to see an increasingly interdependent world politics that favors people who are "identified with others" and "empathetic" rather than "individualistic and egoistic."[18] This suggests that women, as people who exhibit these characteristics (however acquired), may be the people whom world politics needs in order to negotiate, cooperate, and compromise. That is, women may be the rule makers and the peace makers.

Keohane thus welcomed the Feminist critique of international-relations theory because "women's experiences at the margin of political life have given them perspectives on social issues that provide valid insights into world politics."[19] However, Keohane asserted that "feminist perspectives are [not] necessarily superior in an absolute sense to traditional views— only that they contain valid insights into the complex realities of world politics."[20]

This conception sees the Feminist contribution to international relations theory as *additive* rather than *transformative*. Feminist critiques, in Keohane's interpretation, seem to *add women* to the study of world politics. Most Feminist theorists disagree with this interpretation. They argue that women's insights do not merely add to but fundamentally change the current explanations of world politics, as J. Ann Tickner explored in chapter 2 for Realist theory. Feminist theorists say that when we start looking for *women,* we find *gender*—in both its forms—and that gender analysis exposes the gender-based assumptions of the central perspectives on world politics.[21]

Seeing gender-as-difference is an important aspect of gender analysis, but so too is *gender-as-power*. This vision of gender examines the power relations constructed in particular ways in particular historical contexts. Gender-as-power seems to find no place in Pluralist theory. This is because, as Sandra Whitworth has explained elsewhere, Pluralism itself "is ahistorical and denies the material bases of conflict, inequality and power" and thus "fails to recognize the structural features of women's oppression."[22] In the Pluralist vision, women need only make their voices heard—they must network, get organized, form or join NGOs, get hired by and promoted in IOs—and then their perspective is added. This is a strategy of "bringing women in" to places from which they've been excluded in the past, and this is a necessary step.

But is "bringing women in" an easy task? What obstacles do women encounter in trying to make their voices heard? Other chapters in this book address this question in detail. A related question is, What will change when women's voices are heard? Will world politics be "business as usual," or will some fundamental changes take place as a result of the critique that women bring? Recall how J. Ann Tickner sought to redefine "power" in chapter 2. Would this new understanding of power change the kinds of policies that decision makers are likely to adopt?

What happens to Pluralist theory when we look at gender-as-power, when we take gender seriously as a category of analysis rather than look at it as merely another variable or individual characteristic?[23] Then we see international organizations in a different light, not as gender-neutral saviors of the world from conflict, but as gendered institutions, built upon and often reinforcing the distribution of power between men and women, as Nüket Kardam explains in chapter 10. For example, the founders of the UN focused on resolving interstate violence and not ending rape and sexual assault.

In thinking about gender-as-power, we see the growth of multinational corporations affecting women differently from men, as Geeta Chowdhry explains in chapter 11. And we can understand the construction of Pluralist theory itself as gendered, because the transnational relations that it focuses on are still those which occur in the "public" realm, the world of diplomacy and trade. In deciding what "counts" in world politics, Pluralists do not count women or consider gender because they ignore the "private" realm of transnational activities like bride selling and prostitution and the gendered nature of global factory work. Thus, the Pluralist perspective could "bring *women* in" to the study of world politics and could include the analysis of *gender-as-difference* but cannot achieve the level of analysis of *gender-as-power.*

THE CRITICAL PERSPECTIVE

A second alternative to the Realist perspective is the Critical perspective. The label "Critical perspective" encompasses a variety of classical Marxist, neo-Marxist, and non-Marxian theories, including dependency theory, uneven development, world-systems theory, structuralism, and many others. These theories are called "Critical" because each stands "apart from the prevailing order and asks how that order came about" and questions "the origins and legitimacy of social and political institutions."[24] This provides an opening for the analysis of *gender-as-power,* because it would lead us to question the origins of our ideas about *gender-as-difference.* Few Critical theorists, however, have undertaken gender analysis to date.

In general, Critical theorists emphasize the significance of the *context* in which world politics takes place. This context constrains and directs the choices and actions of people engaged in world politics. A leader of a Third World state might like to pursue a foreign policy independent from or in opposition to the United States, but cannot do so without risking severe political and economic repercussions (both personal and national). Seeking independence reveals the depth of dependency, as illustrated by the near collapse of the economy in Jamaica when the United States stopped buying sugar to punish the "anti-U.S. leftism" of Prime Minister Michael Manley. Manley's subsequent electoral defeat and new "moderate" policy orientation since his reelection demonstrate that context constrains policy choices.

Critical theorists also emphasize the *historical process* by which the current context or system has developed: They seek to explain how the system came to be and what it is becoming. The context is not static or "given" or "neutral" as the Realists and Pluralists seem to interpret it, but rather always dynamic and always politically significant. Critical theory perspectives on world politics are, then, both *contextual* and *historical*. Table 4.1, recall, summarizes these differences.

Critical theorists focus on the role of global *social movements* as forces that bring change to the current system of political-economic power. Some examples of social movements are the peace movement, the green movement, the civil rights movement, the human rights movement, the student movement, and the labor movement. Deborah Stienstra has analyzed international women's movements as agents of change. She characterizes social movements as "groups with a self-consciousness or awareness of being a group and having some level of organization, although not all members need participate in that organization."[25] Social movements differ from international organizations in that they have a lower level of formal, bureaucratic organization and have people, rather than states, as members.

Critical theorists assert that political and economic relations are impossible to analyze separately. They see the central characteristic of the international system as neither anarchy nor community but rather *hierarchy* in a "hegemonic order." Currently, this hierarchical order consists of *dominant* and *dependent* states. This hierarchy is based on each state's position in the global political economy or world system. From the Critical perspective, the hegemonic order provides a framework in which developed states dominate underdeveloped states.

Dominant or "developed" states are those with market-based, industrialized or postindustrial economies, such as the United States, Germany, and Japan. These "core" states of the "North" confront, manipulate, and dominate the underdeveloped states of the "periphery" or the "South." Dependent or "underdeveloped" states are those with preindustrial, newly industrialized, or divided economies, or are producers and exporters of primary products, such as Nigeria, Nicaragua, and the Philippines. These underdeveloped states do not merely need to "catch up" with developed states; rather, they have developed already in a particular way, as dependent states in the world economy: The wealth of the few depends upon the poverty of the many, according to Critical theorists.

The goal of the core states is to accumulate capital on a world scale— that is, to gain access to resources and markets and to earn profits. Initially, this was done through direct conquest or imperialism. Later, people of the colonies struggled for and obtained political independence, but their countries remained economically dependent upon former colonizers because of the structural features of their economies. Under this neoimperialism, the trade, production, and financial structures designed and put in place by former colonial masters constrain the choices of Third World leaders and peoples.[26]

One of the earliest Critical theories developed was Marxist theory, which emerged in the writings of Karl Marx and Friedrich Engels in the mid-1800s and of V. I. Lenin in the early 1900s. Marxists argued that their analysis was empirical and scientific in the sense that Karen Feste uses these terms in chapter 3. They claimed that their theory explained how world politics actually worked far better than Realist theory could because it did not separate political from economic relations.

Marxist theorists see the central actors on the world stage as two opposing *classes:* owners versus workers, rich versus poor, haves versus have-nots, with the class division replicated within each state and among all states in the North-versus-South structural framework. For Marxists, the central features of international relations are *conflict* between these classes, both within and between states, and *cooperation* (or potential cooperation or coordination) of working people and of states that are similarly situated in the capitalist world order in the struggle to achieve equality and justice.

What was the context for the development of Marxist theory? In the 1800s, poor and dangerous working conditions in urban factories and wages that kept workers living in poverty prompted Karl Marx to offer his critique of industrial capitalism. During World War I, theorists such as V. I. Lenin objected to the injustice of forcing or tricking working people into dying for causes like colonialism that would only benefit the ruling elites of society. The success of the Bolshevik Revolution in Russia held out the promise that humans could consciously and collectively construct a just and humane society. Since World War II, the decolonization of Africa and parts of Asia, the failure of economic development plans, the growth of the Third World debt crisis, and the rise of many social movements have given Critical theorists—both Marxist and non-Marxist—reason to construct alternatives to the visions offered by both Realists and Pluralists.

Marxism found acceptance among many working people and academics in Europe (and later in the colonial world), but did not find a receptive audience among U.S. scholars for a long time because of its call for radical political change and because its proponents experienced political persecution, as in the congressional "communist hunts" of the 1950s. Hostility to the Vietnam war on many U.S. campuses encouraged a variety of scholars to turn to Critical theories as a way of both understanding American interventionism and preventing its recurrence.

If we consider who is doing this type of theorizing, we find that the Critical perspective is based not in the experiences of those privileged in the powerful states central to the state system, but rather in the experiences of those who are themselves, in some way, on the outside or the "periphery." Many Critical theorists come from the South or Third World, such as Samir Amin or Fernando Henrique Cardoso and Enzo Faletto.[27] Others are from developed or "core" nations but have been political oppositionists or academics, usually from working or middle-class backgrounds, such as Marx and Lenin or contemporary Critical theorists Johan Galtung of Norway and R. B. J. Walker of Canada.

Contemporary critics of this perspective contend that the dissolution of the Soviet Union and the renunciation of a planned economy in the successor states and among Eastern European states invalidate the theory. They also see this perspective as only a partial explanation of world politics because it does not seem to address relations among powerful states or relations among Third World nations but, rather, focuses on relations between the North (developed states) and the South (underdeveloped states). But the Marxists might respond that the Realist focus on East-West relations obscured the real "power game" in world politics, the game of "king of the hill" played by the wealthy in each state and among elites of different states.

Critical theorists explicitly talk about what should be. That is, they offer a *normative* vision of what might be or what ought to be in addition to describing world politics as they see it operating currently. Furthermore, they often attempt to articulate what can be done to bring about this alternative vision. Critical theorists call for an end to the world system's hierarchy by means of political consciousness raising, organization, mobilization, civil disobedience, and, sometimes, armed revolution. Conflict and power remain parts of world politics, as in the Realist perspective. But Critical theorists see economic relations as the source of power and military power as a tool of economic dominance.

Unlike the Realists, some Critical theorists envision a future in which military power and perhaps also states themselves will be obsolete, a future where hierarchy becomes equality and conflict gives way to harmony. And unlike the Pluralists, Critical theorists are not content to build on the Realist vision. Critical theorists offer a *transformative* vision, a complete restructuring, to be accomplished through the challenges presented by global social movements to the existing order. For example, Realist theorists might argue that the end of the cold war, the breakup of the East bloc and the Soviet Union itself, and the rise of the so-called New World Order came about because the United States outspent and economically crippled the Soviet Union in the nuclear arms race. Critical theorists might consider the same events and point to the work of thousands of people in the democracy, human rights, labor, and peace movements as agents of these changes.

As is true for both the Realist and the Pluralist perspectives, the assumptions that underlie the Critical perspective give rise to a number of different theories or explanations of what happens and what "counts" in world politics. The central shared assumption of all theories from the Critical perspective is either that the economic takes primacy over the political or that economic and political are inextricably linked, as in the phrase "political economy."

In general, the Critical perspective provides an opportunity to talk about women and to incorporate gender into the analysis of world politics because, as Sandra Whitworth explains, Critical theory "attempts to theorize about historical variability, power, and the social construction of meaning."[28] Because the Critical theorist "stands apart from the existing order and asks how that order came about," there is room in the Critical perspective to ask how the construction of gender has shaped that order. But most Critical theorists have not yet incorporated gender into their analysis. Whitworth suggests that this may be because as a "newcomer" perspective in the academic community, the Critical perspective is itself "peripheral" and can't risk further marginalization through association with Feminist perspectives. Perhaps its proponents fear that if they take gender seriously their theory will not be taken seriously by the audience of mainly Realist and Pluralist theorists who serve as "gatekeepers" (tenured faculty, journal editors, conference conveners and participants) in the profession.

Critical theory, when it has paid attention to women at all, has analyzed woman-as-worker, woman-as-reserve-army-of-labor, and woman-as-reproducer-of-workers in the production process of the world capitalist system. Thus, some contemporary Critical theorists have looked at where *women* fit into their explanation of world politics, but they do not consider that their perspective may be shaped by their conception of *gender*. For example, in their focus on waged work as evidence of economic activity, Critical theorists miss the economic roles that women play in the "informal sector" or underground economy—such as street vendors, domestics, child-care workers, home health workers, and producers of food for family consumption rather than for market sale. If the political economy is peopled only by "owners" and "workers" who leave home and go to factories, earn cash wages, and join unions, then even most *women* remain invisible to the Critical theorist because most "women's work" happens in the "private" rather than the "public" economy.[29]

What would the Critical perspective look like if it were to take gender seriously? Some Critical theorists such as Maria Mies and Immanuel Wallerstein have worked to analyze the intersection of the hierarchies of gender and of the global economy. They focus on women in households as the support network that enables the capitalist to exploit the waged worker. They take their analysis further than did classic Critical theorists by asking how the social construction of gender makes this possible. That is, they examine the construction of women as "housewives."

But what of women who are not in the "household," that is, women who cannot be described as making an informal economic contribution in raising soon-to-be workers in the home, in traditional gender-appropriate roles and occupations? For example, what about the so-called hostesses hired by corporate executives to entertain foreign clients on business trips? Most

Critical theorists neglect the economic value of the hostesses' "product" of sexual service, yet surely the social construction of gender is at work here as well, with implications for world politics.[30]

Critical theorists almost grasp gender-as-power, but so far they have fallen short. Feminist theories focus on both gender-as-difference and gender-as-power and have much in common with Critical theories. As Table 4.1 indicates, both perspectives share a focus on *historical* and *contextual* analysis as well as on *normative* questions about what should be. Both seek to explain the dynamic of and to promote change in the theory of and practice of world politics. Both commit heresy in "the church of empirical social science" because both urge the examination of "questions about *political identity*—about who the 'we' is that engages in political life" and about "the historical construction of political practice," as Walker has written.[31]

Critical theorists and Feminist theorists both raise questions about *epistemology* or ways of knowing, that is, how we come to know what we think we know. Both reject the notion of "objectivity" and assert that all human knowledge is subjective, that is, contingent upon who is doing the observing, describing, explaining. Both also raise questions about *ontology* or being, and *axiology* or values/value judgments. An ontological focus on world politics asks: How did the current system of world politics come to be, and what is it becoming? An axiological focus asks: What values does the system privilege, protect, or promote? Which does it eliminate, ignore, or neglect?

Critical theorists and most Feminist theorists also agree that world politics is hierarchical. The Critical theorists see a hierarchy grounded in social relations, but define those relations narrowly as material or economic, missing bases of relations like gender and race. Some Feminist theorists argue that not one but several *hierarchies* exist, and that these complex, multiple hierarchies are based on sex/gender, race/ethnicity, class/caste, sexuality, ability, and age. They call these intersecting hierarchies *patriarchy* or capitalist patriarchy.

In exposing the "public"—and thus *political*—nature of women's so-called private work in the home, the Critical perspective opens the possibility of seeing other "private" activities and relations as political as well. It is possible, then, for Critical theory to analyze both *gender-as-difference* and *gender-as-power,* since it asks where social relations come from. But despite the common ground that exists between Critical and Feminist perspectives, few Critical theorists have yet taken gender seriously.

TOOLS FOR EVALUATING THEORY

So far in this book, we have examined theories drawn from a number of different perspectives on world politics: Realism, Behavioralism, Pluralism, and Critical Theory. Each offers different explanations of world politics because each is built upon different experiences and assumptions. How might we evaluate which of these perspectives best explains world politics? As a graduate student in a Ph.D. program, I was told that the criteria of a good theory are parsimony, explanatory power, falsifiability, predictive power, and normative value.

Parsimony means the ability to explain a lot with a little—in this case, to answer the "big questions" of world politics with as few variables as possible.

Explanatory power asks: How much of your research question have you answered? How much have you explained with the variables that you have identified, with your hypothesis about causal relationships?

Falsifiability means that you can think of a case that would prove your explanation wrong and that you would be willing to accept such evidence as a refutation of your hypothesis.

Predictive power asks: Can the theory predict what is likely to happen in the future as well as describe or explain what has happened in the past?

Normative value asks: Does the theory offer a vision of what the future *could* be, if changes are made in the present?

Realists might say that they focus on the "big picture" or explain only what is most important. For Realists, the "big question" in international relations is, Why does war occur? Their critics might rate Realist theories well as far as parsimony is concerned but might say that the theories fare less well on the other criteria because they explain little about what happens beyond interstate interaction and take what "is" as what should be— or fail to ask normative questions at all.

Realist theorists emphasize *continuity* in world politics; they focus on *structure*—the structure of the interstate system, the balance of power. This explanation of world politics is relatively *static:* states are (and always will be) the key actors, power is (and always will be) the central concern, war is (and always will be) the focal point of analysis. The balance of power may shift or destabilize temporarily, but it will reestablish itself. Realist theory describes and seeks to explain a narrow slice of world politics, much like a play synopsis gives only a brief summary of the significance of the drama. Realists tell us that what's important about world politics is international (interstate) relations, and that what's important about those relations is conflict.

Pluralists believe that they improve on the narrowness of the Realist vision. They sacrifice parsimony to increase the explanatory power of their theory. Pluralist theorists begin from the basic vision of world politics depicted by the Realists: They begin with states and add international and nongovernmental organizations; they begin with conflict and add cooperation. Here we get more detail, more of the story line and perhaps some of the dialogue of the play, but not much in the way of evaluation of the drama. The Pluralist perspective is essentially *additive*. Seeing conflict, the

Pluralists also look for (and find) cooperation; seeing states, they look for (and find) nonstate actors. The perspective is normative to the extent that it says we can and should control the conflict among nations. But it is only narrowly so, because it would change only some of the interaction among states, while the basic structures would remain, supplemented by new international institutions.

Critical theorists also sacrifice parsimony for explanatory power, and, they would argue, they provide such power to an even greater degree than do the Pluralists. Critical theorists emphasize *change* in world politics; they focus on *process*—not only what world politics is but also how it came to be and what it is becoming. This explanation of world politics is *dynamic,* or fluid. Critical theory is normative, with its focus on "counterhegemonic order" and alternative visions of what the world might be. Critical theory, then, considers what might be done better, like a play review. But its critics say it is low on predictive power because states have not "withered away" but have instead proliferated and because the Soviet Union and Eastern Europe's experiments with state socialism have failed.

What does Feminist theory offer? Feminist theory offers a critique of these very criteria of theory evaluation! Feminists might ask, Why emphasize parsimony if this means excluding many people's voices and experiences? Why privilege the male-centered scientism of criteria like explanatory power and falsifiability when these are constructed on gendered ideas about what is valuable and what is not?

So, do we want an explanation of world politics that is neat, easy, simple—"parsimonious"—but perhaps inaccurate and incomplete? Or are we willing to deal with an explanation that is messy, complex, and complicated but that acknowledges its shortcomings; reveals its assumptions, suppositions, and starting points; and provides a more expansive and complete picture of world politics? Many opt for parsimony. But as I see the world around me changing rapidly, I am less content with the simple vision of international relations as strategy, conflict, war, and destruction.

Like the Pluralists, I see integrative tendencies, like the formation of economic trading blocs (such as the European Community and NAFTA) and the movement of people, of products, and of ideas across national borders, with the allegedly omnipotent state seemingly powerless to stop or even to regulate the flow. Like the Critical theorists, I see the violence that the Realists miss: structural violence in the poverty and hunger of thousands in the First World and millions in the Third World. And like the Feminist theorists, I also see violence that both Realists and Critical theorists miss: physical and sexual violence in the lives of many people, especially women and children, and environmental violence wasting and destroying the earth's beauty and threatening the survival of not only human beings but of all species. And I see much transnational interaction that is not about violence at all: for example, nongovernmental communications networks. Seeing all these things, I ask: Why are the current theories of world politics silent on these? Can an explanation of world politics ignore these and still tell us anything worth knowing? Do we fix what's wrong with these theories if we include women's voices and experiences and undertake an analysis of gender? What do Feminist perspectives on world politics have to offer?

Realists see states; Pluralists see international and nongovernmental organizations, institutions, and regimes; Critical theorists see social movements and classes; Feminists see people enmeshed in a complex array of social relations. Mainstream theories of world politics see people either as "citizens" of a particular state (Realist) or "human" members of a world community (Pluralist), or as "workers" in a global economy, not as *simultaneously* citizens and humans and workers and partners and parents and so on; they neglect all other human relations beyond these formally acknowledged political identities. Feminists argue that people, not states, make world politics. In the chapters that follow, Sandra Whitworth examines a variety of Feminist theories as each might be applied to the study of world politics, and Hamideh Sedghi offers insight into the experiences of women of the Third World and the variety of perspectives that might be brought to bear on women, gender, and world politics.

NOTES

An earlier version of this chapter was presented at the 34th Annual Conference of the International Studies Association (ISA), March 23, 1993, Acapulco, Guerrero, Mexico; I am grateful to people who offered their comments and suggestions at the conference and to Peter Beckman, Zillah Eisenstein, and Robert Keohane for their insights. Responsibility for any errors of fact or analysis remains my own.

1. This analysis draws upon Sandra Whitworth's essay, "Gender in the Inter-Paradigm Debate," *Millennium: Journal of International Studies* 18:2 (1989): 265–72.

2. Hans Morgenthau, *Politics among Nations: The Struggle for Power and Peace* (New York: Knopf, 1948) and Kenneth N. Waltz, *Man {sic}, the State, and War: A Theoretical Analysis* (New York: Columbia University Press, 1959).

3. James N. Schubert, "Realpolitik as a Male Primate Strategy," (Paper presented at the 34th Annual Conference of the International Studies Association, Acapulco, Guerrero, Mexico, March 25, 1993), 7, 36 (Figure 1).

4. Some might contend that Professor Morgenthau, a Jewish refugee from Nazi rule in Germany, has not always been at the top of all these power hierarchies. His experience of powerlessness as a refugee may have contributed to his understanding of power as domination and, thus, to the formulation of his Realist perspective. Yet even as a German Jew, Morgenthau was not completely powerless: He was still relatively privileged in terms of gender and of socioeconomic class, as his education at some of the finest universities in Germany indicates.

5. J. Ann Tickner, "Foreword," in V. Spike Peterson, ed., *Gendered States* (Boulder, CO: Lynne Rienner, 1992), x.

6. See also Paul R. Viotti and Mark V. Kauppi, *International Relations Theory,* 2d ed. (New York: Macmillan, 1992), Table 1.1, p. 10, and Charles W. Kegley, Jr., and Eugene R. Wittkopf, *World Politics: Trend and Transformation,* 4th ed. (New York: St. Martin's, 1993), Table 2.1, p. 35. Neither text discusses Feminist perspectives on world politics.

7. The paraphrase is from *As You Like It* 2.7.140–67.

8. Viotti and Kauppi, 7–8, 15–16, 228–61.

9. Kalevi J. Holsti, *International Politics: A Framework for Analysis,* 6th ed. (Englewood Cliffs, NJ: Prentice-Hall, 1992), 12.

10. Robert O. Keohane and Joseph S. Nye, *Power and Interdependence: World Politics in Transition* (Boston: Little, Brown, 1977), 8–9, 12–15.

11. See Kegley and Wittkopf, *World Politics,* 297–386.

12. Keohane and Nye, *Power and Interdependence,* 23–29.

13. Ibid., 19.

14. See Kristen Timothy, "Women as Insiders: The Glass Ceiling at the United Nations," and Deborah Stienstra, "Organizing for Change: International Women's Movements and World Politics," Francine D'Amico and Peter R. Beckman, eds., in *Women in World Politics* (Westport, CT: Bergin & Garvey, 1995), chaps. 6 and 9.

15. See Petra Kelly, "Women and the Global Green Movement," Francine D'Amico and Peter R. Beckman, eds., in *Women in World Politics* (Westport, CT: Bergin & Garvey, 1995), chapter 11.

16. Robert O. Keohane, "International Relations Theory: Contributions of a Feminist Standpoint," *Millennium* 18:2 (1989): 245–53. Professor Keohane has told me that he dislikes the "pluralist" label applied to his work, but here I follow the typology of "images" of international relations categorized by Viotti and Kauppi.

17. Ibid., 248.

18. Ibid., 247.

19. Ibid., 245.

20. Ibid.

21. See Christine Sylvester, "Feminist Theory and Gender Studies in International Relations," *International Studies Notes* 16:3–17:1 (Fall 1991–Winter 1992): 32–38.

22. Whitworth, "Gender," 269.

23. V. Spike Peterson, "Introduction," in V. Spike Peterson, ed., *Gendered States* (Boulder, CO: Lynne Rienner, 1992), 17–18; Patricia Lee Sykes, "Women as National Leaders: Patterns and Prospects," in Michael A. Genovese, ed., *Women as National Leaders* (Newbury Park, CA: Sage, 1993), 225.

24. Mark Hoffman, "Critical Theory and the Inter-Paradigm Debate," *Millennium* 16:2 (Summer 1987): 231–49; quoted in Whitworth, "Gender," 269.

25. Deborah Stienstra, "Critical Theory and Feminist Movements in International Politics" (Paper presented at the 33d Annual Conference of the International Studies Association, Atlanta, Georgia, April 1–4, 1992), 6.

26. V. I. Lenin, *Imperialism: The Highest Stage of Capitalism* (Moscow: Progress, 1964); Johan Galtung, "A Structural Theory of Imperialism," *Journal of Peace Research* 8:2 (1971): 81–110; Immanuel Wallerstein, *The Modern World System* (New York: Academic, 1974); idem, *The Modern World System II* (New York: Academic, 1980); idem, *The Modern World System III* (San Diego: Academic, 1988); Samir

Amin, *Accumulation on a World Scale: A Critique of the Theory of Underdevelopment* (New York: Monthly Review, 1987).

27. Fernando Enrique Cardoso and Enzo Faletto, *Dependency and Development in Latin America,* trans. Marjory Mattingly Urquidi (Berkeley: University of California Press, 1979).

28. Whitworth, "Gender," 269.

29. See V. Spike Peterson and Anne Sisson Runyan, *Global Gender Issues* (Boulder, CO: Westview, 1993), especially 79–112.

30. See Cynthia Enloe, *Bananas, Beaches, & Bases: Making Feminist Sense of International Relations* (Berkeley: University of California Press, 1990), and idem, *The Morning After: Sexual Politics at the End of the Cold War* (Berkeley: University of California Press, 1993); Mayra Buvinic and Sally Yudelman, *Women, Poverty, and Progress in the Third World* (Washington, DC: Foreign Policy Association, 1989).

31. R. B. J. Walker, "Gender and Critique in the Theory of International Relations," in V. Spike Peterson, ed., *Gendered States* (Boulder, CO: Lynne Rienner, 1992), 189, 195, 197 (emphasis added).

5

Feminist Theories: From Women to Gender and World Politics

Sandra Whitworth

Feminists share a commitment to uncovering the activities of women and gender relations within world politics. This is important because so much of the study of international relations has assumed that women are naturally absent from world politics or that world politics is somehow gender neutral, or about neither women nor men but rather the ungendered activities of states in intermittent collision within an anarchic system. Feminists challenge this view and argue that much can be said about both women and gender relations within world politics.

However, just as there are many different approaches to the study of world politics, so too have different approaches to Feminist theory suggested different strategies for making women and gender relations visible within world politics.[1] Some Feminists seek merely greater empirical clarity about the role of women in international relations. Others argue that theories must be judged also by the contributions that they make to Feminist *praxis,* that is, to political action aimed at the actual transformation of relations of inequality between women and men. This chapter will critically assess three different approaches: Liberal feminism, Radical feminism, and Feminist postmodernism. I will argue that combining these theories into a Critical/Feminist or "gender-in-International-Relations" approach can develop a successful Feminist politics of international relations.

LIBERAL FEMINISM: BRINGING WOMEN IN

Liberal feminists argue that women have been excluded from many of the most important public spheres of modern social, political, and economic life. They aim, as Alison Jaggar writes, "to incorporate women into the mainstream of contemporary society."[2] Liberal feminists who examine women and world politics outline the extent to which women are underrepresented within traditional areas of international relations activity and seek also to show the ways in which women may overcome barriers to their participation. Maude Barlow and Shannon Selin, for example, have documented the underrepresentation of women in the arms-control-policy process in Canada and throughout the world. In Canada, no woman has ever been a director or deputy director of either the Arms Control and Disarmament Division or the Defence Relations Division of the Department of External Affairs. Further, it is only recently that Canada appointed a female Ambassador for Disarmament. The situation internationally is similar, with only five women occupying the approximately 800 key nuclear weapon decision-making positions identified by the Oxford Research Group worldwide.[3]

Reasons given for the underrepresentation of women in these positions are varied. One popular form of explanation is the socialization of women away from these activities. It is young boys, by this view, who are encouraged to play with guns and military toys, not little girls. By extension, then, arms control and security issues are "a man's topic," about which women are assumed to have neither interest nor expertise.[4] This view is illustrated well by the comments made by Ronald Reagan's White House Chief of Staff Donald T. Regan, when he said in 1985 that women would not be interested in the U.S.–USSR summit at Reykjavik, Iceland, because women could not comprehend "missile throw-weights and other unfathomables."[5]

The socialization argument is also used to explain women's underrepresentation in international decision-making bodies more generally. Betsy Thom suggests that many women within the United Nations system are less ambitious than men, having internalized society's expectations that they are not suited to policy-making positions. Moreover, she argues, women often face a double-day, balancing career and family responsibilities, thus limiting their opportunities for career advancement.[6]

Other explanations for women's underrepresentation look to systemic barriers to their participation. By this view, it is not simply the case that women lack the will to participate in the upper echelons of international relations activities, but that they are systematically discriminated against by men in authority who refuse to promote them and by legislation which limits their opportunities for employment, training, and so on.[7] Even those women who are successful must work harder to be taken seriously by their colleagues. As Jeane Kirkpatrick suggests in the companion volume, *Women in World Politics,* she failed to win the respect or attention of her male colleagues on issues of foreign policy because she was a woman. Proposals for change that emerge from Liberal feminism suggest that societal attitudes, the division of labor within the home, educational and career opportunities must all change before greater numbers of women enter international decision-making positions.

Clearly, it is important to document women's activity in traditional areas of international relations. Such information provides us with a rich data source to demonstrate the absence of women from the activities of world politics. There are, however, a number of problems associated with this form of Liberal feminism. For one, the call to "bring women in" to international relations assumes that women were not there in the first place.[8] That is, it accepts, along with "mainstream" International Relations (referred to elsewhere in this anthology as Realist theory), that the appropriate subject matter of world politics is the so-called high politics of security and peace issues, the *public* realm of policy making, conflict analysis, war and peace, and so on. This assumption neatly removes women, historically awarded the *private* sphere, from the political, and international relations, arena. As Joni Lovenduski writes:

The complication here is that there never was any way that the modern study of politics could fail to be sexist. Its empirical concerns have been almost exclusively those of the exercise of public power, aspects of political elites and aspects of the institutions of government. Such studies are bound to exclude women, largely because women usually do not dispose of public power, belong to political elites or hold influential positions in government institutions.[9]

Liberal feminists accept the distinction between public/private, political/nonpolitical, and thus accept the view that women have traditionally been excluded from international relations because war, diplomacy, and "high politics" have not been about issues which are of interest to women, specifically, children and families.

The Liberal feminist claim that the greater inclusion of women in the public and political realm of international relations will eliminate sexual inequality in this field ignores the structural features of social and political action. In other words, Liberal feminism accepts the prevailing power structures as legitimate. There is nothing, by this view, that is inherently unfair or unequal within politics or international relations (or the educational system, science, medicine or even corporate capitalism) except the historic exclusion of women from these spheres.[10] For Liberal feminists, once women are represented in numbers that correspond to their presence in the general population, equality will have been achieved. For many other Feminists, however, there are important features of the political system that help to sustain the inequality of women, regardless of their participation there. We turn now to these other Feminist critiques of International Relations.

RADICAL FEMINISM: WOMAN NURTURER

Radical feminists argue that relations of subordination and domination between women and men constitute one of the most fundamental forms of oppression.[11] Men seek to control women through controlling their sexuality, their roles in reproduction, and their roles in society more generally. Moreover, much of the way in which society is organized supports patriarchy or male rule, and is informed by a "masculine" worldview. When applied to the study of world politics, the Radical feminist perspective argues that this masculine worldview emphasizes conflict and neglects cooperation. This leads to many of the various "truisms" associated with the study of world politics. In this way, international relations scholars have assumed that foreign policy must be informed by an understanding of national interest defined by military power, and that military security ought to be the primary objective of the state. In a Radical feminist reformulation of these notions from a "feminine perspective," power is defined as empowerment and security as including development and ecological concerns. This is an important first step, according to Radical feminists, toward a better understanding of women and international relations.[12]

Much of the world politics literature developed from a Radical feminist perspective has been devoted to the study of women and war and peace. Unlike Liberal feminists, however, these writers are not concerned with documenting the *activities* of women in war and peace, but with outlining women's different *attitudes* toward war and peace. They argue that both war and peace would have been understood quite differently had it been women, and not men, dominating both the study and practice of international relations.

By and large, these writers suggest that because women are more peace loving, more nurturing, and more connected with life, it is they who may be our only hope of salvation in the nuclear age.[13] According to this view, the basis of wars in general and the nuclear-arms race in particular is masculine behavior. For some writers in this tradition, it is a biological inevitability that men are more aggressive, hierarchical, and territorial than women. Others deny any biological determinism and suggest instead that young boys raised in a society that devalues the work of women come themselves to devalue the attributes that they most closely associate with women: the nurturing, emotive, affective values learned from their mothers. In order to differentiate themselves from their mothers, young boys privilege their more aggressive, conflictual tendencies.

Young girls, by contrast, need not differentiate themselves from their mothers, and so may adopt many of her nurturing characteristics. As Sara Ruddick writes:

There is a real basis for the conventional association of women with peace. Women are daughters who learn from their mothers the activity of preservative love and the maternal thinking that arises from it. These "lessons from her mother's house" can shape a daughter's intellectual and emotional life even if she rejects the activity, its thinking, or, for that matter, the mother herself. Preservative love is opposed in its fundamental values to military strategy. . . . A daughter, one might say, has been trained to be unsoldierly.[14]

If it is masculine values that have created wars, then it is feminine values that can end them, by this view. Women not only privilege their more nurturing values, but as victims themselves of sexism they understand more fully than men the implications of war and militarism. Radical feminists join here with Liberal feminists and issue a call to "bring women in" to nuclear- and arms-control decision making. They do so, however, not to right the historic injustice of women's absence, but rather to bring women's more pacifistic views to international decision making.

Radical feminism makes a number of advances over the Liberal approach. For one, it rejects the distinction between public and private realms, embracing as it does the most important concept of the new women's movement: the personal is the political. In this way, it does not reproduce the Liberal feminist identification of the political with the public and appears, at least, to reject the notion that international relations is concerned solely with the "high politics" of security and war issues.

More important, Radical feminism points to a more profound epistemological critique of mainstream International Relations theory than does Liberal feminism. In demanding that we examine the specifically masculine bias brought to the study of world politics by men, Radical feminists underline the extent to which "theory is always *for* someone and *for* some purpose."[15] In this way, Radical feminists reject the assumption that social science methodology can ever be value neutral, and demand instead that all scholars, at a minimum, be explicit about the particular biases with which they operate.

The Radical feminist notion of a "feminine perspective," however, also has numerous limitations. For one, while it appears to widen the purview of legitimate world politics inquiry beyond those questions concerned solely with security and war, this is precisely the type of issue on which most radical feminists concentrate. While they explore these issues in a way far removed from that of traditional International Relations scholars, bringing in as they do the more personal analytical methods described here, their substantive focus thus far has been precisely the same as their more traditional counterparts, and it is as yet unclear just how widely they may begin to move the parameters of International Relations inquiry.

In addition, the epistemological critique is not as radical as it first appears, for while Radical feminists acknowledge the different "perspectives" that emerge from different material and historical conditions, they privilege the perspective of women over that of men. By virtue of her being oppressed, according to this view, a woman's "feminine perspective" provides her with a less distorted and more truthful account of the world than a man's "masculine perspective" can. Such a claim is tenuous at best, and directly contradicts the Radical feminist observation that theory is always *for* someone and represents *some* interests, whether they be gender interests, class interests, or race interests.

More importantly, the idea of a "feminine perspective" contrasts "woman" as nurturing, virtuous, and natural with "man" as aggressive, power seeking, and arrogant. This suggests that these differences are essential, fundamental, and unchanging. Such an essentialist view not only cannot be sustained empirically, ignoring as it does important differences amongst women (and amongst men), but it is dangerously apolitical.[16] As Lynne Segal writes: "A feminism which . . . insists upon the essential differences between women's and men's inner being, between women's and men's natural urges and experience of the world, leaves little or no scope for transforming the relations between men and women."[17] A biologically determined relationship between women and men fixes those relationships firmly across time, place, and culture. Feminist politics in this context becomes a concerted effort to limit the damage inevitably done, to make the best of a bad world, and to hope that the more peaceful norms of "woman" may one day inform the practices of international decision makers.

Other Radical feminists claim no biological determinism and argue instead that social practices such as mothering produce fundamental differences between women and men. They also universalize those practices, creating yet again an essentialist vision of feminine and masculine characteristics. One single activity such as mothering, by this view, produces the same characteristics in women and men across time, place, culture, class, race, and sexual orientation.[18] Except for a few incomplete attempts to imagine what might happen if men participated equally with women in parenting, these visions of masculine and feminine are practically inviolable, and the only politics left to Radical feminists is to privilege what previously has been made subordinate: the "feminine" values of nurturance, passivity, and peacefulness.

Indeed, the notion of "woman" described by Radical feminists not only ignores important differences among women, but it also reproduces exactly the stereotypical vision of women and men, feminine and masculine, produced under patriarchy: woman as emotional, passive, and nurturing; man as competitive, aggressive, and calculating.[19] Those women who do not fit the mold—who, for example, take up arms in military struggle—are quickly dismissed as expressing "negative" or "inauthentic" feminine values (the same accusation is more rarely made against men who demonstrate "inauthentic" values such as pacifism and nurturance).[20] Radical feminists find themselves defending the same account of women—as nurturing, pacifist, submissive mothers—that one hears from men under patriarchy, from antifeminists, and from the New Right. As some writers suggest, this in itself should give Feminists pause to reconsider this position.[21]

FEMINIST POSTMODERNISM: DECONSTRUCTING "WOMAN"

Largely as a response to the essentialism of Radical feminism, some Feminist scholars are pursuing a Postmodernist or poststructuralist approach. Many hail it as the most promising avenue for the development of a feminist international relations theory, and some suggest that it is the only viable place in which to locate such work.[22] Feminist Postmodernists take as their point of departure the attempt by Radical feminists to define *woman*. As Jane Flax writes: "Any feminist standpoint will necessarily be partial. Thinking about women may illuminate some aspects of a society that have been previously suppressed within the dominant view. But none of us can speak for 'woman' because no such person exists except within a specific set of (already gendered) relations—to 'man' and to many concrete and different women."[23]

Postmodernists reject the suggestion that subjects have an authentic core or essential identity. They argue that any attempt to define an individual must necessarily exclude some important feature of that person's identity in a way that will be constraining.[24] Radical feminists reject the definition of women made by men, but not the process of definition itself. In this way, according to Postmodernists, Radical feminists reinvoke the fundamental mechanism of oppressive power used to perpetuate sexism in their efforts to overcome it.[25]

A Feminist Postmodernist project aims at deconstructing the fiction of the category of "woman." *Deconstruction* entails exploring, unraveling, and rejecting the assumed naturalness of particular understandings and relationships. As Julia Kristeva writes: "A woman cannot be; it is something which does not even belong in the order of being. It follows that a feminist practice can only be negative, at odds with what already exists so that we may say 'that is not it,' and 'that is still not it.'"[26] Political struggle for the Feminist Postmodernist entails rejecting "everything finite, definite, structured, loaded with meaning, in the existing state of society."[27]

Postmodernist insights are useful in a number of ways. They seem first to hold out the promise of an increased freedom for women, not involving any preconceived gender identity as determined by either women or men. In this way, there is no single and generic "woman" of a particular class, race, and sexual orientation, but the possibility of many women crosscut by these and other differences. Second, and more importantly, Postmodernism begins to theorize the construction of gendered identities, highlighting the ways in which meaning is contingent and socially constructed.[28] The ways in which knowledge about gender relations is organized becomes the focal point for this type of analysis. This opens up the possibility, at least, of examining the way in which this knowledge is organized by international institutions and by the discipline of world politics itself.

Despite these advances, however, there are numerous problems associated with Feminist Postmodernism. Chief among these is the political paralysis that it creates. According to critics, if the category "woman" is fundamentally indeterminate, then there is no rational way in which a positive alternative or vision of an alternative world order can be suggested, for each such attempt can (and should, according to Postmodernists) itself be deconstructed.[29] Indeed, the very idea of feminism becomes highly problematic:

If gender is simply a social construct, the need and even the possibility of a feminist politics becomes immediately problematic. What can we demand in the name of women if "women" do not exist and demands in their name simply reinforce the myth that they do? How can we speak out against sexism as detrimental to the interests of women if the category is a fiction? How can we demand legal abortions, adequate child care, or wages based on comparable worth without invoking a concept of "woman"?[30]

This points also to the serious limitations involved in Feminist Postmodernist understandings of "social construction." While acknowledging that identities and meanings are never natural or universal, Postmodernists locate the construction of those meanings almost exclusively in the play of an ambiguously defined power, organized through discourse. This means that identities and meanings are constructed in the absence of knowing actors. More importantly, it means that there is very little that knowing actors can do to challenge those meanings or identities. The ways in which power manifests itself, the particular meanings and identities that emerge, seem almost inevitable. They are unrelated to prevailing material conditions or the activities of agents and institutions. Critics, then, may describe the play of power in the construction of meaning, but cannot participate in changing it.[31]

Postmodernists are equally postfeminist, a title that they sometimes adopt, for their analysis loses sight of the political imperatives that inform Feminism: to uncover and to change inequalities between women and men. As Ann Marie Goetz suggests, when many of the issues surrounding women and international relations are ones that concern the very survival of those women, Postmodernism's continued backpedaling and disclaimers are not only politically unacceptable but are, more importantly, politically irresponsible.[32]

CRITICAL/FEMINIST INTERNATIONAL RELATIONS:
FROM WOMEN TO GENDER

There are, then, a number of important problems associated with Liberal feminism, Radical feminism, and Feminist Postmodernism, but this is not to say that there is nothing of value in any of these attempts to produce a Feminist theory of world politics. Each makes a contribution toward uncovering the ways in which women have not been absent from international relations and the ways in which world politics have always been gendered. Combining the best of each theory will help us move from an examination of *women* to an analysis of *gender* in world politics. I call this combination "Critical/Feminist Theory," or a "gender-in-International-Relations" perspective.

Liberal feminists have underscored the absence of women from both the practice and study of international relations. This absence has been used in the past to defend the supposed gender neutrality of the study of world politics. Criticizing it is therefore important. Liberal feminists challenge that claim and effectively give voice to women scholars and previously silenced practitioners of world politics, as well as expand the boundaries of the field.

Similarly, Radical feminism not only challenges the assumption that mainstream International Relations theory has been produced in a value-neutral way, but also points to the importance of expanding the arena of legitimate inquiry in world politics beyond its traditional focus on war and peace. Along with other critics of this tradition, Radical feminism insists on exploring the constitutive elements of all international activity, not merely the surface appearance of interstate rivalry, which has been privileged through Realism.

Finally, Feminist Postmodernists have emphasized the ways in which identity and meaning are contingent and socially constructed. This is important in International Relations because it underscores the ways in which the topics that are considered important, the ways of posing questions, and the approach to studying them, are created rather than natural.

A Critical/Feminist account of world politics that is sensitive to *gender relations* should attempt to incorporate many of the insights of the above types of feminist theorizing while overcoming their limitations. Like Liberal feminists, we are interested in documenting the underrepresentation of women in particular spheres, or describing the unfair burdens borne by women as a result of particular legislative practices. An analysis sensitive to gender, however, calls for more than simply including women in areas closed to them, or righting previously unfair legislation, as Liberal feminists demand.

In part, *gender* means knowledge about sexual difference.[33] In examining gender as sexual difference, we begin to incorporate some of the insights generated by Radical feminists. We are interested, for example, in notions of masculine and feminine, but avoid any singular and essentialized vision of *a* feminine perspective. Instead, we ask: What ideas and practices about gender have been used to create, sustain, and legitimize the underrepresentation or unfairness we have documented, and where do these ideas come from? What ideas about the appropriate relationship between women and men, about the appropriate role of women in society, about what it is to be a man or a woman, feminine or masculine, inform the practices of particular actors and institutions? And what material conditions and social forces contribute to the reproduction of those practices? Finally, are material conditions such that attempts to alter those understandings and practices are facilitated or hindered?

A Critical/Feminist International Relations theory also, then, picks up on the Postmodernist idea that gender is a socially constructed inequality between women and men. However, this approach departs from Postmodernism and argues that understandings about what are considered appropriate relationships between women and men can be discovered through an examination of particular material conditions and the habits, practices, and discourses of particular international actors and institutions. Thus, meanings do not simply "emerge" from the play of power, but from the play of actors operating within particular circumstances. At the same time, and precisely because of this, these understandings are fluid and historically variable. They are not universalizable because they are constantly created anew and, more importantly, are often open to challenge.[34] Thus "social construction" can be discovered without slipping into the indefinite regress and political paralysis that characterizes Postmodernism.

A "gender-in-International Relations" analysis must explore how these notions are created, sustained, and legitimized by international institutions. Gender relations do not fall from the sky; they are socially constructed through the social definitions of gender as developed by women and men and as constructed in and affected by international economic and political institutions (among other things).[35] Robert Cox has written: "human institutions are made by people—not by the individual gestures of 'actors' but by collective responses to a collectively perceived problematic that produces certain practices. Institutions and practices are therefore to be understood through the changing mental processes of their makers."[36] To this it can be added that these institutions, practices, collective responses, and changing mental processes include understandings of gender relations. As Cynthia Enloe writes, contemporary power relations depend upon sustaining certain notions of male and female, masculine and feminine, and the appropriate roles associated with each.[37] It is this claim that informs the questions that we ask here.

"Gender-in-International Relations" accounts of women and war have already been developed. These seek not only to document the activities of

women during war, as Liberal feminists would do, or women's feelings
about war, as Radical feminists would do, but also to document the ways
in which governments and militaries use, and alter, prevailing understandings about gender for their own ends. Work in this area demonstrates a
coincidence of militarist and mysogynist rhetoric in mobilizing both
women and men to perform various wartime functions.[38] The processes of
military "manpower" acquisition have been premised on ideological beliefs
about the different and stratified roles of women and men. The distinction
between "battle front" and "home front," for example, has been used to
mobilize men into battle and women into taking up their positions in the
production process back home. Moreover, the assumption that women are
not appropriately a part of that production process, but are there only for
"the duration," is sustained throughout war to ensure that they will relin-
quish those positions to the returning heroes at war's end.[39]

The study of women and development has also begun to transform its
focus by examining gender. In chapter 10, Nüket Kardam, for example,
notes that despite the proliferation over the past twenty years of Women
in Development (WID) programs in all of the major development agencies,
few WID policy proposals have ever been implemented. She suggests that
the reason for this is that the WID discourse does not exist in a vacuum,
but rather coexists and comes into conflict with other prevailing development discourses and practices. These include understandings about the appropriate role of women in developing countries and the appropriate role
of development in general. When there is a congruence of these discourses,
policy emerges. So, for example, when WID policy coincides with the most
recent development priority (basic human needs in the 1970s), women become part of the development agenda much more easily. Similarly, when
development projects involving women do not threaten the assumed roles
of women, they too are accepted more easily. Thus, projects providing
training in sewing, cooking, knitting, and gardening proliferate.[40]

International organizations more generally are also involved in promoting
and sustaining particular assumptions around gender relations. The International Labor Organization (ILO), for example, has always made explicit reference to women workers throughout its history, but always in very specific
ways. Women have required special attention, according to the ILO,
whether in the form of protective legislation or through various promo-
tional efforts. While such instruments have sometimes benefited women,
they also reinforce particular views about women in the work force, for they
begin with the assumption of the male worker as the "norm." This view
often reproduces the assumption that because women workers differ from
the norm they are not "real workers" and, thus, not entitled to the same
rights, remuneration, and obligations as men. Such policies also promote
particular assumptions about men, most important of which is their general
exclusion from protective legislation based on their role in reproduction,

which is virtually ignored through ILO policy. More recently, ILO policies have begun to reflect the struggles of those concerned with women's equality, and have begun to reassess the effect that previous policies concerning women may have on their role in the family, work force, and society.[41]

CONCLUSIONS

This chapter has argued that the most fruitful point of departure for Feminist International Relations theory is one that takes into account gender relations. Such an analysis permits us to assess not only the particular institutional and policy biases that affect the lives of women and men, but also the manner in which these biases were created, the effects that they have, and the possibilities for change. In this way, we combine the strengths of Liberal feminism, Radical feminism, and Feminist Postmodernism. This kind of synthesis of theories not only improves our understanding of the empirical world, but it also addresses some of the political imperatives of feminism because it understands gender as relational and historically specific. It sees that gender is organized and is not simply some natural category defined by the terms "woman" and "man." What is constructed can be reconstructed, and what is made can be remade.[42]

Contrary to the mainstream vision of despair that depicts world politics as both inaccessible and unchangeable, this vision sees international relations as both accessible and subject to change. While a consideration of gender underscores the profound complexity of international practices, it is precisely because of that complexity that these practices are subject to change. And contrary to the view of monolithic states' engaging in occasional anarchic collision, the understanding of world politics presented here is one whose international relations affects us in the most basic ways, including the constitution of gender relations. If international relations can affect us in the most basic ways, then so too can it be affected. In this way, we see the extent to which we are all engaged in international practices, at all times. In this way, too, sites of resistance are always available to those who oppose the status quo. World politics is both personal and possible.

NOTES

This is a revised version of chapter two from Sandra Whitworth, "Feminism in International Relations: Gender in the International Planned Parenthood Federation and the International Labour Organization" (Ph.D Thesis, Carleton University, Ottawa, Ontario, Canada, 1991), 21–64. I would like to thank Susan Boyd, Jane Jenson, Michael Dolan, Eleanor MacDonald, John Sigler, Oran Young, and the editors of this anthology for their comments about and criticisms of earlier versions of this work.

1. See, for example, Christine Sylvester, "The Emperors' Theories and Transformations: Looking at the Field through Feminist Lenses," in Dennis C. Pirages and Christine Sylvester, eds., *Transformations in the Global Political Economy* (London: Macmillan, 1990), 234, and Anne Sisson Runyan and V. Spike Peterson, "The Radical Future of Realism: Feminist Subversions of IR Theory," *Alternatives* 16 (1991).

2. Alison Jaggar, *Feminist Politics and Human Nature* (Sussex: Harvester, 1983), 181.

3. Maude Barlow and Shannon Selin, *Women and Arms Control in Canada,* Canadian Centre for Arms Control and Disarmament, Issue Brief No. 8 (Ottawa, 1987), 2–3.

4. Ibid., 8–9.

5. "Little Women, Little Man," *New York Times,* November 20, 1985, A30.

6. Betsy Thom, "Women in International Organizations: Room at the Top: The Situation in Some United Nations Organizations," in C. F. Epstein and R. L. Coser, eds., *Access to Power: Cross-National Studies of Women and Elites* (London: George Allen & Unwin, 1981), 175–79.

7. Barlow and Selin, *Women and Arms Control,* 10.

8. Sarah Brown, "Feminism, International Theory, and International Relations of Gender Inequality," *Millennium* 17:3 (Winter 1988): 464.

9. Joni Lovenduski, "Toward the Emasculation of Political Science: The Impact of Feminism," in Dale Spender, ed., *Men's Studies Modified: The Impact of Feminism on the Academic Disciplines* (Oxford: Pergamon, 1981), 89.

10. Brown, "Feminism," 462.

11. Rosemarie Tong, *Feminist Thought: A Comprehensive Introduction* (Boulder, CO: Westview, 1989), 71.

12. J. Ann Tickner, "Hans Morgenthau's Principles of Political Realism: A Feminist Reformulation," *Millennium* 17:3 (Winter 1988): 430–37.

13. See, for example, Betty A. Reardon, *Sexism and the War System* (New York: Teachers College Press, 1985).

14. Sara Ruddick, "Pacifying the Forces: Drafting Women in the Interests of Peace," *Signs* 8:3 (1983): 478–79.

15. R. W. Cox, "Social Forces, States and World Orders: Beyond International Relations Theory," in Robert O. Keohane, ed., *Neorealism and Its Critics* (New York: Columbia University Press, 1986), 207.

16. See Teresa de Lauretis, "Feminist Studies/Critical Studies: Issues, Terms, and Contexts," in Teresa de Lauretis, ed., *Feminist Studies/Critical Studies* (Bloomington: Indiana University Press, 1986), 9, and Biddy Martin and Chandra Talpade Mohanty, "Feminist Politics: What's Home Got To Do with It?" in ibid., 193.

17. Lynne Segal, *Is the Future Female?* (London: Virago, 1987), 37.

18. Nancy Fraser and Linda J. Nicholson, "Social Criticism without Philosophy: An Encounter between Feminism and Postmodernism," in Linda J. Nicholson, ed., *Feminism/Postmodernism* (New York: Chapman & Hall, 1990), 29–30.

19. Judith Grant, "I Feel Therefore I Am: A Critique of Female Experience as the Basis for a Feminist Epistemology," *Women and Politics* 7:3 (1987): 103.

20. For a critique of this, see Christine Sylvester, "Some Dangers in Merging Feminist and Peace Projects," *Alternatives* 12 (1987): 499.

21. Marja ten Holder, "Women in Combat: A Feminist Critique of Military Ideology; or, Will Amazons Cause Armageddon?" (Master's thesis, Carleton University, Ottawa, Ontario, Canada, 1988).

22. See, for example, Christine Sylvester, "Reginas and Regimes: Feminist Musings on Cooperative Autonomy in International Relations," in Christine Sylvester, ed., *Feminist Theory and International Relations in a Postmodern Era* (Cambridge: Cambridge University Press, 1994).

23. Jane Flax, "Postmodernism and Gender Relations in Feminist Theory," in Nicholson, *Feminism/Postmodernism,* 56.

24. Michel Foucault, "Why Study Power: The Question of the Subject," in H. L. Dreyfus and P. Rabinow, eds., *Beyond Structuralism and Hermeneutics: Michel Foucault* (Chicago: University of Chicago Press, 1983), 212.

25. Linda Alcoff, "Cultural Feminism Versus Post-Structuralism," *Signs* 13 (Spring 1988): 407, 415.

26. Julia Kristeva, "Woman Can Never Be Defined," in Elaine Marks and Isabelle de Courtivron, eds., *New French Feminisms* (New York: Schocken, 1981), 137.

27. Julia Kristeva, "Oscillation Between Power and Denial," in ibid., 166.

28. Alcoff, "Cultural Feminism," 418.

29. Ibid., 419; Anne Marie Goetz, "Feminism and the Limits to the Claim to Know," *Millennium* 17:3 (1988): 489.

30. Alcoff, "Cultural Feminism," 420.

31. Eleanor M. MacDonald, "The Political Limitations of Postmodern Theory," (Ph.D diss., York University, North York, Ontario, 1990), 131.

32. Goetz, "Feminism," 490–91.

33. Joan Wallach Scott, *Gender and the Politics of History* (New York: Columbia University Press, 1988), 2.

34. Alcoff, "Cultural Feminism," 431.

35. Joan Wallach Scott, "Rewriting History," in Margaret Randolph Higonnet, Jane Jenson, Sonya Michel, and Margaret Collins Weitz, eds., *Behind the Lines: Gender and the Two World Wars* (New Haven: Yale University Press, 1987), 153.

36. R. W. Cox, "Postscript," in Keohane, *Neorealism and Its Critics,* 242.

37. Cynthia Enloe, *Bananas, Beaches & Bases: Making Feminist Sense of International Politics* (London: Pandora, 1989), 4.

38. Scott, "Rewriting History," 27.

39. See Cynthia Enloe, *Does Khaki Become You? The Militarization of Women's Lives* (London: Pluto, 1983), chap. 1; idem, "Tie a Yellow Ribbon 'Round the New World Order," *Village Voice,* February 19, 1991, 37; Rebecca Isaacs, "The Implications of Militarism, An Interview with Cynthia Enloe," *Out/Look* (Summer 1991): 22–24.

40. See also Nüket Kardam, "Social Theory and Women in Development Policy," *Women and Politics* 7:4 (Winter 1987): 75–76.

41. Sandra Whitworth, "Gender, International Relations and the Case of the ILO," *Review of International Studies* 20 (1994).

42. Enloe, *Does Khaki Become You?,* chap. 1.

6

Third World Feminist Perspectives on World Politics

Hamideh Sedghi

"Saudi Women Take Driver's Seat in Protest" and "Rebels in Arabia" were titles of articles in major American newspapers during the Desert Storm phase of the 1990–1991 Persian Gulf War.[1] "In daring defiance of the Saudi tradition against women driving," one journalist wrote, "about 70 veiled Saudi women gathered . . . in Riyadh, dismissed their drivers and drove a convoy of [luxury] cars before being stopped and detained by the police a short time later."[2] Another columnist concluded that "this is really an inexplicable development, or nondevelopment."[3]

Who were those Saudi women drivers? Were they opposing what Western reporters saw as the women's subordination to men, or were they opposing the war and the presence of foreign forces in the land? Did they place their gender interests ahead of nationalist considerations during that international crisis? To what extent did their actions parallel other Third World women's responses and perceptions in times of strife?

The Western press generally ignored and misunderstood the complexities of Third World women caught by domestic conditions and international crisis. Instead, the media reinforced the view that American women were superior to their cohorts in the Middle East. Writing in the *Washington Post,* Judy Mann observed that the rape of Kuwaiti women by Iraqi soldiers "underscores the tremendous cultural differences that exist between the United States and the countries in the Persian Gulf with which we have made common cause. Nowhere are these differences more fast and troubling than the way women are treated. They are generations behind American women in approaching anything remotely similar to economic, social and political equality."[4] Journalists were also quick to point out the differences between Arab women and American women who were serving in the armed forces. A reporter quoted a U.S. woman major as saying, "I'm thankful I'm not a Saudi woman. I just don't know how they do it."[5]

Third World women captured world attention as "victims," but Western reporters saw them subjugated only by their own cultures and *not* by international conflict. By contrast, Western women acquired a "liberated" status as though they were not subject to rape, sexual harassment, physical abuse, prostitution, commercialization of women's bodies in advertisements, and sexual subjugation as it exists within the U.S. military. Also absent from the media was any discussion of discrimination against Third World women in the West: the differential treatment of Middle Eastern women in American higher education or the controversy over restricting Muslim girls from wearing their veils in French schools. Reporters, like many Western academicians, resort to general categories to explain East-West cultural differences. By so doing, they dismiss the importance of class and of ethnic, local, and national variations among Third World women; and they fabricate false notions, such as the superiority of Western women juxtaposed to the inferiority of women in "backward" Third World countries.

This study focuses on Third World women's perspective on world politics. It avoids falling in the reporter's trap of thinking that Third World women's histories and perspectives are the same as each other's or that they are similar to the histories and perspectives of Western women. It thus elaborates on the historical specificity and varied perspectives of Third World women and argues against the monolithic perception of Third World women. At the same time, the study sketches a theory of world politics from the perspectives of Third World women. These perspectives, illustrated by the experiences described here, give rise to a theory that sees world politics as a struggle against domination by class, race, the state, and gender. These multiple layers of struggle may be engaged in individually or simultaneously.

This theory of a Third World Feminist perspective suggests that the central characteristic of world politics is the struggle for the control over life, the ability to make life choices, or to have the "power to" make those choices. The main "actors" in world politics are the women and men involved (sometimes together, sometimes not) in the struggle against domination, whether exercised by class, race, the state, or gender. This perspective expands the parameters of world politics far beyond Realist theory, which views world politics as a struggle for supremacy among sovereign states. While conflict is a central characteristic of the world political system, the Third World Feminist perspectives see the resolution to conflict not, as some would have it, by the imposition of a supranational authority to maintain the international hierarchy, but rather by the elimination of that hierarchy. Moreover, unlike many Western Feminist and Marxist perspectives, the Third World Feminist perspectives reject either gender or class oppression as the primary form of domination against which to direct the struggle for a more just world order. This theory views the systems of oppression as interconnected or overlapping. The goal of the struggle for Third World women remains the eradication of multiple forms of domination both at the national and international level.

Furthermore, this study of Third World women's perspectives on world politics considers the inherent tension that exists between the quest for specificity about women's experiences and theory's need for generality. The focus on specificity, though illuminating, impairs theory building, which by definition requires an inquiry into commonalities. However, the search for generalizations may lead to misperceptions. The suggestion that veiled Saudi women drove their cars in defiance of tradition says little about these women and much less about nonparticipating Saudi women, the millions of veiled and unveiled women in the Muslim world, or Third World women in general. The theory of world politics articulated here will be based on the premise that there are a multitude of Third World women's responses to world politics, responses that are specific to time and place. But there are also universal and common grounds that transcend such variations. Based on my own experiences as a woman born, raised, and educated in the Third World, and as a Third World woman scholar whose voice resonates throughout this study, I suggest that the quest for such a theory calls for the study of specific categories rather than the universal ones invented by Western scholarship.

Those theoretical categories will be drawn from the experiences and perceptions of Third World women involved in four specific conflicts: the Turkish nationalist movement, the Algerian national liberation struggle, the Iran-Iraq regional war, and the Persian Gulf War. This attempt, though very partial, will be based on the limited resource materials that are available. Thus far, the disciplines of Third World women's studies, comparative politics, and international relations have ignored Third World women's perspectives on world politics.

THEORETICAL CONCERNS

A theory of world politics from Third World women's perspectives can be constructed not only on the basis of experiences specific to Third World women but also on more universal experiences of women. Such a construct, however, necessitates a critical appraisal of the terms "Third World" and "Third World feminism." The "Third World" as a social-scientific category stems from asymmetrical global power relations. Defining the "First World" as the "developed," capitalist Western societies and the "Second World" as the state-planned economies and communist societies of the former Soviet Union and its Eastern European allies meant that what was left over was the "Third World." These definitions ignored the varied experience of Third World inhabitants. They also implied a hierarchy in which the Third World was last. Inherent in those definitions was the distortion of the Third World: It was "underdeveloped," "inferior," "uncivilized," "backward," and "traditional." Given the end of the cold war and the disintegration of most of the "Second World" states, it is increasingly irrelevant to designate a large portion of the world as the "Third World," without even having a second one! As problematic as the concept of the "Third World" may be, I will use it, not in those ethnocentric or orientalist ways,[6] but in reference to societies whose contemporary histories include resistance to colonialism, national liberation movements and revolutions, and survival in the age of the internationalization of capital and labor.

Similar concerns are justified when speaking of "Third World feminist" perspectives. In the West, there is a Eurocentric view that women's movements are purely European and North American and not indigenous to Asia or Africa. It is inarguable that "feminism" as a concept is a Western construct. In its variety of forms, Western feminism began to challenge patriarchal and/or capitalist structures effectively during the twentieth century, although such movements had their roots in European liberal and radical thought almost a century earlier. While not called feminism, diverse Third World women's movements manifested themselves much earlier in history than did their Western counterparts.[7] As early as the eighth century, for instance, women of the Sufi sect of Islam contested the established male hegemony and its effect on them. In eighteenth-century China and nineteenth-century India, there were movements in support of women's rights and education. Many Third World women's movements have merged with or emerged from various local resistance movements, a large number of which, especially during this century, questioned colonial and imperial domination, such as those in Algeria and Palestine during the nineteenth and early twentieth centuries.

In the later twentieth century, some of these movements included specific demands for the improvement of women's position, such as those in Egypt and Iran. Other movements, while anti-imperialist, were less gender specific: for example, the struggles during the 1970s in Guinea-Bissau and South Yemen and during the 1980s in Nicaragua. Other Third World women's movements with anti-imperialist and revolutionary overtones were divided on issues related to women's sexuality. These included movements in post-1979 Iran and in the Palestinian Intifada. In Guatemala and Bolivia, grassroots women's organizations have articulated voices against internal repression, class inequalities, and capitalist development. These movements did consider gender issues to be the focal point of their struggles. In South Africa, women participating in the antiracist and anticapitalist struggles have at times incorporated their own gender interests into their battles. The eruption of devastating wars throughout the contemporary Middle East has caused many Lebanese, Iranian, Kuwaiti, Palestinian, Kurdish, Afghan, Iraqi, and Saudi women to vocalize their opposition to ethnic conflict and international wars as well as to gender oppression.[8]

The diverse women's movements make it difficult to talk about a *common* perspective about gender among Third World women. There were a variety of "feminisms" among them, few of which may correspond to the Western conception of "feminism." Indeed, many Third World women, ranging from conservatives to leftists, have rejected Western feminism by associating it with Western cultural decadence.

The diverse experiences of Third World women do suggest, however, two major, yet complementary, propositions that illustrate *common* patterns that in many ways transcend women's differences but are linked to gender. The first proposition is that women have expressed an oppositional voice and have participated in resistance movements. To be sure, not all Third World women have taken an oppositional position. Many have chosen the status quo and pacifism. Some in areas distant from resistance centers have remained inactive, while numerous others have decided to be a "sack of potatoes"[9] and remain apolitical. The theory proposed here builds on the response of oppositional women to world politics and considers nonoppositional women outside its area of concern.

Depending on the nature and the context of their resistance, women's responses were articulated either against internal forces or external powers, or simultaneously against both. Women's opposition to *internal* factors has been generated by their opposition to national patriarchal structures, to class, to race, and to ethnic inequalities. *National patriarchy,* despite its cultural variations, denotes male dominance over women's sexuality and labor, both in the private and public spheres. When women responded to the *external* world, they opposed *international patriarchy,* as manifested by foreign interference, intervention, and domination. By international patriarchy, I mean male dominance of world political conduct with far-reaching consequences for the control of women on a global scale. Whether or not women were responding to internal or external enemies (or to both), they have at times combined their oppositional voices with their own gender-specific interests.

Third World women confront and resist the dilemma of a double-edged sword of internal and international patriarchy. On the one hand, siding with national patriarchy in defense of the nation against international enemies betrays women's demands for the degenderization of national politics. On the other hand, by demanding degenderization of national politics, women may appear to betray the nation during the onslaught of foreign powers. This is a dilemma that reflects conflicting national and international imperatives as experienced and expressed most intensely by many Third World women who participate in international conflicts.

The dilemma of women who experience the double-edged sword of domestic and international patriarchy leads to the second proposition that is derived from the common experience of women: Women's interests are often subordinated to the interests of states, statesmen, or male revolutionaries. Many women are mobilized on behalf of the state or the nation. Many have echoed the voice of the male elite or of male revolutionaries. But only a few have expressed their own interests as women.

A state's mobilization of women, especially during conflict, is not unique to the Third World. Italy and Germany under fascism, the former Soviet Union and China under communism, the United States during World War II, and Israel are other examples. Similarly, male revolutionaries' mobilization of women is not specifically a Third World phenomenon, as indicated by earlier periods of mobilization policies in both capitalist and socialist states. What is peculiar to many Third World women's movements is that the structural inequalities that are inherent in the global political economy shape women's perception. Outraged by the devastating effect of wars of colonialism and imperialism, many Third World women may perceive uniting with men as a goal and as a choice of their own—one that they themselves make during those specific moments of struggle. Domitila Barrios de Chungara, a revolutionary Bolivian woman involved in household organizations to resist both imperialism and class domination, did not consider gender oppression as the focal point of her struggles. "For us," she said, "the first and main task isn't to fight against our *compañeros,* but with them to change the system we live in for another, in which men and women will have the right to live, work, and organize."[10] Not all Third World women share this view. Unlike many Intifada women, the Palestinian novelist Sahar Khalifa maintains, "I don't want to be a heroine for the sake of the nation. I don't want my body to be the bridge for the state; I want to undergo a transformation, to have the experience of changing, to reap the benefits of the struggle."[11]

Any attempt to develop a theory of world politics from Third World Feminist perspectives must respond to the complexities and specificities of women's varied voices and historical experiences. At the same time, such a theory must build not only on diverse experiences of women, but also on the commonalities that transcend those diverse experiences. By focusing on women's involvement in wars, this theory presents the dilemma of conflicting national and international imperatives as experienced and expressed by Third World oppositional women, those who sided with men during the struggle and those who articulated their own specific interests as women.

WOMEN, NATIONALISM, AND NATIONALIST MOVEMENTS

The twentieth century has been a period in which many Third World countries have challenged colonial or imperial domination. Resistance took many different forms, one of which was manifested in the creation of a national identity for the purpose of uniting and mobilizing people to combat external forces. Nationalism is defined here as a phenomenon determined by a shift from a "simple gut reaction to foreign interference" to "an articulate political doctrine."[12] Women's dilemma in the national context is most clearly revealed precisely when this "gut reaction" is transformed into the "political doctrine" of the nation.

In modern Turkey, nationalism was precipitated by World War I. The war brought about the disintegration of the Ottoman Empire of which Turkey was a part and the occupation of parts of Turkey by the French, Italians, Greeks, and British. Under the nationalist leadership of Mustapha Kemal Attatürk, women fought alongside men until the Turkish army drove out the Europeans and Attatürk announced the formation of the Turkish Republic. During the war, Attatürk called on women to join the army since he had been impressed by women's militancy during the earlier Balkan wars and his army was facing massive male casualties at the front. Many militant women protested against the invaders, joined the army voluntarily to liberate their country, served as nurses at the front, or worked in ammunition factories, hospitals, or other public places. Among those who joined Attatürk's forces were women who synthesized their nationalism with their "feminism."[13]

As nationalists, Turkish women opposed and resisted European intrusion, just as Iranian nationalist women had done against the Russian and British incursion in Iran at the turn of the century. In the defense of the motherland, Turkish women acted on their own will. Women's "consciousness may be deemed to exist whenever [they] act as self-conscious subjects of their own struggle,"[14] although that struggle may be an integral part of the movement that attempts to defend the nation against the outside world. In the words of one observer, Turkish women had indeed become the "female counterparts of the core group of Mustapha Kemal's bureaucrats, soldiers, and merchants."[15]

Turkish women from different class backgrounds joined the nationalist struggle. The most active women resisters were the wives, daughters, and sisters of notables. These women formed the Anatolian Women's Association for Patriotic Defense, with branches all over Turkey. A central figure in this organization was Halidé Edib Adivar (1883–1964), a European-educated writer, poet, and journalist who synthesized nationalism with women's rights. Adivar recalled that "on my own childhood, polygamy and its results produced a very ugly and distressing impression," which led her to describe herself as a "believer in monogamy, in the inviolability of name and home."[16] These experiences became the basis for her voice on behalf of women and their oppression. She advocated education for women and their increasing participation in national life. Adivar's own involvement in national politics and in Ojak, a Turkish nationalist club, resulted in modifying the club's constitution to permit other women to participate.

Whether or not Adivar's intense involvement in the Turkish army, Turkish nationalism, and the Turkish women's movement influenced Attatürk's projects for the emancipation of Turkish women remains unknown. It is clear, however, that his reforms regarding women were quite radical when compared to contemporaneous Middle East norms. Some of these reforms included the abolition of polygamy, the restriction of veiling, the right to vote and hold public office, the requirement of woman's consent to marriage, as well as equal rights in divorce, inheritance, and child custody. Women became "citizens" and received their rights as legal members of their own society.

The "emancipation" of Turkish women was, however, a strategy of state building. Attatürk's interest lay in building a nationalist, secular, Western-style state—one that would, paradoxically, claim its roots in pre-Islamic Turkish culture. The specific image of women as citizens served as an important symbolic statement to the outside world and invited other countries to accord legitimacy to the new Turkish state because it appeared modern and European.

Reforms were also class bound. Only a few urban and wealthy women were actually affected, and the masses of Turkish women remained untouched by them. Elite women, whose labor and material resources benefited both themselves and the nationalist cause, organized and directed the women's movement. Activism was confined to the elite and failed to incorporate the interests of other women, possibly because their elite background prevented these women from acting on behalf of other women. Adivar herself had a contemptuous attitude toward less-privileged women.

In all, the reforms failed to break the cultural roots of women's oppression, and as Deniz Kandiyoti argues, a gap remained between the formal "emancipation" of Turkish women and their "liberation" from "Islam as an ideological system [that provided] some unifying concepts that influence women's experiences of subordination."[17] In this way, the nationalist-secular state emancipated Turkish women but subsumed their specific interests as women. Patriarchal power continued to be perpetuated, albeit in a new way.

WOMEN, COLONIALISM, AND NATIONAL LIBERATION STRUGGLES

While both nationalist movements and *national liberation* movements aim at the liberation of the motherland from foreign domination, the latter involves more intense and violent struggles because of the physical occupation of the native land. Turkish women fought to repel foreign invaders. Algerian women actively participated in the struggles to drive the French from the latter's 125-year hold on Algeria. The response of Algerian women to French colonial control is one of the classic case studies of women's involvement in armed struggles in the world and one of the most significant in African history.

Unlike the Turkish case, the Algerian nationalists espoused socialism. As a consequence, the anticolonialists held radical views on gender equality, while paradoxically committing themselves to the preservation of the national culture. The intensive participation of women in the resistance movement no doubt influenced the movement's advocacy of gender equality. Unlike the Turkish case, no distinct women's organization was ever formed during the 1956–1962 struggle for national liberation. Frantz Fanon, the most vocal anticolonialist, insisted at the time, "It is not a war waged with an active army and reserves. Revolutionary war, as the Algerian people is waging it, is a total war in which the woman is at the heart of the combat."[18]

Nevertheless, Fanon's own views on the centrality of women were contradicted by his own report on the reasons for their actual participation. The male leadership of the FLN (the Algerian National Liberation Front) needed to create reserve groups to back up the active, revolutionary cells of male activists. "After a final series of meetings among leaders," he wrote, "and especially in view of the urgent daily problems that the Revolution faced, the decision to concretely involve women in the national struggle was reached."[19] The FLN needed the support of women's labor for anticolonial warfare, but in the majority of cases *"utilized,* entirely willingly, . . . [women] as auxiliaries and adjuncts."[20]

Like other opposition forces, the top male leadership of the FLN controlled the voice of women and mobilized them in the interest of the national patriarchy. Despite their expressed commitment to gender equality, the FLN failed to incorporate a coherent ideology capable of recognizing women's autonomy and voices during the struggles. Such a failure is undoubtedly an important reason for the sex-segregation policies of the postcolonial Algerian state, as it was in the postrevolutionary Iranian state of 1979.

Algerian women had perspectives similar to the FLN leadership. Jamilah Buhrayd (1937–), a daughter of a businessman, is the most celebrated revolutionary heroine. In her anticolonial struggles, she carried bombs in her handbag and planted them at various sites occupied by the French. She was finally arrested and tortured horribly. Buhrayd explains the development of her own perspective in the following way:

When I was fifteen, . . . I began to realize that there was something else besides this French identity which I had all along. There was something called Algerian identity; it was different, it was ours, but we had no clear picture of it. I don't know exactly when I began to realize about a freedom, independence, but I think it was the death of my friend Aminah that changed me, from Jamilah the schoolgirl with the long braids who wanted to be a seamstress to a . . . [revolutionary fighter].[21]

Many women militants who, like Buhrayd, "were arrested, imprisoned, and tortured [were] made into 'national heroines' . . . to prove to international opinion that the struggle they were carrying on was 'progressive' even regarding women."[22] Attatürk took a similar approach in Turkey. Both the use of women to legitimate the anticolonial struggle and the silencing of their voices are in no way revolutionary; together they perpetuated the subordination of women by adjusting their position to fit new circumstances. Women, on the other hand, because of their intense involvement in oppositional and violent anticolonial struggles sided with men (or national patriarchy) in defense of the nation against the enemy (or international patriarchy). By so doing, women acted in the interests of the nation and not in the interests of their own gender—a dilemma that Third World women experienced widely when they mobilize in times of conflict and voluntarily participate in such conflicts.

It is interesting that in postindependence Algeria, Buhrayd saw herself, *not* as a different person, but as one who wanted different things. She said, "We are still in a struggle to make our new country work, to rebuild the destroyed family, to preserve our identity as a nation. In the future, perhaps, we will arrive at a kind of life where men and women relate on a more friendly, equal, and open basis."[23] Some Western feminists have been quick to state their ethnocentric evaluations of this stance. For example, Juliette Minces criticized the Algerian revolutionaries' view that women's "participation in the fight . . . should aid in accelerating the process of decolonization, after which they should again take their place in the home, which they should never have been forced to leave."[24] Minces misses the possibility that women could have chosen to go back into the home. Algerian women like Buhrayd *chose* to resist colonialism. In an independent Algeria, she *chose* to become a "committed wife and mother, and a nurturant human being," which to her was "above all other aspects of her existence."[25] Buhrayd had *not* given up the struggle; she was involved in the same war but in a different battle. She became a leader of a neighborhood organization that worked to improve its social and economic condition.

WOMEN AND REGIONAL WARS

Regional wars, such as the Iran-Iraq War of 1980–1988, exhibit characteristics comparable to other kinds of conflicts. All these wars are commanded and organized by patriarchs who recruit and draw on women and men as laborers of war. In regional wars, however, the states sponsor the conflicts and have monopolies over coercive powers as well as over the mobilization of the warriors. As a result, a larger number of women and men are absorbed into the orbit of these states' activities and greater destruction ensues. Another difference is that in contrast to nationalists and anticolonialists who strive to achieve national and international legitimacy by capitalizing on women's issues, states involved in regional wars display great power by silencing voices of dissent.

Iraq invaded Iran almost eighteen months after the Shah of Iran had been ousted through a revolutionary upheaval. As the war began, many Iranians volunteered to defend the nation and the revolution. The new Iranian state also incited many, including women, through *Basij-e Umumi* (public mobilization) to defend Islam in one of the bloodiest wars of modern history. The war proceeded and intensified horribly. Many women opposed the war in silence, others went into exile, and a group of almost 300,000 women participated in the war. These women warriors, trained by the state as guerrillas, were sent off to the front to serve as cooks and nurses. Although we have no hard evidence on the perceptions of the mobilized women, it seems likely that they fully supported the state and its "Islamic" ideology as it was specifically derived from the Iranian tradition and culture. They were the urban poor and identified with a state that claimed to represent their class interests as *mosta'zafin* (the oppressed).

The voices of the mobilized women echoed the voice of the state: It was "Islamic" and nationalist at the same time. Iraq was perceived as the enemy that was destroying Islam, *their* nation, and their sons, brothers, fathers, and husbands. Hence, in sharing with men their religious and nationalist ideologies, mobilized women responded to the calls of the charismatic leader, Ayatollah Khomeini, and prepared themselves to liberate Islam and Iran.

Other devout women contributed to the war indirectly. Some responded to the state's encouragement to marry the wounded or injured war veterans. In return, women received financial compensation from the state. The war strengthened the institution of *mot'eh* (temporary marriage), which inspired *Shi'i* men to marry as many wives as they wished for a designated period of time and money; and the economically needy women contributed to the war by offering their labor and sexual services to soldiers upon their return from the battlefields.

Another group of women, however, became active in various Islamic women's movements and expressed their voices to save the country in a war that seemed supported by the Western world to promote its colonial and "hegemonic aims." These Iranian women considered both the Western world and Iraq to be the enemies of Islam. Like their male counterparts, the devout Muslim women believed that Islam had to be defended and that Westernism and cultural imperialism had to be defeated. Such women believed in the Islamic tenets of human liberation as a whole, not in notions of equality and rights in the Western sense. Theoretically and in practice, Islam asserts that social differences between women and men are due to biological differences.

On the Iraqi side, Saddam Hussein called on women to defend the nation. The available information suggests that owing to repression, both

Iraqi women and men lived in fear of the state before and during the wars. Like the leaders involved in nationalist struggles, Hussein sought legitimacy by capitalizing on women's issues. He consistently stated his support for women: "Unless the woman is liberated, there is no freedom in Iraqi land. When the Iraqi woman is well, the Iraqi people are also well, and when her position is disturbed, the disturbance reaches all Iraqi people." [26] Women were mobilized to work for the domestic economy and to occupy the positions that had been held by their sons, husbands, and fathers who had been sent to the front. This was stipulated by the Iraqi president: "The conditions of war caused the woman to play an unusual leading role in the family, and she ought not to let this chance get away. The man is fighting in the battle fronts . . . and the woman has two roles: the role of the man, family management and . . . leading the family. This is a rare chance in history which is to be put into action by the Iraqi women." [27]

Not only were women mobilized by the state, they were actively recruited and trained by the only women's organization, the General Federation of Iraqi Women (GFIW). GFIW was one of the official organs of Hussein's Ba'th Socialist Party, not an independent organization. It was fully supported by Hussein, and it gave full allegiance and "love and admiration" [28] to him and his policies. Outspoken and active GFIW women such as S. Al-Musavi endorsed and echoed Hussein's plans and precepts as she stated that women's obligations were twofold: "achieving on the home front" and "turning the wheel of production." [29] The more intensified the conflict became, the more women were called upon by GFIW to lend their efforts to the war buildup.

Unlike Iranian women volunteers who were mobilized by religious leadership, Iraqi women were mobilized by a secular leader who espoused socialism and secularism and, at times, nationalism and Islamism. It is interesting that during the Iran-Iraq war, Iraqi women actively organized unaffiliated women in the service of destruction, a task generally assigned to men. This is not, however, a perplexing phenomenon given the repressive and authoritarian character of Saddam Hussein's regime. Women's voices could not contradict the voice of the state and the male elite leadership. It is hard to conclude that Iraqi women *exercised* a choice like that of their sisters in Turkey, Algeria, and Iran (Iranian women participated in the war voluntarily). Iraqi women were *forcibly* mobilized by the state. They feared not to be, or to have perceptions different from those that were state mandated and male endorsed.

WOMEN AND INTERNATIONAL WARS

The perspective of women involved in recent international warfare has been somewhat different. During the Persian Gulf War of 1990–1991, two distinct yet interrelated women's perspectives could be observed: (1) the nationalist view that sided with the national patriarchy and (2) the defiant voice that attempted to break new ground by articulating its own gender-specific interests. Both of these views were expressed by Saudi women as the deployment of U.S. forces in Saudi Arabia began after Saddam Hussein's invasion of Kuwait. These different perspectives contradict the "subordinated" and "backward" images of Saudi women portrayed and presented by the American media. Saudi women's perspectives and activities during a major international crisis illustrate significant linkages between gender and world politics.

Seen from a sociohistorical context, substantial changes have occurred in the lives of Saudi women, especially in family relations, sex-segregation traditions, education, and employment.[30] Saudi men continue to control political decisions, particularly at institutional levels. Elite women find it hard to challenge male domination, although both educated women and men have recently played more active roles in expressing "choices that they themselves make, to interpret or to otherwise modify patterns of meaning featured in the established ideology."[31] Elite Saudi women have increasingly exercised political power in controlling property rights and in arranging marriages or participating in marriage negotiations that have important political and economic consequences. Their increased influence is a consequence of wealth and status—their social class—rather than changing definitions of gender.

In the early months of Desert Shield, Saudi women, especially the well-to-do, were called upon to contribute their services in civil defense. The Saudi monarch encouraged women volunteers to work in hospitals in anticipation of the war and the shortage of manpower that would result, and to capitalize on the nationalist fervor. It was also a response to pressure from the more liberal members of the elite who advocated a more open society. A poll of 130 Saudi women from a cross-section of Jeddah, Riyadh, and the Eastern Provinces revealed that most Saudi women felt they could manage life while men were away at the front, and that most of them advocated an increased role for women, especially during the war. The women, however, held different views on women's position in the society and on the war. For example, one woman contended, "The crisis has created the condition of change for women and women have the opportunity to define the role." Another argued, "Social conditions in the country are not favorable for women; it is up to men to decide."[32] The appearance of women in the U.S. armed forces stationed in Saudi Arabia evoked mixed but critical opinions: "I am glad not to be an American woman," commented a Saudi woman doctor in speaking about U.S. Army women. "Women are not made for violence with guns." Another Saudi woman said it was "a little strange that American women should want to become soldiers, though . . . [they] have the right to choose for themselves."[33]

Saudi women's activities and views during the war illustrate Third

World women's perspectives on world politics. Despite their nationalism, some Saudi women expressed their gender-specific concerns, for example by driving their cars without male chauffeurs, even at the expense of antagonizing the hegemonic state. These women acted because of their class interest. Wealthy, Western educated, and professional, these Saudi women had been pressing for a wide variety of rights for some time. They chose to protest openly and express themselves during a major war so that they could "be heard by the authorities loudly and clearly." [34] I was told by one of the Saudi women protestors that they wished to pressure their government into relaxing certain laws while world public attention was noticing them.

At the same time, a number of the protestors indicated that they meant "to do no harm to Saudi Arabia and strongly defended their actions as 'patriotic' and 'necessary.' " [35] In coping with their gender oppression, the women sought to use the oppressor's principles against them. In such a religiously devout society as Saudi Arabia, women used, but did not challenge, Islam to promote their own gender interest. One of the demonstrators commented,

It is important for the authorities to understand that as educated women who have driven themselves abroad while we pursued graduate studies, we cannot be reduced to being dependent on strangers to drive us. . . . In addition to being humiliating, this is anti-Islamic. . . . Islam says that a woman should not be left alone in the company of a man who is not her relative and that is exactly what happens every time [we are] driven in a car by a . . . driver. . . . [We] would repeat [our] actions again. [36]

The Saudi women's defiance of national patriarchy during that international crisis might have been symptomatic of women's attempts to negotiate their own gender interests with their governments. They publicly defied the state during an international crisis, and found a way to ward off criticism of being unpatriotic and a threat to the state's existence and to defend their behavior within the precepts of their religion. Even though they failed to subvert the system to their own advantage, they broke new ground. Their protest against the state during the time of a global conflict stands in contrast to the Turkish, Algerian, Iranian, and Iraqi cases where oppositional women allied themselves with national patriarchs during wars.

CONCLUSION

National and international politics are gendered, along with wars and conflicts. Wars, as a consequence of foreign policy, are imbued with masculine ideology. Third World wars often silence the voice of women while at the same time veiling women's visibility. It is therefore difficult to determine and learn about Third World women's specific perspectives during conflicts. What little information is available on Third World women's views and voices during wars warrants greater attention.

This discussion of Third World women's perspectives on world politics has demonstrated that the perspectives are neither monolithic nor homogeneous. Rather, they are historically specific and varied. In contrast to the common Western conceptualization of Third World women as "subordinated" and "victimized" I have offered an alternative explanation that negates single-sided presentations and that focuses on women through the complex interaction between class, culture, ethnicity, nationality, and race, on the one hand, and the hierarchial global relations in which women are situated and through which their lives and struggles are defined, on the other.

This approach has argued for the centrality of the multiplicity and diversity of Third World women's perspectives. It has also contended that two general themes have appeared in these perspectives, particularly those of the oppositional women: (1) women who sided with the national patriarchy in defense of the nation and (2) women who used events in world politics to break new ground by articulating their own gender-specific interests. It is true that historically, owing to tensions arising from their colonial, semi-, and postcolonial status, more Third World women have allied themselves with men in the liberation of their countries. This assertion need not mean that all Third World women have been mobilized in the interest of national male warriors and politicians or in the interest of the nation or the state.

Nor does it mean that they will continue to be so in the future. When not silenced, many women have presented themselves as subjects of their own gender-specific struggles, while others have expressed their voices against both national and international politics. Even when silenced, many women have dared to articulate their concerns. Third World women have defined themselves in their *own* world—the world that they alone see and the world that they choose to live in. The nations and inhabitants of the "Third World" are diverse. They are linked by women who share, confront, and resist a double-edged sword: national patriarchy and international patriarchy.

NOTES

I am grateful to Peter Beckman and Francine D'Amico for their useful and careful comments on earlier drafts of this study. Thanks also to Madeleine Tress and Anuradha Seth for their helpful suggestions. Part of this research was presented at the Annual Meeting of the International Studies Association, Acapulco, Mexico, March 23–27, 1993.

1. Youssef M. Ibrahim, "Saudi Women Take the Driver's Seat in Protest," *New*

York Times, November 7, 1990, A18; Richard Cohen, "Rebels in Arabia," *Washington Post,* November 20, 1990, A23.

2. Ibrahim, "Saudi Women," A18.

3. Amy Goldstein, "Crossing the Gulf Culture," *Washington Post,* August 23, 1990, D1.

4. Judy Mann, "Kuwaiti Rape: A Doubly Savage Crime," *Washington Post,* March 29, 1991, C3.

5. James LeMoyne, "Army Women and the Saudis: The Encounter Shocks Both," *New York Times,* September 25, 1990, A1.

6. Edward W. Said, *Orientalism* (New York: Pantheon, 1978), and Stewart Schaar, "Orientalism at the Service of Imperialism," *Race & Class* 21:1 (1979): 67–80. For a feminist discussion of ethnocentrism, see Chandra Mohanty, "Under Western Eyes," in Chandra Talpade Mohanty, Ann Russo, and Lourdes Torres, eds., *Third World Women and the Politics of Feminism* (Bloomington: Indiana University Press, 1991).

7. Leila Ahmed, *Gender in Islam* (New Haven: Yale University Press, 1992); Kumari Jayawardena, *Feminism and Nationalism in the Third World* (London: Zed Books, 1986); and Maria Mies, *Patriarchy and Accumulation on a World Scale* (London: Zed Books, 1986).

8. Julie M. Peteet, *Gender in Crisis: Women and the Palestinian Resistance Movement* (New York: Columbia University Press, 1991); Diana Russell, *Lives of Courage* (New York: Basic Books, 1989); Jane Jaquette, ed., *The Women's Movement in Latin America* (Boulder, CO: Westview, 1991); Farah Azari, ed., *Women of Iran* (London: Ithaca, 1983); Stephanie Urdang, *Fighting Two Colonialisms: Women in Guinea Bissau* (New York: Monthly Review, 1979); Mervat Hatem, "The Politics of Sexuality and Gender in Segregated Patriarchal Systems: The Case of Eighteenth and Nineteenth Century Egypt," *Feminist Studies* 12 (Summer 1986); Maxine Molyneaux, "Socialist Societies: Progress Towards Women's Emancipation?" *Monthly Review* 34 (July–August 1982); and Hamideh Sedghi, "Women, State, and the Islamic Revolution in Iran" (Paper delivered at the Annual Meeting of the American Political Science Association, San Francisco, 1990).

9. This is Marx's characterization of peasants in revolutions. See Karl Marx, "The Eighteenth Brumaire of Louis Bonaparte," in Robert Tucker, ed., *The Marx-Engels Reader* (New York: Norton, 1978).

10. Domitila Barrios de Chungara, *Let Me Speak!* (New York: Monthly Review, 1978), 199.

11. Sahar Khalifa, interviewed by Maya Rosenfeld, "I Don't Want My Body to Be a Bridge for the State," *Challenge* 2:6 (1992): 27.

12. Edward Mortimer, *Faith and Power: The Politics of Islam* (New York: Vintage, 1982), 122.

13. Jayawardena, *Feminism and Nationalism,* 38; Mortimer, *Faith and Power,* 122; and Deniz Kandiyoti, ed., *Women, Islam, and the State* (Philadelphia: Temple University Press, 1991).

14. Deniz Kandiyoti, "Emancipated but Unliberated? Reflections on the Turkish Case," *Feminist Studies* 13 (Summer 1987): 337.

15. Abadan-Unat, quoted in Jayawardena, *Feminism and Nationalism,* 35.

16. Halidé Edib Adivar's memoirs, quoted in Elizabeth Warnock Fernea and

Basima Qattan Bezirgan, eds., *Middle Eastern Women Speak* (Austin: University of Texas Press, 1977), 168, 177, 181.

17. Kandiyoti, "Emancipated," 320.

18. Frantz Fanon, *A Dying Colonialism* (New York: Grove, 1965), 66.

19. Ibid., 50–51.

20. Juliette Minces, "Women in Algeria," in Lois Beck and Nikki Keddie, eds., *Women in the Muslim World* (Cambridge: Harvard University Press, 1978), 162.

21. Walid 'Awad, interview with Jamilah Buhrayd, quoted in Fernea and Bezirgan, *Middle Eastern Women Speak,* 256.

22. Minces, "Women in Algeria," 163.

23. Fernea and Bezirgan, *Middle Eastern Women Speak,* 261.

24. Minces, "Women in Algeria," 164.

25. Fernea and Bezirgan, *Middle Eastern Women Speak,* 252, 262.

26. Quoted in Jennifer Freedman, "Women in Iraq," *Arab-American Affairs* 29 (Summer 1989): 44.

27. Ibid., 42.

28. Suad Joseph, "Elite Strategies for State-Building: Women, Family, Religion, and State in Iraq and Lebanon," in Kandiyoti, *Women,* 176.

29. Quoted in Freedman, "Women in Iraq," 42.

30. Soraya Alturki, *Women in Saudi Arabia: Ideology and Behavior Among the Elite* (New York: Columbia University Press, 1986).

31. Eleanor Abdella Doumato, "Gender, Monarchy, and National Identity in Saudi Arabia" (Paper presented at the annual meeting of the Middle East Studies Association, Washington, D.C., 1991), 1.

32. Khaled Nazer, "Women Able to Answer Country's Call," *Arab News,* December 4, 1990, 2.

33. LeMoyne, "Army Women," A1.

34. Ibrahim, "Saudi Women," A18.

35. Ibid.

36. Ibid.

Part II _____

POLICIES

❖ 7 ❖

Thinking about Women and International Violence

Jean Bethke Elshtain

In order to think critically about women and international violence, the student and scholar alike should spend some time reflecting on the story of men, women, and war. War stories are pervasive in the long march of Western culture—indeed, of all complex, long-lived traditions. The question, then, is how we treat the stories that have been deeded to us. What stories remain resonant and resiliant? War historically has served to sustain sex-based social and political identities and claims.

JUST WARRIOR AND BEAUTIFUL SOUL IMAGES

Let me offer an example of what I have in mind. One powerful image of the male as war fighter, a figure central to the story of war and politics in the West, is the ideal of the *just warrior*. The just warrior fights by a code of honor that permits violence but also limits it to certain situations. Further, the way in which a war is fought is also restricted. The just warrior must not intend to kill noncombatants and must do all that he can to limit the damage to civilians. As well, there is a powerful female ideal that I call the *beautiful soul*. She is the woman who waits at the home front, who prays before the battle, but who is not herself deeply immersed in the bone-crunching, body-destroying business of war. Notice that these two images of men and women serve to reinforce one another. They further serve as underpinnings for action. They locate men and women in particular relations to the wars that their countries fight. The cultural anthropologist, Clifford Geertz, calls such images "constellations of enshrined ideas."[1]

When we think about women and war, therefore, we must consider the social identities of men and women, since these have mutually defined one another and have sustained the historical status of the woman as noncombatant, the man as warrior. We grant social authority to these identities and to the sex-linked ideals that they both reflect and sustain. When we speak of women, men, and war, therefore, we are not talking about easily sloughed-off superficial notions. Instead, we are talking about socially constructed identities. We continue to be shaped by these deeply encoded images, but at the same time we are free to ask if they continue to define war for us and to animate and tap contemporary male and female ideals in relation to war and war-fighting.

Let us briefly consider the just warrior and beautiful soul as symbolic constructions that help to sustain our main narratives of war and politics. Remember that we are not talking about an *essential* male or female identity; rather, we are interested in how certain ideals function to re-create and to secure women's social location as noncombatants and men's identities as warriors constrained in our culture and history by the rules of fighting a just war.

The power of these deeply rooted stories and ideals is such that they make it difficult to fend off evidence that might disentangle the standard linkages: woman = nonviolent, nurturing, compassionate; man = violent (either eagerly and inevitably or reluctantly and tragically), dutiful, brave. Locked in a deep symbiosis, perceived as beings who have complementary needs and who exemplify gender-specific virtues, *real* men and women give way in cultural memory and narrative to mythical Man and Woman who, in time of war, take on the personae of just warriors and beautiful souls. No conscious bargain was struck by our collective forefathers and foremothers to ensure this outcome; rather sedimented lore, stories of men fighters and women home keepers and mourners of wars' inevitable tragedies, spill over from one epoch to the next, shaping future possibilities by constraining consideration of alternatives.

There are some who suggest that these traditional notions of the just warrior have been shattered by certain cruel experiences, such as the Vietnam War that seemed to many dishonorable. Furthermore, contemporary American culture no longer puts a heavy premium on notions of duty, honor, and sacrifice. And what about the woman as beautiful soul in an era when approximately 12 percent of the 2.2 million soldiers in the U.S. All Volunteer Force are women? As well, in modern *total war,* the distinction between combatants and noncombatants has been blurred. In World War II, strategic bombing aimed *specifically* at civilians, not at combatants.

But there is something tremendously seductive about just warriors and beautiful souls. Wartime's beautiful soul is a woman who is needed civicly as well as familially. Wartime's just warrior is someone who is fighting for a purpose higher than self-interest. As I did the research for my book, *Women and War,* I was struck by the fact that men and women alike both love and hate war. J. Glenn Gray, in his masterwork *The Warriors,* recounts the story of a French woman whom he had known in World War II, a time of danger and suffering, and whom he then met later in a time of peace and comfort. The woman told Gray, "You know that I do not love war or want it to return, but at least it made me feel alive as I have not felt alive before or since."[2] A nurse and veteran of Vietnam, an activist organizing readjustment counseling for the nearly 8,000 women who were stationed in Vietnam, many of whom suffer from the delayed-stress syndrome widely recognized in Vietnam combat vets, acknowledges all the horror, but then tells a reporter for the *New York Times,* "I think about Vietnam often and I find myself wishing I was back there. There was no such thing as a black or white, male or female, we dealt with each other as human beings, as friends. We worked hard, we partied hard, we were a unit. A lot of us, when we left, wished we didn't have to come home."[3]

It is this complex seduction of wartime that reminds us that we are up against something very powerful: a narrative that shapes our thinking, often unconsciously. Other cultures have their parallel traditions—stories of nationhood achieved and freedom gained through fighting in war. War is interesting to us. People are put in extreme situations. We learn how men and women respond to or enact those extreme situations.

CITIZEN-WARRIORS AND CIVIC VIRTUE

Perhaps we can understand why we are drawn to war stories if we look to how it all began in Western history, with the Greek *polis* or *city.* In ancient Greek political organization there were not nation-states but cities that were warrior communities. War opened up for the male warrior a field of honor, of glory, of virility, of virtue. The woman occupied a different field of honor. Hers was the realm of the *oikos,* the household. With the shift to settled city life from the Homeric warrior ideal, we find a partial tempering of the warrior ideal in the work of the founders of Western political thought, namely, Plato and Aristotle. Aristotle, for example, criticized those Greek city-states whose politics aimed at domination over others. Such domination is a goal that elevates war over all other forms of human activity. He chastised the Spartans because they "never accustomed themselves to any discipline other and better than that of war."[4] Once war becomes habitual, whether among the Greeks or any other people, and highest honor is paid to military prowess, then, Aristotle fretted, the laws of a city will be directed to a single object: conquest. Nevertheless, his ideal of the citizen remained the ideal of the *citizen-warrior.* But this warrior is not to be driven by a passion for war; rather he is to fight only when the city requires it and only when the city's ends will be served, not for his own glory.

An interesting complication emerges in our dominant war narratives when Aristotle's tempering of the warrior ideal was strengthened by the emergence of Christianity in the West, even as the Spartan ideal of the strong warrior-citizen got picked up in early modern Europe by theorists like Machiavelli, who wrote to urge the Prince to take power and to hold it by any means necessary. In his book *The Art of War,* as well as in *The Prince,* Machiavelli reappropriated the Spartan warrior ideal of male valor and adapted it to a notion of civic virtue. The word *virtue* itself comes from the Latin word for man, *vir.* Machiavelli was insistent that *this* civic virtue is essential in preparing citizens to defend and to die for the city or principality. He wrote,

When it is a question of saving the fatherland, one should not stop for a moment to consider whether something is lawful or unlawful, gentle or cruel, laudable or shameful, but putting aside every other consideration one ought to follow out to the end whatever resolve will save the life of the state and preserve its freedom: *si vis pacem, para bellum,* If you seek peace, prepare for war.[5]

Where does woman fit into this tough world of *Realpolitik,* a world that binds civic and martial virtue together? The woman becomes a character whom I tag the Spartan mother. Sparta serves as the ideal for both the male and the female citizen. The sayings of Spartan mothers were recorded by Plutarch and later picked up by Western European civic republicans, most importantly Jean-Jacques Rousseau. Rousseau honored Spartan mothers, those who are pleased to hear that their sons died in battle. Plutarch recounts one mother, as she buried her son, telling a would-be sympathizer that she has had good luck, not bad: "I bore him that he might die for Sparta and this is the very thing that has come to pass for me."[6] For Rousseau, virtuous polities require virtuous families. Children must imbibe love for *la patrie,* the fatherland, with their mother's milk. In his book, *Emile,* Rousseau elaborates his ideal of the female citizen by telling the story of the Spartan mother who was awaiting news of the battle in which all five of her sons were engaged. A slave arrives, he approaches her and says, "I have terrible news. Your five sons were killed." The Spartan mother slaps him fiercely and shouts, "Base slave, did I ask you that? Who won the battle?" And the slave replies, "Sparta." The mother goes to the temple and gives thanks to the gods. The Spartan mother, then, along with the strong ideal of the armed citizen-warrior, is one powerful strand in the Western tradition. Men, women, politics, and war are part of a complex set of mutually defined relations.

ARMED CIVIC VIRTUE AND JUST WARS

With the creation of the *levée en masse* (the mobilization of men, women, *and* children as part of the French Revolution), noncombatants are drawn directly to the wartime task. The ideal of the nation-at-arms emerges in the writings of the French revolutionaries, themselves indebted to Jean Jacques Rousseau. What emerges is a strong notion of nationalism, of a unified body politic, *la Peuple,* elaborated at its most uncompromising in the work of the theorist G. W. F. Hegel. Hegel articulated an ideal of the nation-state as a war-state, a *Kriegstaat.* To Hegel and other celebrants of Western nation building, men and women have an active but very *different* part in the story. This tradition of *armed civic virtue* is one aspect of our historic inheritance with which we continue to struggle. We are forced to ask ourselves just how closely we wish to associate war and politics, citizenship, and war fighting.

There is a "disarmed" tradition that cuts across, commingles with, and sometimes conflicts with that of armed civic virtue. Its serious beginnings can be traced from the New Testament Jesus who challenges the powerful metaphor of the warrior central to previous Greek narratives as well as those of the Hebrew Testament. The Prince of Peace dreams of a peaceable kingdom: In the Sermon on the Mount, Jesus blesses the peacemakers, "for they shall be known as children of God." His followers, to be sure, never completely realized that ideal. They entered into a world geared toward war and imperialism, domination by the stronger over the weaker. This was, remember, the time of the *Pax Romana,* or Roman Peace.

The upshot of the Christian injunction against violence was the creation, over time, of a body of teaching that came to be called the teaching of a *just war.* This tradition begins with the presumption that the burden of proof for the justification of war must be placed on those who would take up arms rather than those who refuse. Social life is to be evaluated not from the standpoint of the victors, but from the standpoint of the suffering, of the potential or actual victims of violence. Appended to this new set of images that deemphasizes war, we find new ideals of community and what might be called a feminization of ideals of fellowship. The model for Christian love, *agape,* is based on the mother's unconditional love for her child. The Church itself is mother, *mater ecclesia.*

Female ideals came to the fore and men and women alike could be soldiers for Christ, *milites Christi.* For example, early women martyrs were honored for their heroism and their glorious examples as they faced death in the arena. Women got linked to the image of the Madonna and, thus, to values and virtues at odds with war making. The Madonna is often a *mater dolorosa,* or sorrowing mother, because of the death or suffering of her children. Unlike the stern Spartan mother, the suffering mother is cast in the role of a victim of war. She may support the war of her country but she mourns rather than exults over the death of sons. At times, the Spartan mother and the mourning beautiful soul come together in the image of "Mothers of Martyrs" who died for a just cause. The fighter was reborn in the image of the just warrior who takes up arms reluctantly and only if he must to prevent a greater wrong or to protect the innocent from certain harm. His is a tragic task, not an occasion for civic celebration.

As we move into what are the European Middle Ages, we find a world of conflict and confusion, a mingling of ancient notions, Christian ideals and experiences of community, Germanic tribal codes, many diverse peoples and principalities, and more or less constant warring or skirmishing by a warrior class of medieval knights who devoted their lifetime to training for fighting. The vast majority of human beings were not involved in this war making. It was the purview of a noble class. Total war, as we understand it, did not exist. And there were official campaigns against violence. The Church promulgated the so-called Peace of God and the Truce of God in the eleventh century, limiting the days on which fighting could take place and restricting those who were to be involved in conflicts. One did see, alas, an excess of moralistic fervor helping to fuel the Crusades against the so-called foreign infidel. But despite the Crusades there remained a strong presumption against a resort to violence, combined with the insistence that violence was always tragic and involved sin even when it was justified.

WOMEN AND WAR

Throughout the complex epochs from the medieval period into the early modern, we find a clash, then, of two powerful traditions: armed civic virtue and an at least partially disarmed tradition. When we arrive at the nation-state in its modern form, we also find congealed the notion of the woman as a collective beautiful soul. By the late eighteenth century, strong distinctions between men and women in regard to violence had come to prevail. Male violence had been moralized into the fighting of a just "war," but "female" and "violence" had no such relation. Female violence lay outside the boundary of normal expectation. When it occurred, it was seen as disruptive and personal. Male violence could be orderly and rule governed. Very sharp cleavages emerged between personal life and public life, between family and state: Women were guardians of the family; men, protectors of the state.

Since the eighteenth century, women in the West have often devised means to strengthen their cultural definition as the ethical guardians of culture. There are both strengths and weaknesses in this tradition. It can take generous forms or narrowly constricting ones, such as various hygienic crusades against vice, for example. For the beautiful soul, wartime presents many perplexities. The beautiful soul is drawn to the task of modern war yet tries to uphold the image of one not sullied by politics, without dirty hands. Thus, we find over and over again women defining themselves in opposition to men, engaging in self-congratulation about women's superior virtue, and then seeking to suffuse political and social life with an image of private virtue. What we see when we look at history is that women, cast as society's beautiful souls, have not only *not* succeeded in stopping the wounding and slaughtering of sons, brothers, husbands and fathers, but have more often than not exhorted men to the task and honored them for their deeds. They share responsibility for war, for destruction.

Thinking about women and war in the present means that one must go back over the historical separation of enshrined male and female identities and consider their current power. For wars both destroy *people* and bring into being men and women of a *particular* kind. War is productive destructiveness, not only in the sense that it shifts boundaries, defines states, and alters balances of power, but in a more profound sense. War has created images of "the people." But the way in which we think of female violence remains formless. Because such violence falls outside the boundaries of our received narratives, stories of women fighters, for example in the Soviet Army, the Yugoslav partisan resistance, or other resistance movements, are little known. We know a lot about the beautiful soul and the Spartan mother, but very little about the female warrior.

When we read what these women fighters have to say, they explore what they are doing in the pure logic of war. They speak as soldiers. They describe their wartime activities as personally liberating, despite pervasive fears and almost paralyzing anxieties. None regrets her choice to fight or be in the thick of fighting and each would, to the woman, do it all over again, if they were called upon. Nadya Popova, a Soviet bomber pilot, has recounted her wartime experience in the classic language of force that Clausewitz, the supreme Western theorist of war, would recognize and endorse: "They were destroying us and we were destroying them. That is the logic of war. I killed many men but I stayed alive. I was bombing the enemy. War requires the ability to kill among other skills, but I don't think you should equate killing with cruelty. I think the risks we took and the sacrifices we made for each other made us kinder rather than cruel." [7]

Or, consider the words of Major Rhonda Cornum, a flight surgeon attached to the 101st Airborne Division during the 1991 Persian Gulf War. Shot down and taken prisoner, Cornum reflects on her experiences in a memoir. She writes her family that she is prepared to die. "I was proud of what I was doing . . . if anything happened to me, they should remember that I chose to be here." [8] Cornum didn't want to stay home and "be a wimp." She concludes that, in the army, "we're so busy doing our jobs, it doesn't matter to anyone if I'm a woman or a man. We're all soldiers; or as they say in the army, we're all green." [9]

Finally, however, it is to the woman as noncombatant that one must turn, for women have been, and remain, the prototypical noncombatants.

Women are designated noncombatants, remember, not only because of the part that they play in the reproductive process, but because women have been linked symbolically to images of suffering victims and nonviolence. Many noncombatant women have used war to break out of the narrow confines (perceived by themselves as such) of the home or of social life into a wider civic arena. Eleanor Roosevelt called World War I her emancipation and her education. In World War II, in the United States, a staggering 99 percent of American women led "private lives." But the vast majority of these women were mobilized as civically virtuous citizens, heroines of the home front. We find the reemergence of the image of the Spartan mother as well as the beautiful soul—or, perhaps one could say, of a woman who combines them. Take, for example, Mrs. Aleta Sullivan, the champion gold-star mother of World War II whose five sons were killed when one ship went down. She mourned them but she also toured the country selling war bonds. Indeed, she was the champion war-bond salesperson during World War II.[10]

Just as there are many ways through which women have inhabited the world of war, there are all sorts of ways to be a soldier. J. Glenn Gray writes of those who are brutally dehumanized and those who attain a cama-raderie that would have been unthinkable in civilian life, a preparedness to sacrifice themselves for others. This is the identity that I call the compassionate warrior. Not so much the bloodthirsty militant, but a person reluctantly drawn into combat, dying for others, and sacrificing himself so that others might live. Indeed, when one turns to the literature of war, the primary theme is not killing but sacrifice. Male combat veterans have invented a modern, bitter approach to writing about war. Women, who have not experienced battle themselves, can more easily picture war as a realm of freedom and glory rather than a terrible place where, in the words of the poet Wifred Owen, men die as cattle.[11]

CHASTENED PATRIOTISM

This brings us to the complexity of the present. Can we create an image of men, women, and civic life that links men and women alike to the social and political world and narrows the gap between them? Here feminism's encounter with war comes to the fore. Feminists have been and are divided on whether to fight men or to join them, whether to be inside the circle of war or to be in some presumably purer condition outside. It is no doubt ironic that even as a feminist tradition that recalls Virginia Woolf's injunction to a secret society of pacifist "outsiders" proliferates, more and more women are joining the warriors and seeking to embrace this identity by overturning the so-called combat-exclusion rule. The United States now has a higher percentage of women in its armed forces than does any other industrial nation. We have yet to assimilate this fact. We have yet to ask ourselves what the implications of this transformation are. We have yet to settle as a society whether any of our young people in the future should be called to combat or whether we are going to reserve that civic duty to those who, because of race, class, and, yes even gender, are drawn into the armed services as a secure job with certain opportunities attendant upon it.

Even as the United States debated combat exclusion limits on female participation in war, in other parts of the world women as noncombatants are victimized in ruthless wars of "ethnic cleansing." Despite the fact that rape in time of war is punishable by death (Section 45, Article 120 of the Uniform Code of Military Justice), current estimates are that 20,000 Muslim women have been raped as part of a planned war strategy in the fighting in Bosnia. Noncombatant status has not spared women the worst depredations of war, past or present.

Finally, how do we struggle with the problem of peace? Is it the absence of armed conflict? Is it some ideal of perpetual world harmony? Is it world order? Is it the end of the need for any sort of defense? Like the just warriors reject total war, it is important to reject sentimentalized notions of peace, especially the idea that human beings might somehow create a completely disarmed world. This is not a realizable civic possibility. The twenty-first century promises to be one of continuous disruption and upheaval. To explore this problem, we must look at the strengths and weaknesses of our own tradition, for example, the just war insistence that there are moral limits to action that must be articulated and respected. Perhaps we can move to a civic identity for men and women along the lines of what I call *chastened patriotism.* The chastened patriot loves his or her country but is also concerned about other countries and acknowledges the dangers of nationalistic excess. The chastened patriot is the man and woman who keeps alive a remembrance of the way in which patriotism can shade into the excesses of warlike nationalism. This means that he or she is a critic of *armed civic virtue* as an ideal and that he or she supports, instead, efforts to disarm civic virtue and, hence, to find nonviolent ways of fighting. We will always have tension, disagreement, conflict. But perhaps the best way in which we can honor our just warrior and beautiful soul forebearers is by trying to find ways to stop the killing and the dying and the mourning, however worthy and honorable.

NOTES

1. See the collected essays of Clifford Geertz, *The Interpretation of Culture* (New York: Basic Books, 1973).

2. J. Glenn Gray, *The Warriors* (New York: Harper Colophon, 1970), 217.

3. Georgia Dullea, "Women Who Served in Vietnam Emerge as Victims of War Strain," *New York Times,* March 23, 1981, 1, B-12.

4. Aristotle, *Politics,* ed. and trans. by Ernest Barker (New York: Oxford University Press, 1962), bk. 2, 79.

5. Machiavelli's *Discourses,* quoted in J. R. Hale, "Machiavelli and the Self-Sufficient State," in David Thompson, ed., *Political Ideas* (New York: Penguin Books, 1966), 22–23.

6. Plutarch, *Moralia III,* 459, 463, trans. Frank Cole Babbitt (Cambridge: Harvard University Press, 1931).

7. Shelley Saywell, *Women in War* (New York: Viking, 1959), 132, 149.

8. Rhonda Cornum as told to Peter Copeland, *She Went to War* (Novalto, CA: Presidium Press, 1992), 14.

9. In ibid., 14.

10. Jean Bethke Elshtain, *Women and War* (New York: Basic Books, 1987), 191.

11. Ibid., 140.

❖ 8 ❖

The Cold War and the Feminine Mystique

Rebecca Grant

"America in the 1950s" is a phrase that conjures up competing images: the danger of atomic bombs, the fantasies of carefree girls with ponytails and boyfriends in chinos and leather jackets. For Feminist scholars, the 1950s bred the stereotypes of gender roles that drove later generations to intellectual and political rebellion. For international relations, this was the early cold war period, when foreign policy and the role of the military in peacetime transformed from the pre–World War II model of sporadic internationalism to a permanent commitment to global power. Literature analyzing the cold war has sought to understand the domestic roots of this transformation, but the question of whether gender relations reflected or affected the cold war period has seldom—if ever—been raised.

The same is true in reverse: Literature concerned with gender issues and feminism has not focused on the early cold war period as one of particular interest in gender relations. Studies of women in Nazi Germany and of aristocratic women in the Renaissance establish that fluctuations in the nature of the state and its security often parallel changes in the status of women. However, for the most part, few Feminist scholars have enquired into the 1950s with the objective of tracing gender relations and the transformation of America's international role.

Recently, one particular coincidence suggested to me that the 1950s might be fruitful ground for exploring the links between concepts of gender and concepts of security. The first time that I read Betty Friedan's book, *The Feminine Mystique*, I was struck by her offhand references to the atomic bomb and other aspects of cold war life in the United States throughout the text.[1] Thinking about it again years later, it occurred to me that the coincidence might be significant. The references and historical atmosphere of the book hinted at something more. *The Feminine Mystique* was not only one of the pioneering books of popular feminism, but it emerged from and was rooted in the early cold war period. Underneath the main story of her text was evidence of an elaborate structure of concepts of gender woven into and around the international role of the state.

The Feminine Mystique was researched and written between 1957 and 1962, the peak phase of the cold war. 1957 was the year in which the Soviet Union orbited the world's first satellite, Sputnik, and touched off U.S. fears of a long-range nuclear strike from the Soviet Union. October 1962 brought those fears to a crisis point when Kennedy faced Khrushchev during the Cuban missile crisis. Linking the time period to Friedan's evolving thesis on women in America forms the core of this chapter. The trends described by Friedan portrayed a changing pattern of gender relations that shaped and was shaped by the cold war. The resurgence of a feminine stereotype in U.S. popular culture paralleled the evolution toward superpower status and permanent global security commitments—a transition that broke with ingrained historical attitudes toward peacetime military forces and with patterns of U.S. foreign policy.

At first glance, international politics seldom played more than an anecdotal role in Friedan's account of the interplay of femininity and society. However, on closer inspection, the core of Friedan's arguments about the origins of the feminine mystique depended on the post–World War II setting. It seemed to me that the same domestic and international events that shaped foreign policy and national security concerns in the early cold war period also played a role in creating the *feminine mystique.* Indeed, the mystique was part of the intellectual history of the cold war.

THE FEMININE MYSTIQUE

What was the feminine mystique? Friedan used the label to describe an ideal of femininity that flourished in the late 1940s and throughout the 1950s. Friedan's consciousness-raising descriptions of American women were situated within a society that had moved away from the relative increase in opportunities for women in education and employment during World War II. Though she postulated that the war made women vulnerable to the mystique, it was after the war that, according to Friedan, a more repressive stereotype of femininity gained prominence in popular culture and permeated institutions ranging from the family to colleges and universities.

Under the terms of what Friedan called the mystique, women's highest commitment was "the fulfillment of their femininity."[2] Because it described a stereotype, the mystique centered on the experiences of white, middle-class women—the narrow image associated with the popular ideals of the 1950s as portrayed in the mass media. The problem with the mystique at its worst was that it did not value the creativity and intelligence of women outside a narrow definition of femininity that revolved around the home. Yet far from being a stereotype forced on women against their will, elements of the mystique were embraced by women and men alike. As Friedan saw it, women persuaded themselves that clean floors or home-baked biscuits were the real way to fulfillment. Many of the women whom Friedan interviewed gave up educations and career goals in order to live up to the mystique's ideals of how to fulfill the feminine self.

Ultimately, it was frustration with the mystique that brought the phenomenon to Friedan's attention. She first called the symptoms "the problem that had no name," a yearning by women for sources of fulfillment beyond what the mystique prescribed. College-educated women were a particular subject. Friedan found that the lesson for women college students between 1945 and 1960 was "*not* to get seriously interested in anything besides getting married and having children" if they wanted to be "normal, happy, adjusted, feminine."[3] One graduating senior said her friends did not want to be serious about their studies or undertake careers in something "peculiar" and "unfeminine" like research: "I guess everybody wants to graduate with a diamond ring on her finger. That's the important thing."[4]

But living out the mystique as housewives brought as much frustration as fulfillment. Women who met socially talked of home and children. As Friedan wrote: "Nobody argued whether women were inferior or superior to men; they were simply different. Words like 'emancipation' and 'career' sounded strange and embarrassing; no one had used them for years."[5]

The feminine mystique was (constructed from) a mixture of Freudian psychoanalytic theory, trends in sociology and education, and the conditions of postwar society. While the mystique had many sources, Friedan's characterization made clear that chronologically the mystique was a phenomenon of the cold war period. Friedan's thesis (and much of her controlled outrage in the book) was that the feminine mystique was not an inherent feature of U.S. society but a phenomenon that developed in the aftermath of World War II. *The Feminine Mystique* documented a transformation in the role of women based on social and economic conditions. In the historical context, two broad factors—national security and economics—combined in the creation of the mystique.

First, part of the impetus for both women and men to subscribe to a more traditional view of the feminine role may have been a response to the aftermath of World War II and to the new conditions accompanying the evolution of the cold war. Friedan's text singled out some compelling examples of a sociological transformation underway in U.S. society after the war. One aspect was a shunning of broader concerns with the fate of the world in favor of a focus on the feminine realm of domesticity. After the trauma of the war and the development of the atomic bomb, both women and men "sought the comforting reality of home and children," Friedan postulated, and women "went home again just as men shrugged off the bomb, forgot the concentration camps."[6]

Friedan argued that from that human turning back to the home, women also took a path toward a mystique of feminine fulfillment in the domestic realm. Changing economic conditions and societal attitudes melted opportunities for women in the workplace and in education. By the late 1950s, more women dropped out of college, married younger, forsook careers, and suffered isolation in the suburbs. This was the crux of Friedan's thesis—namely, that society's views of femininity and women's views of themselves were bound up with the mystique of feminine fulfillment based on family, children, and even sexuality, rather than on active discovery of a self beyond these commitments. Historically, the phenomenon could not be analyzed apart from underlying postwar conditions. Friedan wrote that in the years after World War II, "this mystique of feminine fulfillment became the cherished and self-perpetuating core of contemporary American culture."[7]

If international events from 1945 to 1960 created some of the conditions for the growth of a mystique of femininity, what effect did it have on international policy in turn? Marshaling a heightened national image of the feminine role was part of the process of legitimizing the military and cultural foundations of America's superpower status. The United States' role in the cold war required domestic society to adapt to complex ideological and military challenges stemming from the international environment. The status of gender relations in U.S. society fluctuated as part of this broader process of adaptation.

Friedan never explicitly addressed international politics in language familiar to students of international relations. However, *The Feminine Mystique* offered some explanation of the historical context of the changing views about women. Attempting to explain the origins of the mystique, Friedan broadened responsibility for the growth of the feminine mystique to encompass a societal apathy characteristic of the early cold war. The issues raised by the beginning of a global military confrontation provoked denial on a wide scale. She theorized that what happened to women was "part of what happened to all of us in the years after the war." Friedan explained that "it was easier, safer, to think about love and sex than about communism, McCarthy, and the uncontrolled bomb. It was easier to look for Freudian sexual roots in man's behavior, his ideas, and his wars than to look critically at his society and act constructively to right its wrongs."[8]

The loss of interest in social problems beyond the individual and family may have reflected disillusionment in the aftermath of war and the new reality of nuclear confrontation. Friedan cited a researcher who suggested that early marriages were on the increase in the 1950s in part because young people "saw no other true value in contemporary society."[9] Friedan noted that the postwar "baby boom" took place in other countries but was not "permeated . . . with the mystique of feminine fulfillment" as it was in the United States.[10]

These hints and allusion suggested to me that the feminine mystique flourished in part because it filled a gap in what might be described as national identity. As the U.S. adapted to a more taxing international environment, the process required new confirmation of fundamental principles—the values that legitimize war and international violence—inherent in the political contract. At one level, the feminine mystique buttressed the image of masculinity and eased the remilitarization of American society in the early 1950s. To adapt to the demands of the cold war, U.S. society drew on and cultivated a heightened view of femininity.

A second source for the feminine mystique of the 1950s may have been rooted in economic trends. World War II gave women in the United States unprecedented access to well-paying jobs in the defense sector. Women served in all branches of the armed forces during the war. While they had been segregated initially into special women-only organizations attached to the service branches, such as the WAVES, the WAACs, and the SPARS, they also ferried bomber aircraft, deployed to combat zones in Europe and the South Pacific, and performed tasks that still cause controversy today.

The economic opportunities did not last. Few women remained in the defense sector, either as civilians or as military personnel, after demobilization began. Returning to home and family put women in a different position in a relatively short period of time. Part of the record of the feminine mystique was the decline of professional interests among women in favor of taking on the challenges of the housewife. These findings paralleled Friedan's interviews with young women who saw college not as a training ground for a career but as a route to marriage.

Another aspect of Friedan's analysis centered on documenting how advertisers rushed to push the appliances and products to make women more feminine through the excellence of their housework or by keeping them youthful and attractive. One could suggest that encouraging domestic consumption related in a complex way to the economic growth in the 1950s that made it possible for the federal government to spend a relatively large share of the gross national product on defense.

One chilling example came from Friedan's analysis of advertising in a chapter titled "The Sexual Sell." A 1945 study surveyed attitudes of women toward electric appliances, grouping women according to how much of their lives and interests revolved around the home. Advertisers used such studies to target their pitch for everything from cake mix to clothing, based on their findings about women's views of their own femininity. As Friedan noted, the 1945 study was of interest to companies that "were going to have to make consumer sales take the place of war contracts."[11] Thus did war, economics, and popular culture combine in this instance to fuel a feminine mystique that limited roles for women but valued their purchasing power.

The blatant interests of manufacturers tailoring new markets had a more subtle counterpart in validating a greater role for the peacetime military than Americans had accepted previously. The image of the woman as ultra-feminine and dependent invigorated the need to protect her and what she stood for. The feminine mystique, then, was part of an image of gender relations that provided legitimacy for the state's activities abroad. The classic image of men marching off to war to defend their property, wives, and children is one simple example. The feminine mystique magnified the feminine component and, by extension, reinforced the image of masculinity central to the basic Western political contract.

What shocked Friedan was the timing—namely, that an enlightened, modern society that permitted women greater freedoms in the Depression and in wartime could again turn to a more restrictive image of femininity. The explanation lies in the magnitude of change that cold war foreign policies extracted from the U.S. body politic. The dominant features of the early cold war were ideological competition between American capitalism and Soviet communism, the struggle for economic dominance in a global market, and the special challenges of security in a nuclear world. In the area of international security in particular, responding to the challenge tapped the construction of images of masculinity and femininity in U.S. society. Gender relations were part of the foundation that shaped the character of the state's policies in the international arena.

During the early phases of the cold war, the role of the military in American society was in flux. While with hindsight this transition is taken for granted, it was not an easy or smooth process in the late 1940s and early 1950s. Taking on the mantle of global security interests ran counter to previous U.S. experience.

Becoming a global military power—with the investment in national resources and *manpower*—placed unprecedented demands on the relation between the military and civilian society in the United States. Traditions of isolation and aloofness from long-term involvement in European power politics were more in character for the historical policy line of the U.S. in peacetime. After World War I, the United States refused to join the League of Nations, Congress set up commissions to investigate war profits by arms manufacturers, and American diplomats promoted fashionable idealism such as the 1928 Kellogg-Briand Pact to outlaw war. Yet after a brief flurry of peacemaking diplomacy in the late 1940s, exemplified by hopes for the United Nations Organization, the United States went against the historical grain to rebuild and maintain a large peacetime military and to finance the industrial base to equip it.

The process required deliberate action and debate for the decade after the end of the war. In 1948, when the first Berlin crisis began, the United

States did not have many forces based overseas. About 100,000 troops were stationed in Europe, a minimal occupation force stretched by policing duties and not ready for prolonged combat. At home, force levels for all the services reached their postwar low. Even with the stimulus of the Korean war, rearming was a difficult transition. Heated debate accompanied the decisions in the early 1950s to deploy U.S. troops to Europe on a permanent basis. By 1951, six army divisions were on their way to permanent posts in Europe to fortify NATO, and another eight army divisions were in Korea.

My point here is that the changing direction of international policy had consequences for the status of gender relations because the roots of those policies ran deep into American culture and society. The interplay of images of masculinity and femininity at the most fundamental social and economic levels cannot be separated from the foreign policy decisions. By the time that Truman ordered forces to Korea in the summer of 1950, the Soviet Union was seen as an enemy of colossal proportion. Communism embodied by the Soviets appeared to—and actively aspired to—threaten the American way of life.

To mount the defense against potential Soviet aggression, the United States had to present its most masculine image to legitimize the military component necessary for national security. The *policy of containment* articulated in the late 1940s and early 1950s relied on masculine symbolism. George Kennan, frequently cited as the conceptual architect of containment, wrote: "Should the Western world . . . muster up the *political manliness* to deny Russia either moral or material support for the consolidation of Russian power throughout Eastern and Central Europe, Russia would probably not be able to maintain its hold successfully for any length of time over all of the territory over which it has today staked out a claim." [12] This quotation illustrates Kennan's impeccably subtle argument that political containment, rather than military force, should be the backbone of U.S. foreign policy in the cold war. That makes it all the more interesting that he should talk about the "political manliness" of Western states in an argument for shrewd diplomacy, not war. The term unintentionally expressed the concepts of gender underneath the new concepts of postwar security.

To muster the political resolve that Kennan described as "manliness," the West, and the United States particularly, emphasized traditional concepts of femininity to generate more of the public "political manliness" through contrast. The women who lived out the feminine mystique may or may not have been conscious of choices and alternatives as individuals. They may or may not have seen their lives as part of a societal phenomenon. However, to a degree, the feminine mystique was a response to the international climate.

One of the most intriguing overlaps of the cold war and the feminine mystique centered on the way in which U.S. society came to terms with the atomic bomb. To most Americans in 1945, the bomb was a wonder of technology, a terrible agent of destruction, yet a force that might also be harnessed for good. Popular literature and articles for the first few years after Hiroshima and Nagasaki often reflected a certain optimism about nuclear technology and its benefits. As late as 1948, *U.S. News & World Report* published an article entitled "Atom: Key to Better Farming," extolling the virtues of atomic fertilizer. Other articles speculated about atomic home appliances or atomic locomotives. These mundane examples illustrated a belief that atomic power could be an engine of social change for individuals and perhaps for society itself. Another topic of debate was whether the destructive power of the atom would force nations toward a world government in order to avoid atomic war.[13]

By the late 1950s, as Friedan began work on *The Feminine Mystique,* more was known about the dangers of radioactive fallout and nuclear testing. Public enthusiasm for fanciful atom projects had cooled. However, now the perils of the atomic age made an appearance as defining features of the social environment. Houses constructed in the 1950s often boasted fallout shelters. In some towns, children drilled at school on what to do in a nuclear attack. Friedan wrote with clinical horror about an article published in 1957 on how to give birth in an atom bomb shelter. The mystique suggested that women "might be interested in the concrete, biological details of having a baby in a bomb shelter, but never in the abstract idea of the bomb's power to destroy the human race."[14] Implied was that the mystique could be powerful enough to distract mothers from thoughts of Armageddon.

In addition to these incursions into domestic life, the cold war underlined traditional divisions of labor supporting the mystique. Friedan quoted an American educator who suggested that women not be admitted to colleges because "the education which girls could not use as housewives was more urgently needed than ever by boys to do the work of the atomic age."[15] She also quoted a similar remark made by Democratic candidate Adlai Stevenson in 1955 as he prepared for his second presidential campaign against Dwight D. Eisenhower. Stevenson told an audience at elite, all-women Smith College in Massachusetts that "there is much you can do about our crisis in the humble role of housewife."[16] Another trend was what Friedan termed "sex-directed education" where the top priority for educators was to "adjust" curricula for women to their anticipated role as housewives. In a quick reference buried in a discussion of the ups and downs of sex-directed education, Friedan mentioned that no one asked whether adjustment should be the aim of education until the Russians had put men in space and orbited the moon, referring to Sputnik and other Soviet space successes.[17]

IMPLICATIONS FOR GENDER ISSUES
AND INTERNATIONAL SECURITY

What does the combination of the cold war and the feminine mystique tell us about how images of masculinity and femininity affect international politics? As Simone de Beauvoir wrote in *The Second Sex* in 1948, "Most female heroines are oddities. . . . Joan of Arc, Mme. Roland, Flora Tristan . . . are exemplary figures rather than historical agents," and the masses of women "are on the margin of history, and circumstances are an obstacle for each individual, not a springboard."[18] Here de Beauvoir enters Friedan's territory. Women are seen as a group, and the effects of their constrained—oppressed—identity become the agent of history. In the United States in the 1950s, the mystique named the passive but critical role of women in playing to the image of enhanced femininity as part of the social contract for a state of cold war to exist.

De Beauvoir's next point suggests why the feminine mystique was bound up with the cold war: "Because of woman's marginal position in the world, men will turn to her when they strive through culture to go beyond the boundaries of their universe and gain access to something other than what they have known."[19] For American society, entry into the cold war and the realm of nuclear confrontation was a step beyond the boundaries of the previous foreign policy universe. De Beauvoir's larger point in this excerpt was about how women's success had been bound up with arts and letters, not war and politics. But the portrait of the feminine as creative muse applies to other activities that stretch out the boundaries of the "universe" of the body politic at a particular point in time. The need to gain access to a different way of perceiving the world applies to international politics as well as to art. It applied with force in the early cold war period; here, the feminine mystique may be said to have been a source for viewing the world in a way different from past political traditions.

Friedan's "sign-posting" of the historical context provides compelling evidence that concepts of gender were part of a transition to different concepts of security. The growth of the feminine mystique was not an inevitable consequence. For example, the first steps of the United States into global empire at the turn of the twentieth century were not shadowed by a feminine mystique of the same proportions as in the 1950s. America's rapid victory in the Spanish-American War in 1898 led to prolonged U.S. involvement in the Philippines and to a searching national debate on imperialism. To Jane Addams, a prominent social reformer and founder of Hull House in Chicago, the Spanish-American War sparked an interest in the peace movement that led her to a prominent role in the women's peace movement during World War I.[20] Addams' responses to the dawning global interests are in contrast to the period of the feminine mystique and the early cold war.

Addams drew on her experience with the plight of labor—especially women and children—to argue in her 1907 book that a woman should have a right to vote because "she is essential to the normal development of the city of the future, and because the definition of the loyal citizen as one who is ready to shed his blood for his country, has become inadequate and obsolete."[21] To Addams, feminine values were a force for reform powerful enough to *sublimate* martial values. Popular psychological theories of the time advocated channeling the will to war into games and other forms of "combat" regulated by society as a way to end war. Addams took a cue from these theories. Her substitutes for war and the military spirit required an egalitarian regard for the role of women as workers and citizen-leaders for the "city of the future." Instead of turning inward to support man and the family, women had a social responsibility to fulfill in civic and international politics—as part of the process of evolving beyond violence in cities or between states. The feminine mystique Friedan described did just the opposite. In the 1950s, a heightened image of femininity served to reinforce nationalism and make martial values more prominent through the force of contrast—just the reverse of what Jane Addams theorized in her era.

CONCLUSION

The overlap of the feminine mystique and the cold war opens a different way to understand the phenomenon of the cold war and the concepts of a gender that were part of it. To do so within the international relations field, however, is complicated by terms of reference. Feminist perspectives, in all their diversity, offer transformation, not adjustment. And this crosses two taboos for international relations scholars. The first is the unacceptable tackiness of prescribing action. The second is that arguing for a different way of looking at sexual imagery and national security smacks of wide-eyed idealism, of not being realistic enough about the cold barren surfaces of *Realpolitik.*

Now that the cold war is apparently over and Feminist literature has grown beyond *The Feminine Mystique,* are there new lessons to uncover about gender relations and international security? Does the greater emphasis on equality and empowerment for women or the recent trends identified as a backlash against women relate to current-day security issues? Moving beyond the parallels of the mystique and the cold war, does exploring the dimension of gender relations suggest conclusions of value to students of international politics? These questions are up to you. As you consider them, you may find a new book titled *The Morning After: Sexual Politics at the End of the Cold War,* in which author Cynthia Enloe has begun to examine these possibilities, a useful starting point.[22]

NOTES

1. Betty Friedan, *The Feminine Mystique* (New York: Norton, 1963).
2. Ibid., 43.
3. Ibid., 156.
4. Ibid., 153.
5. Ibid., 19.
6. Ibid., 186.
7. Ibid., 19.
8. Ibid., 186–87.
9. Ibid., 188.
10. Ibid., 183.
11. Ibid., 209.
12. George Kennan, *Memoirs, 1925–1950* (New York: Bantam, 1967), 581; emphasis added.
13. Paul Boyer, *By the Bomb's Early Light* (Berkeley: University of California Press, 1983).
14. Friedan, *Feminine Mystique*, 51.
15. Ibid., 23.
16. Ibid., 67.
17. Ibid., 159.
18. Simone de Beauvoir, *The Second Sex* (London: Picador, 1988), 162–63.
19. Ibid., 163.
20. See Sybil Oldfield, "Jane Addams: The Chance the World Missed," in Francine D'Amico and Peter R. Beckman, eds., *Women in World Politics: An Introduction* (Westport, CT: Bergin & Garvey, 1995).
21. Allen F. Davis, *The Life and Legend of Jane Addams* (New York: Oxford University Press, 1973), 173.
22. Cynthia Enloe, *The Morning After: Sexual Politics at the End of the Cold War* (Berkeley: University of California Press, 1993).

❖9❖

The United Nations and Women's Issues

Margaret E. Galey

When the victorious Allies created the United Nations at the end of World War II, their principal concern was to promote peace and prevent another world war. They also aimed at promoting economic and social progress and human rights without discrimination as to race, sex, nationality, or religion. These goals, reflected in the UN Charter, were agreed upon by the fifty-one delegations at the San Francisco Conference in 1945. Almost immediately, however, "women's issues" began to appear on the UN's agenda. What are women's issues? How did they reach the UN? How has the UN dealt with them? Why is the UN's involvement in women's issues important?

An *issue* is a point in question or a matter in dispute between contending parties whose resolution has special public, political importance.[1] In the UN, issues are raised, debated, and resolved by official representatives of governments (delegates) within the institution's principal political organs: the General Assembly (GA), the Economic and Social Council (ECOSOC), and the Security Council (SC).[2] Delegates act under government instruction and articulate national foreign policy positions that differ, sometimes dramatically, on points of substance or procedure. Debates among delegates mirror conflict as well as cooperation among governments in world politics. In working out differences, delegates reach decisions called resolutions by majority vote or by consensus.[3]

Historically, men who have participated in the public arena—of which the UN is an example—have taken women's voice for granted, according to some scholars.[4] In contrast, women traditionally relegated to the private sphere of the home, family, child bearing and child rearing have had to work to gain a voice in the public arena and to obtain their rights even before the UN was established. In voicing their interests, women came into conflict with existing custom or law and created issues over their right to own property or to vote. Men in positions of power dubbed women's concerns "women's issues." In nineteenth-century England, a bundle of women's issues—suffrage, participation in parliament, property ownership, and better working conditions and wages—constituted what members of parliament and journalists called "the woman question."

WOMEN AND THE UN

When the UN was established in 1945, determined women aimed at making known their views in this new international intergovernmental arena, and the goals of the UN Charter, an international treaty, enabled them to do so. Its three major goals were: (1) to prevent future war and promote peace and security, (2) to foster economic and social progress, and (3) to promote and protect the fundamental freedoms and human rights of peoples and individuals without distinction as to race, sex, nationality, or religion.

The third goal, in particular, known as the "equality clause," offered a handful of interested women delegates a legal-constitutional justification for creating a UN Commission on the Status of Women (CSW) at the first session of the ECOSOC in 1946. The Commission, comprised of women appointed by governments, made recommendations to ECOSOC, its parent body, in order to improve women's political, economic, social, and civil status. Its members met regularly to discuss and resolve issues of women's status, and over the years built a creditable record of achievement with the help of a supporting UN Secretariat and the participation of interested international nongovernmental organizations (NGOs). ECOSOC in turn transmitted the recommendations to the General Assembly and its Third Committee on Social and Humanitarian Affairs for discussion and ultimate decision.[5] The Commission and the GA's Third Committee soon became known as the "women's committees" because of their emphasis on "women's issues" and because more women were represented there than in any other UN commission or committee.

The Commission decided to commemorate its twenty-fifth anniversary in 1972 by calling for an International Women's Year (IWY) to take place in 1975 and then for a conference of governments to commemorate IWY. The historic 1975 conference held in Mexico City endorsed the "World Plan of Action" and recommended a UN "Decade for Women" to publicize the importance of improving women's status in countries throughout the world. A second conference of governments met in Copenhagen in 1980 to approve a "World Program of Action." A third conference convened in Nairobi in 1985 to review and appraise progress achieved and to approve the "Forward Looking Strategies to the Year 2000." Together with the parallel unofficial conferences of nongovernmental organizations, the government conferences provided a place for women from all UN member governments to meet, resolve issues, and agree on strategies to advance their status worldwide. A fourth UN–sponsored women's conference is scheduled for Beijing, China, in 1995. Nüket Kardam discusses these conferences in this anthology; Kristen Timothy and Deborah Stienstra do so in the companion volume, *Women in World Politics.*

WOMEN'S ISSUES

Beginning in 1946, the Commission on the Status of Women first discussed issues of legal equality: the right to vote, to stand for and to hold public office, and to obtain equal pay in employment as well as equal treatment by civil authorities. Then in the 1960s, women's role in economic and social development became a priority. By the late 1970s and 1980s, the CSW began to emphasize women's contribution to peace and security. Thus, over its historical development, the CSW has addressed three major categories of women's issues that parallel the UN's major purposes: (1) peace and security, (2) economic and social development, and (3) human rights without distinction as to race, sex, nationality, or religion.

Equality

To address the *equality* category of women's issues, the CSW sought to define and recommend narrow and specific and then more comprehensive measures to improve women's legal status. In doing so, the commissioners relied upon the UN Charter's "equality clause" and their own awareness of women's inequality in political, economic, educational, and civil spheres.

Commission members began their campaign for women's equality with formal political rights because in 1945 only about half the then-sovereign states granted women the right to vote or to hold public office. They discussed how best to influence governments to grant women their political rights. They considered a legally binding international treaty, known as a convention, as well as nonbinding recommendations to governments to enact national legislation. The majority decided on a convention or treaty, the Convention on the Political Rights of Women, which ECOSOC and the GA approved in 1952.[6] This treaty required states that ratified it to grant women the right to vote, to stand for election, and to hold public office.

Another formal political right defined by the CSW was women's participation in the UN Secretariat staff, particularly in professional and higher-level posts. To this end, members made numerous recommendations to governments urging them to nominate qualified women to such Secretariat posts.

Meanwhile, the CSW worked to advance women's equality in employment and education. Members discussed the universal need for applying the principle and practice of equal pay for work of equal value and encouraged the International Labor Organization (ILO), a UN Specialized Agency, to prepare the Convention on Equal Pay. The ILO responded and approved the convention in 1951. Similarly, after studying educational opportunities for women and girls, CSW members spurred the UN Educational Scientific and Cultural Organization (UNESCO), also a UN Specialized Agency, to prepare and approve the Convention on Eliminating Discrimination against Women in Education by 1961.

Besides its work in education, employment, and political rights, the CSW also aimed at correcting inequalities in civil and family law. One example was marriage. In many countries, marriages were arranged and child brides common; girls were married at age eleven or twelve. Bride price and payment of dowry were practiced in some territories. Often marriages were not even recorded. Members advocated delaying the age of marriage to enable young women to gain education and prepare for marriage and family, eliminating bride price and dowry, and registering marriages and divorces to give women legal standing in the community.

After deliberating on these matters for more than a decade, the CSW recommended a Convention on the Consent to Marriage, the Minimum Age of Marriage, and Registration of Marriages, which the General Assembly approved in 1962. It provided that no marriage should be entered into without full and free consent of both parties, that states should prescribe a minimum age for marriage and that all marriages should be registered. Subsequently, the CSW sponsored studies on the legal conditions and effects of annulment, judicial separation, and divorce on women and recommended measures to support equal treatment of women before the law. It then initiated studies of the relation of family planning and the status of women. Despite initial objection of several predominantly Roman Catholic countries, members soon defined and agreed on a new women's right to obtain information on family planning and to decide on the number and spacing of children.

After preparing several specific conventions and numerous resolutions to advance women's equality, in the late 1960s the CSW began work on two comprehensive measures. Members first recommended a non–legally binding Declaration and then the Convention on the Elimination of Discrimination against Women (CEDAW). The latter, called the Women's Convention, the first comprehensive international treaty on women's rights, imposed legal obligations on governments that ratified it to incorporate its provisions into domestic law and practice. This is particularly important because it for the first time defines and prohibits discrimination based on sex in all spheres, public and private. The Women's Convention was approved by the General Assembly in 1979. By 1981, after twenty states ratified it, it came into force as law for UN members who signed it. An international committee established by the Women's Convention annually reviews reports from governments that have ratified it.

Economic and Social Development

In the 1960s, an increasing number of new states from Africa and Asia joined the UN, and the GA approved the First UN Development Decade, making economic growth a major priority. The Commission on the Status of Women responded by considering women's role in development. UN representatives had defined economic development in reference to increasing per capita/GNP but had neglected the role of women in development.

The challenge for the CSW was to define women's role in development in all societies. Its members assessed UN programs, women's role in community development and the relation of family planning to women's status. By 1970, members recommended a Long-Term Program for the Advancement of Women. That year, Ester Boserup's now famous book, *The Role of Women in Economic Development,* appeared and spurred further CSW deliberations. Boserup demonstrated that women were not only reproducers of children, but also producers of goods and services. For instance, women were primary food producers. She also asserted that GNP-based economic-development programs changed production patterns from family-subsistence production to specialized production of goods for sale or export and shifted the division of labor between men and women, which in turn affected women's role adversely.[7] Her analysis is discussed elsewhere in this book by Nüket Kardam and by Geeta Chowdhry.

This thought-provoking book helped CSW members as well as participants in UN-sponsored conferences to recognize the need for research and data gathering on women and development as a basis for policy and program development. Resulting studies and reports affirmed existing problems, such as women's invisible work, that is, work that was unpaid and/or unrecognized. These studies also helped the UN staff prepare development strategies to assist women, and identified new problems, such as the feminization of poverty and the increasing number of female-headed households.[8]

The growing emphasis on development also led to several new international institutions following the 1975 conference on IWY. One was the UN Development Fund for Women (UNIFEM). Funded by voluntary contributions of governments, UNIFEM provided direct, practical assistance and training to women in developing countries. For instance, UNIFEM provided seed monies to help women acquire income-generating skills, such as making and marketing handicrafts, and for projects to reduce women's need to carry water long distances by drilling wells near households or farming areas. UNIFEM is headed by a director and is governed by a five-member Consultative Committee to screen requests for project funding. UNIFEM has been autonomous from, but located within offices of, the UN Development Program (UNDP) in New York.

Another new institution is the Institute for Training and Research for the Advancement of Women (INSTRAW). Like UNIFEM, INSTRAW is also an autonomous body within the UN, funded by voluntary contributions from governments and private sources. INSTRAW is located in the Dominican Republic and is headed by a director working with an international board of trustees. Its program has concentrated on two priorities: research and training. Its research activities aim at making women visible by defining their situation comprehensively. INSTRAW has contributed to major statistical compilations, *World Survey on the Role of Women in Development* and *World's Women: Statistics and Indicators.* INSTRAW has also designed ways to monitor and evaluate programs and projects on women and development and has sponsored a global study on financial and credit policies and their effect on women's access to credit. Its training program concentrates on seminars and workshops to train development officials, UN field staff, nongovernmental organizations, and women's organizations in development planning, women in development, and statistics.[9]

A nongovernmental institution affiliated with the UN, the International Women's Tribune Center was established to maintain communication with participants at the 1975 unofficial conference, La Tribuna. The Center has circulated newsletters and published and disseminated handbooks on various topics, for instance, on organizing community-action groups, improving fuel efficiency in cooking, and starting cooperatives. As a result, the Center has developed a worldwide network of individuals and groups interested in supporting women's activities.

Despite these new institutions and a growing number of women and development programs in national governments, lives of poor women in developing countries have not improved as some development specialists had hoped. However, as useful as such studies and reports have been, development planners, because of their own gender bias, have not always heeded their recommended strategies to assist women. Newer studies aim to correct such bias and redress adverse or unintended effects of several programs.[10]

Peace and Security

Women have historically worked for peace and security, as Sybil Oldfield illustrates in her chapter about peace activist Jane Addams in the companion volume. In the nineteenth century, many women joined peace societies in the United States and Western Europe. By 1915, the Women's International League for Peace and Freedom (WILPF) was established. After World War I, women in the United States convened a series of Conferences on the Causes and Cure of War. Various American women's groups such as the American Association of University Women (AAUW), the League of Women Voters, Zonta International, Business and Professional Women (BPW), and the Young Women's Christian Association (YWCA) actively supported U.S. ratification of the UN Charter as a path to peace. Their international affiliates served as observers at Commission meetings. East

European women created the Women's International Democratic Federation (WIDF) to support various peace initiatives.

Within the UN itself, many individual women and women's groups have endorsed peace and security measures. These measures include arms control and disarmament and promoting mediation, conciliation, and adjudication of international disputes between states. Other measures that women have supported are defining aggression and developing international law prohibiting the use of force by states. Women and women's groups have also supported peacekeeping operations to prevent the spread of war.

After concentrating on measures of equality and development, CSW members began to define dimensions of peace and security that affected women and children. For instance, they discussed women and children as victims of armed conflict and eventually recommended a declaration on the subject, which the General Assembly approved in 1972. They also determined that 80 percent of the world's refugees were women and children who required special protection and assistance against rape and assault. Subsequently, the CSW recommended that the UN High Commissioner for Refugees sponsor measures to ensure these refugees' personal safety as well as adequate housing and training.[11]

Perhaps the most stunning contribution by the CSW to the notion of peace and security has been their discussion of physical and sexual violence against women. For years, women themselves had avoided acknowledging physical violence despite its destructiveness and growing incidence within the privacy of marriage, home, and family. Fear and humiliation motivated suppression. But in the 1980s, women in the CSW as well as in the 1985 official and unofficial conferences began to raise the matter; to define its practice as rape, forced prostitution, exploitation of women workers or prisoners, or wife beating; and to devise ways to end the violence. Following the 1985 Nairobi Conference, the General Assembly approved Resolution 40/36 recognizing the importance of violence in the home. The CSW sponsored a special seminar on domestic violence in 1986, raising awareness and publicizing the subject. Currently, the commissioners have been discussing a draft Declaration on Eliminating Violence against Women and may consider an international treaty on the subject that, once ratified by governments, would oblige them to prohibit such practices and to punish violators. Meanwhile, NGOs have been active publicizing domestic violence. The Overseas Education Fund International, for instance, sponsored a major study containing a series of thoughtful strategies to combat physical and sexual abuse of women in personal relations.[12]

EFFECT AND IMPORTANCE

What difference has the UN's involvement in women's issues made? Have resolutions recommended by the Commission and approved by the

General Assembly had an effect on governments, the UN Secretariat and the perspectives of UN and government officials as well as ordinary citizens? Has the UN's discussion and resolution of women's issues altered the nature of multilateral diplomacy or the configurations of world political power?

These questions merit further study, but several points can be made. First, as this brief discussion indicates, matters previously encapsulated in the traditional, private domain of woman's world—home, family, children—as well as those already on national public agendas, such as formal political and economic rights, have been moved by women onto the international public agenda for discussion, decision, and implementation by governments. This is a significant political development itself and is symbolized by the retitling of the *Handbook on the Work of the United Nations,* called *Everyman's UN* since its initial publication in 1946, to *Everyone's UN* in 1979.[13]

A related aspect of this political development is that women through their own efforts to internationalize their issues have expanded traditional notions of equality, development, and peace to define dimensions particular to their gender. Several of these dimensions, discussed here, illustrate that women do speak "in a different voice" and demonstrate that women's issues are not only social issues, but are integral to the range of issues before the UN General Assembly.[14]

A third point regarding effect is that the UN, a voluntary association of member governments, has no authority to compel its member governments to accept its decisions. Rather, its members must persuade each other of the importance of accepting decisions. To complicate the matter of effect, UN decisions are aimed at governments, UN agencies as well as its Secretariat or staff. Those decisions directed by member governments to the UN Secretariat are usually, but not always, carried out. Thus, for example, the UN Secretariat staff, has, as discussed here, prepared important studies on various aspects of the status of women for nearly 50 years. Recent studies include *The World's Women: Trends and Statistics* and *Women in Politics and Decision-Making.*[15] These studies have identified trends, such as the feminization of poverty, the increasing number of female-headed households, and women's limited participation in politics and decision making, and have thus been sources for defining new issues for discussion. Importantly, they have helped make women visible in national societies as well as in the public international arena of the UN.

However, the UN Secretariat has not always implemented decisions recommended by members of the CSW and the General Assembly. For instance, it has not yet fulfilled targets for hiring women professional staff. By 1990, the Secretariat failed to achieve the target of hiring 30 percent women in professional posts by 1990. Few women have been appointed to high-level posts as undersecretaries or assistant secretaries general, and no woman has yet served as secretary general.

Yet, such considerations evidence a growing expectation of equality in employment within the UN staff. Undersecretary General Margaret Anstee's career shows that change is underway; she tells her story in the companion volume. In addition, the efforts of the CSW to improve women's political, economic, and civil status have helped change the traditional expectation by UN member governments of women's role within national societies over the last five decades. Recommendations by the CSW and the General Assembly assert the principle of equality and recognize women's contribution to development and peace. This has helped transform traditional views of the role of women and has emphasized the importance of their equal treatment. Even though governments implement UN decisions voluntarily, the CSW and the GA have created the expectation that national governments must treat women citizens accordingly.

Various UN treaties, most notably the Convention on the Elimination of Discrimination against Women, have been especially important to this development. Almost 120 nations, or about two-thirds of the UN's membership, have ratified this first comprehensive treaty on women's rights and have taken steps to implement its provisions in domestic law. The high number of ratifications appears to signify governments' intent to end discriminatory laws and practices. Yet, about forty ratifying states have had reservations, stating that they will not be bound by certain provisions, thus raising the issue of the universality of the Convention's application.

Meanwhile, several governments have signed but not yet ratified the Convention. One is the United States, where there has been a historically active women's movement and whose government boasts a record of legislation that aims at eliminating sex discrimination. This is not to say that the U.S. government should not ratify the Convention, but that there are factors other than government ratification that may promote adherence to the Convention's principles.

There are many more questions to think about in relation to women's issues and the UN. A systematic assessment of the impact of UN decisions on women's issues on governments, UN agencies, and the Secretariat is needed to explain fully the UN's role in improving women's status worldwide. It could also help explain the role of women's issues addressed by the UN within the larger context of world politics. For instance, has the resolution of women's issues affected the nature and practice of multilateral diplomacy? Have women who have become professional diplomats and members of the UN staff thanks to the efforts of the Commission on the Status of Women and women's groups made a difference in solving problems and promoting cooperation among nation-states? Does the evidence of their participation confirm or expand existing Feminist critiques of international relations theories of *realpolitik* and interdependence? Keep these questions in mind as you read on.

NOTES

1. *Webster's Third New International Dictionary,* 1981 ed. s.v. "issue."

2. The other principal organs of the UN are the Trusteeship Council (TC), which oversees the administration of trust territories, the Secretariat, which deals with the administrative burden of the organization and plays an increasing role in efforts at conflict resolution, and the International Court of Justice (ICJ), or World Court, which issues advisory opinions and decides contentious cases.

3. H. K. Jacobson, *Interdependence and the Global System* (New York: Knopf, 1979), especially pt. 2, 81–144.

4. Jean Bethke Elshtain, *Public Man, Private Woman* (Princeton: Princeton University Press, 1981), and Rebecca Grant and Kathleen Newland, *Gender and International Relations* (Bloomington: Indiana University Press, 1991).

5. United Nations, *The UN and the Status of Women* (New York: United Nations, 1964), 3–11.

6. The text of this and subsequent conventions appear in United Nations, *Compendium of International Conventions Concerning the Status of Women,* ST/CSDHA/3 (New York: United Nations, 1988).

7. Ester Boserup, *Women's Role in Economic Development* (New York: St. Martin's, 1970).

8. United Nations, *Compendium of Statistics and Indicators on the Situation of Women* (New York: United Nations, 1986); idem, *1989 World Survey on the Role of Women in Development* (New York: United Nations, 1989).

9. Margaret Shields, "About INSTRAW," *Women and Development News* 18 (Autumn 1992): 3–7.

10. Jodi L. Jacobson, *Gender Bias: Roadblock to Sustainable Development,* World Watch Paper 110 (Washington, DC: World Watch Institute, September 1992). See also Irene Tinker, ed., *Persistent Inequalities* (New York: Oxford University Press, 1990).

11. Pamela A. DeVoe, "The Silent Majority: Women as Refugees," in Rita Gallin, Anne Ferguson, and Janice Harper, eds., *Women and International Development Annual* (Boulder, CO: Westview, 1993), 3:19–51.

12. Margaret Schuler, ed., *Freedom from Violence: Women's Strategies from around the World* (Washington, DC: OEF International, 1992), especially 18–45.

13. United Nations, *Everyone's United Nations,* 9th ed. (New York: United Nations, 1979).

14. For a discussion of the range of issues before the General Assembly, which treats "women's issues" as "social issues," see John Tessitore and Susan Woolfson, eds., *Issues before the 42nd UN General Assembly* (Lanham, MD: University Press of America, 1991).

15. United Nations, *The World's Women, 1970–1990: Trends and Statistics,* ST/ESA/STAT/SER.K/8 (New York: United Nations, 1991); idem, *Women in Politics and Decision-Making in the Late Twentieth Century* (Dordrecht, Neth.: Martinus Nijoff, 1992).

❖ 10 ❖

Women and Development

Nüket Kardam

Development assistance, as an important aspect of world politics, affects women's roles and women's power within societies of the developing world in many ways. Development assistance provides new resources; access to these resources may or may not go to women. It is accompanied by new ways of defining the process of "development," with the potential to alter relationships within society, including gender roles. Although development-assistance efforts have undeniably influenced women, we also need to understand how women have responded to development and have attempted to shape world politics in light of that experience. Not until the rise of an international women's movement with a developmental agenda were issues related to women and development treated in a systematic way by donors and recipients of assistance.

Developing countries have traditionally sought development assistance in the form of financial capital and technical aid. Large-scale capital flows from official sources have become a phenomenon of the post–World War II period. Official development assistance (ODA) consists of loans made to developing countries at favorable interest rates, as well as outright grants by individual states to developing countries and to international organizations, which in turn allocate those funds for development. Technical cooperation and assistance are another part of ODA.

Such assistance often comes from countries that operate under a collective umbrella. Two of the most notable collective-aid providers are the Organization for Economic Cooperation and Development (OECD) (which includes the United States, Western Europe, and Japan) and the Organization of Petroleum Exporting Countries (OPEC) (which includes states such as Kuwait, United Arab Emirates, and Venezuela). According to the *World*

Development Report, 1992, official development assistance from these two sources is approximately $55 billion.[1] This sum was 0.36 percent of the gross national product (GNP) of the member nations, falling short of the 0.7 percent that had been set as an internationally agreed target. There is considerable variation in aid as a proportion of GNP among countries. For example, in 1991, Norway allocated over 1 percent of its GNP while the United States contributed only 0.15 percent. The general trend in the 1980s has been a decline in ODA available to developing nations. In spite of the decline, ODA plays an important role in the economic life of many nations, especially the poorest. In fact, in some forty countries, ODA was more than 10 percent of their GNP.

Although ODA is meant to exclude purely military assistance, the borderline is sometimes blurred. Bilateral development assistance tends to follow the foreign policy priorities and definitions of the donor country and may include military assistance. For example, about 60 percent of U.S. foreign aid consists of military and security assistance, while 40 percent is development assistance. The top recipients of U.S. aid in 1991 were Egypt and Israel, followed by Turkey, Nicaragua, and the Philippines. The five "neediest" nations, in terms of GNP per capita, were Mozambique, Tanzania, Ethiopia, Somalia, and Nepal.[2]

Besides the ODA delivered by donor governments and multilateral development agencies, international nongovernmental organizations (NGOs) provide development assistance as well. Such organizations include the Ford Foundation, CARE (Cooperative American Relief Everywhere), Catholic Relief Services, Working Women's Forum in India, and Development Foundation of Turkey. There are approximately 2,200 NGOs, whose assistance during the 1980s was equivalent to 8 percent of official development assistance. They have generally focused on social priorities such as education, health, and community development. Beyond their financial role, NGOs also act as innovators in development issues and do much to mobilize public support for international cooperation and development.

THE RISE OF AN INTERNATIONAL WOMEN'S MOVEMENT

Development has traditionally been understood as the industrialization of a developing country and its integration into the world capitalist economy. According to economic analysts in the 1950s, the growth of developing countries was constrained primarily by insufficient savings and/or foreign exchange. External financial assistance, it was argued, would fill this resource gap. Capital flows and technical assistance to improve the use of both domestic and external capital would create the conditions for self-sustaining growth.

Most development theorists writing in the 1950s and 1960s assumed that industrialization would liberate women, offer them employment opportunities, and make them citizens of young democracies in the Third World with rights equal to men's. Since the early 1970s, however, it became increasingly clear that most development projects had either ignored women or had made their situations worse.

Initially, development projects were designed to increase GNP; they therefore promoted cash crop agriculture while neglecting subsistence agriculture. Men came to dominate cash-crop farm production, while women dominated subsistence agriculture. Many studies demonstrated how women's status actually declined as a result of development efforts because development planners treated women mainly in their reproductive roles and as unpaid volunteers, failing to take into account women's economic productivity and failing to provide them with such resources as access to credit and to new technology, even in activities traditionally performed by women.[3] For example, when tractors were first introduced to India, males in the family were first taught to drive them; the tractors displaced women in some of the activities for which they had been responsible.

Expansion of cash-crop acreage may add to family income, but it still may mean that women must assist their husbands while they continue to do unpaid work in order to produce subsistence crops for family consumption. Women are not necessarily compensated for their cash-crop labor either; even when they have performed such tasks as seedbed preparation and transplanting, all of the income from sales may go to the men. Under a World Bank project in the Bolivian Altiplano, where women have responsibility for livestock, training in livestock care was nevertheless given to the men, who passed the information on to their wives with inevitable and costly omissions. When modern laundries were installed in connection with a World Bank project in Mexico, men were employed to operate the facilities; the women who had washed and ironed tourists' laundry by hand lost their income.[4] Women in urban areas displaced by such "development" became the main participants of the so-called informal sector, primarily petty trading and often prostitution.

In the 1970s, "development" emerged as the primary concern of the United Nations (UN) as developing countries became the majority and sought to redefine both concepts and agencies of development. Development was redefined to focus on equity and poverty issues as it became apparent that the poor—in most developing countries a majority of the population—had been excluded from the benefits of economic growth. Instead of measuring development by increased national income or GNP per capita, new measurements such as the Physical Quality of Life Index (PQLI) examined literacy, infant mortality, and life expectancy to reflect the treatment of basic human needs. The U.S. government responded with the 1973 "New Directions" legislation that required focusing assistance programs on food, nutrition, health and population, education, and human resources.

These developments provided fertile ground for women's groups in the

United States and abroad to link women with development issues. The term *women in development* (WID) was coined by the women's committee of the Washington, D.C., chapter of the Society for International Development.[5] This group moved to influence the policy of the U.S. Agency for International Development (USAID) by testifying at the congressional hearings that frame U.S. foreign assistance policies. From this group came the concepts that underlie the Percy amendment to the 1973 "New Directions" legislation. This amendment stipulated that bilateral and multilateral assistance programs "be administered so as to give particular attention to those programs, projects, and activities that tend to integrate women into the national economies of foreign countries" and mandated that USAID implement the guidelines.[6]

Beginning in 1970, WID activities within the UN system also increased substantially. Members of the UN, its specialized agencies, and all organs and agencies within the system were invited to cooperate in achieving WID objectives and to make available adequate staff and resources for the advancement of women.

The impetus to include women's issues in UN conferences came from the informal WID network, particularly from supporters in nongovernmental development agencies such as the International Tribune Center, Development Alternatives with Women for a New Era (DAWN), the Association for Women in Development, International Council of Women, and Zonta International.[7] This network is reported to have organized "countermeetings" because women and women's issues had been excluded from UN conference agendas before 1970.

The 1970 resolution of the General Assembly on International Action for the Advancement of Women led to the organization of an Interregional Meeting of Experts on the Role of Women in Economic and Social Development by the UN Division of Social Development in June 1972. In 1974, an International Forum on the role of Women in Population and Development was held as part of the activities of the World Population Year. In 1975, the World Conference of the International Women's Year was held in Mexico, and the period 1975–1985 was declared the UN Decade for Women. The Mexico conference was followed by a middecade conference in Copenhagen in 1980 and an end-of-decade conference in 1985. By the close of the Nairobi conference, an international women's movement on a global basis was evident. In fact, overlapping the official intergovernmental conference in Nairobi, NGOs sponsored Forum '85, which drew 14,000 people. Margaret Galey discusses the UN conferences and Decade for Women in greater detail, as does Kristin Timothy in the companion volume, *Women in World Politics*. I focus on the 1985 conference because at Nairobi, for the first time, the gendered aspect of development was acknowledged by the international community.

The outcome of the Nairobi conference was the publication of a document that treated a number of issues such as legal equality for women, access to economic resources, women's rights to control their own bodies, and the achievement of international peace. The guidelines, called the *Nairobi Forward Looking Strategies for the Advancement of Women,* stipulated that bilateral and multilateral agencies' policies for WID assistance should involve all parts of donor organizations and that programs and policies for WID should be incorporated into their operations. This publication formulated guidelines for national governments and international agencies to implement gender-sensitive strategies in areas such as employment, health, education, food, water, agriculture, industry, housing, and the environment. For example, the economic contributions of rural women to family survival in subsistence economies were emphasized, and ways were sought to reduce their drudgery through appropriate technology, including water pumps, food grinders, and cookstoves, and to provide greater access to productive employment and education. Furthermore, efforts were made to set up compliance mechanisms whereby UN development agencies could be held responsible for the implementation of WID policy.

The Nairobi strategies were adopted by 157 countries. During the next two years, various meetings were convened by international development agencies to develop guidelines for the implementation and monitoring of the guidelines in *Forward Looking Strategies.*[8] At the same time, pressure from government donors encouraged much greater attention to women's issues within the UN system. As a result, there is now general agreement that women are affected differently by development policies and programs. However, there is considerable difference of opinion on *why* women have been disadvantaged by the development process and *how* to rectify the situation.

THE THEORETICAL APPROACHES TO WOMEN'S ISSUES IN DEVELOPMENT

There are a number of theories on how and why women have been disadvantaged in the development process. Depending on the reasons given, policy recommendations vary. Two approaches, the antipoverty approach and the efficiency approach, come under the WID framework. Two others, the neo-Marxist approach and the empowerment approach, offer alternative visions.

The antipoverty approach focuses on low-income women and aims at increasing their employment and income-generating options through better access to productive resources. The assumption is that women's inequality with men is attributable to women's lack of access to private ownership of land and capital and to sexual discrimination in the labor market. Integral to the antipoverty approach was the basic-needs strategy, with its primary purpose of enabling women to provide more effectively for their families the most fundamental human needs (food, shelter, clothing, medical care). At the same time, it was intended as a strategy to ease women's work burdens, to enable them to become more independent economically and to allow them to participate more actively in community-development activities.

Recommended programs and projects for women included increasing literacy, providing loans for small-scale enterprises, and providing upgraded technology to reduce hours of work. While the antipoverty approach may have been based on a desire to ensure that the poor had some control over their own lives, it did not challenge existing patterns of inequality, including the sexual division of labor within households. Many programs attempted to organize women into groups; to provide human development training and/or training in stereotypical female skills such as sewing, knitting, and gardening; and to have group activities through which women attempted to apply the skills that they learned to income-generating activities. Many such programs, in fact, have increased the number of hours that women work. Projects directed exclusively at women and operating in a sex-segregated environment were acceptable as long as there was no possibility of competition for scarce resources between women and men. Mayra Buvinic argues that development projects involving women have mostly been those that do not threaten the "public/private distinction."[9] While the number of antipoverty projects for low-income women have increased since the 1970s, the projects generally have remained small in scale, are developed by nongovernmental organizations, and are assisted by grants rather than loans from international-development agencies.

The efficiency approach is now the predominant one within the WID framework. As developing countries grappled with world recession, falling export prices, and mounting external debt from the mid-1970s onward, development theories reemphasized efficiency and the restoration of economic growth rates. The efficiency approach, in the case of women, rests on the assumption that 50 percent of the human resources available for development are being wasted or underutilized. This approach focuses on the contribution of women to economic growth. It is argued that discrimination is not economically rational; if women are marginal to development programs, it is at the cost of greater productivity. Thus, the economic contributions of women to development are the means to achieve the goals of economic growth and efficiency. As the World Bank has noted: "Leaving questions of justice and fairness aside, women's disproportionate lack of education, with its consequences in low productivity, as well as for the nutrition and health of their families, has adverse effects on the economy at large."[10]

Women generally have less access to resources, such as education and agricultural extension training, provided for development, and they are less likely to be consulted for projects, such as the placement and design of water pumps, related to their traditional activities. A lack of consideration of these issues may lead to inefficient projects that either end in failure or in diminished rates of economic return.

There are many examples of projects in which women have been ignored or their activities have been misperceived. For example, in rubber plantation projects in the Ivory Coast, women were found to be better tappers than the average male; since output was suffering from high turnover among the labor force of single males, a deliberate policy of recruiting and training couples was introduced.[11] In Nepal, women are traditionally responsible for watering trees and, at least near the homestead, protecting the trees against foraging livestock. In a village tree nursery, where women were not specially targeted to receive extension, mostly men took seedlings for planting around their homesteads. Most of the trees died because the women were not aware of the planting program.[12]

The antipoverty and efficiency perspectives represent the approaches that have guided development assistance. They both begin from an acceptance of existing social structures. These perspectives assume that women fared less well because they were overlooked or because their needs were not being addressed. As a result, the perspectives focus only on *how* women could be better integrated into ongoing development initiatives and how they could attain more equal participation in education, employment, and other spheres of society. Two alternative visions, the neo-Marxist and the empowerment perspectives, on the other hand, start by questioning the existing political and economic structures of society.

The neo-Marxist perspective suggests that women's integration serves primarily to maintain existing international structures of inequality. This literature has demonstrated how capitalism (whether it is called the international division of labor, international capitalism, or dependent development) has had a major role in shaping the experience of women from different classes in the agricultural subsistence sector, the urban informal sector, and in certain industries like textiles, electronics, or tobacco.[13] For example, women's intermittent employment in the paid labor force—at low wages—creates a "reserve army of labor." Multinational firms seeking the cheapest, most docile labor have turned to employing young, unmarried women, notably in Hong Kong, Singapore, Korea, and Taiwan, and more recently *maquiladoras* along the Mexican border.[14]

Since social class is an important unit of analysis within the neo-Marxist perspective, policy recommendations include the differential treatment of women from different socioeconomic backgrounds, with different policies for urban middle-class women, urban factory workers, domestic servants, or rural peasant women. Ultimately, however, the implication of this perspective is that, given the nature of capitalist development, women's subordination cannot be overcome unless international and class inequalities are overcome.

The empowerment approach that emerged in the 1980s concentrates on gender and development rather than women and development. Using "gender" instead of "women" emphasizes the social relations of gender and questions the validity of roles ascribed to both women and men in different societies. This approach attempts to combine analysis of women's roles in reproduction with production: This approach "analyzes the nature of women's contribution within the context of work done both inside and outside the household, and rejects the public/private dichotomy that commonly has been used as a mechanism to undervalue family and household maintenance work performed by women."[15]

"Empowerment" broadly means Third World women's achieving control over their own lives by expanded choices, self-reliance, and internal strength. The specific policy recommendations that would flow from this view deal with ways of resolving conflicts between women's reproductive and productive roles. Issues in need of resolution are child care, men's share in the maintenance of the family, and women's participation overall in the redefinition of gender relations and the meaning of development itself. Projects using this approach are rarely found in the program of most mainstream development agencies because the projects emphasize fundamental societal change, including an examination of the social relations of gender. As one author has indicated:

The more common strategy is to provide women (and men) with labor-saving technologies and to assume that women's burden will become sufficiently lightened to enable them to carry out their productive/reproductive responsibilities with less effort. This approach may have an important impact on the lives of individual women but it does little to break down existing stereotypes and male-oriented culture patterns.[16]

The origins of the empowerment approach are derived from grassroots organizations of Third World women. An example of such an organization is DAWN (Development Alternatives with Women for a New Era), a loose formation of individual women. Deborah Stienstra discusses similar groups in her chapter on international women's movements in the companion volume. This newer approach no longer sees women as objects of development assistance but rather as actors in their own right; it sees women as agents of change rather than as passive recipients of development assistance and calls for women to organize themselves for a more effective political voice.

MOVING TOWARD EMPOWERMENT

The international women's movement, as an international social movement, tried to influence world politics by changing the policies of governments and international development agencies. To change these policies, women urged, first, that studies of women's situations be undertaken, and second, that governments demonstrate their commitment to change by providing an institutional base for the design and implementation of new policies.

Research conducted under UN auspices shows that women in developing countries work longer hours, earn less money, have greater responsibilities, are less literate and numerate, and have lower caloric intake in proportion to body weight than men. This knowledge is now in the public arena through the efforts of many activist groups that make up the international women's movement.

Governments in different parts of the world have established ministries of women's affairs or women's bureaus to institutionalize and legitimize a concern for the status of women.[17] European donors such as Sweden, Norway, and Denmark have taken the lead by implementing projects for women and by cofunding women's components of large projects undertaken by multilateral agencies such as the World Bank. Initiatives have also come from nongovernmental organizations in the North and the South. Usually, programs succeed that are formulated and implemented by a coalition of gender-sensitive donor agencies, development practitioners in donor and recipient countries, and Third World women's organizations. There is clearly greater recognition of women's concerns than ever before.

How can one evaluate the efforts of the international women's movement in bringing women's position in development to the international agenda? One way to evaluate development programs for women is to determine the extent to which these programs contribute to women's empowerment. Researcher Karin Himmelstrand has suggested that progress toward empowerment may be estimated in terms of a "scale of empowerment" (see Table 10.1). On this scale, stages of empowerment are ranked from "low"

Table 10.1
A Scale of Empowerment

		Criteria
	High	Control
Degree		Participation
of		Conscientization
Empowerment		Access
	Low	Welfare

Source: Karin Himmelstrand, "Can an Aid Bureaucracy Empower Women? The Case of SIDA," *Issue: A Journal of Opinion* 37:2 (1989):41.

(provisions of welfare) to "high" (giving women control over their choices), depending on the degree to which women are involved in decisions about and implementation of development policies and programs.

The "welfare" category is the earliest criterion of development assistance: It is relief aid for socially vulnerable groups. Traditionally, while capital-intensive industrial and agricultural production focused on increasing the productive capacity of the male labor force, welfare provision for the family was targeted at women and provided by NGOs, such as the mothers' clubs created in many developing countries. This approach assumes that women are passive recipients of development and that their reproductive roles are their most important roles in society. The "access" criterion (corresponding to the WID framework discussed earlier) suggests that women should be provided resources in order to overcome poverty and contribute to economic development.

Development agencies have not generally invested their energies beyond providing women with "welfare" and "access." As women gain consciousness of their position and potential, they want to participate actively in decisions that affect them and then to increase control of their productive and reproductive lives. The steps toward empowerment in Table 10.1 imply changes in social, political, and economic structures that most governments and development agencies are unwilling or unable to address. A few projects, however, have begun to combine "access" with higher stages of "empowerment" in women's conscientization and participation in project design. Moser gives an example:

In the Philippines, GABRIELA (an alliance of local and national women's organizations) ran a project which combined women's traditional task of sewing tapestry with a non-traditional activity, the discussion of women's legal rights and the constitution. A nation-wide educational tapestry making drive enabled the discussions of rights in communities, factories and schools, with the end product, a tapestry of women's rights seen to be a liberating instrument.[18]

There are some good reasons why steps toward empowerment have been difficult. First, women's issues may be used by political leaders as a means to achieve other political goals. In recipient nations, gender issues are easily manipulated by political actors for their own interests. The proponents of even the WID approach often lack political power; thus, resources given to WID turn out to be minimal. When women are considered, it is usually for the purpose of mobilizing them to support male-dominated political parties. In developing countries, the ruling elites usually consider women's issues as an instrument in the competition for power. Women's rights may be granted to send a particular message to competing elites and other states in the international system. Even when rights are granted by law, implementation suffers because Third World states sometimes cannot achieve compliance from all parts of society. Moreover, poor, illiterate, Third World women may not be in a position to exercise their rights, especially if such rights clash with traditional perceptions of gender roles.

At times, women's issues are transformed into a much larger debate on the foundations of society. In Turkey, for example, the discussion on the bill to set up a women's unit within the government in response to the Nairobi conference recommendations was transformed into a much larger debate on the virtues of secularism versus religious conservatism. As Rathgeber suggests, traditional religions and cultures often consider women's roles as a fundamental component of their world-view and strongly resist attempts to change the status of women.

In many ways, the issue of women's rights has accentuated the constant tension between tradition and modernity. Women have been classically regarded as the bearers of tradition from one generation to another. The transformation of their role in society is seen as an erosion of the foundation of traditional cultures. When the alternative to tradition is westernization, there is an in-built cultural prejudice which is often the justification of the denial of equal rights for women.[19]

A second reason why the road to empowerment is difficult has to do with implementation of policies for women. Even though guidelines and institutional structures may be in place, implementation of policies for women may still suffer. The international women's movement, like all social movements, has been more successful in bringing women on the international agenda than in implementing policies. The very characteristics that help a social movement succeed as a movement may often inhibit it once it enters the political and institutional realm. Social movements frame issues broadly and ambiguously in order to gain acceptance, and they are on the outside rather than inside. Agencies, on the other hand, require clearly formulated policies that fit their particular goals and procedures, and appropriately trained staff to implement them. Whether women's issues are introduced in a way consistent with the goals and procedures of an organization may determine the organization's response. Staff members who act as "policy advocates" for women's issues can contribute to successful implementation. Yet, most staff members in international donor agencies as well as recipient government agencies are not necessarily gender sensitive.

Ultimately, the redefinition of gender relations and of development will depend on the women and men in developing countries. Development assistance agencies like USAID or the World Bank act primarily as "brokers" of development. These agencies are usually tightly constrained by the policies of governments they are accountable to and have only a limited capacity or even interest in changing practice in the developing countries where they work. At times, they may, in fact, help to reinforce the traditional or existing gender relationships.

Genuine development cannot take place solely by the infusion of resources from the outside. Instead of downplaying the importance of the political and economic motivations of the major actors that provide development assistance, progress will require uncovering and analyzing how their motivations sustain particular relations of gender and a particular definition of what constitutes development. Once the empowerment of women is recognized as central to development and the power relationships that put limitations on this goal are revealed, the first step toward change has been made. We no longer see existing gender relations and institutions as natural but as changeable, and we can begin focusing on how these institutions can be reorganized so as to include women and on how women can take control by acting as agents of change themselves.

NOTES

1. International Bank for Reconstruction and Development/World Bank, *World Development Report, 1992: Development and the Environment* (Washington, DC: World Bank, 1992), 254–57.

2. *Statistical Abstract of the U.S.* (Washington, DC: U.S. Government Printing Office, 1993); IBRD/World Bank, *World Development Report, 1992,* 218.

3. See Ester Boserup, *Women's Role in Economic Development* (New York: St. Martin's, 1970); Irene Tinker and M. B. Bramsen, eds., *Women and World Development* (Washington, DC: Overseas Development Council, 1976); Barbara Lewis, *Invisible Farmers: Women and the Crisis in Agriculture* (Washington, DC: USAID, 1981); Mayra Buvinic, Margaret A. Lycette, and William P. McGreevey, *Women and Poverty in the Third World* (Baltimore: Johns Hopkins University Press, 1983).

4. W. C. Baum and S. M. Tolbert, *Investing in Development: Lessons of World Bank Experience* (Oxford: Oxford University Press, 1985), 488.

5. Irene Tinker, "Women in Development," in Irene Tinker, ed., *Women in Washington: Advocates for Public Policy* (London: Sage, 1983).

6. U.S. Department of State, Agency for International Development, "Integration of Women into National Economies," Policy Determination 60 (September 16, 1974).

7. Patricia Maguire, *Women in Development: An Alternative Analysis* (Amherst, MA: Center for International Education, University of Massachusetts Press, 1984).

8. For the response of development agencies to WID issues, see, Kathleen Staudt, ed., *Women, International Development, and Politics* (Philadelphia: Temple University Press, 1990).

9. Mayra Buvinic, "Projects for Women in the Third World: Explaining Their Misbehavior," *World Development* 14:5 (1986): 653–64.

10. World Bank, *Recognizing the "Invisible" Women in Development: The World Bank's Experience* (Washington, DC: World Bank, 1979).

11. Baum and Tolbert, *Investing in Development,* 488.

12. Augusta Molnar and Gotz Schreiber, *Women and Forestry: Operational Issues,* Policy, Planning and Research Working Paper Series 184 (Washington, DC: World Bank, 1989), 15.

13. See, for example, Cynthia Enloe, "Women Textile Workers in the Militarization of Southeast Asia," in Jean O'Barr, ed., *Perspectives on Power: Women in Africa, Asia, and Latin America* (Durham, NC: Center for International Studies, Duke University, 1982); Annette Fuentes and Barbara Ehrenreich, *Women in the Global Factory* (Boston: South End, 1983); June Nash and M. P. Fernandez-Kelly, eds., *Women, Men, and the International Division of Labor* (Albany: SUNY Press, 1983); Maria Mies, "The Dynamics of the Sexual Division of Labor and the Integration of Rural Women into the World Market," in Lourdes Beneria, ed., *Women and Development: The Sexual Division of Labor in Rural Economies* (New York: Praeger, 1982).

14. Jane Jaquette, "Women and Modernization Theory: A Decade of Feminist Criticism," *World Politics* 34:2 (1982): 267–84.

15. Eva Rathgeber, "WID, WAD, GAD: Trends in Research and Practice," *The Journal of Developing Areas* 24 (July 1990): 494.

16. Ibid., 499.

17. See S. E. Charlton, J. Everett, and K. Staudt, eds., *Women, the State, and Development* (Albany: SUNY Press, 1989); Sonia Alvarez, *Democracy in Brazil: Women's Movements in Transition Politics* (Princeton: Princeton University Press, 1990); Kathleen Staudt, ed., *Women, International Development, and Politics* (Philadelphia: Temple University Press, 1990).

18. Caroline O. N. Moser, "Gender Planning in the Third World," in Rebecca Grant and Kathleen Newland, eds., *Gender and International Relations* (Bloomington: Indiana University Press, 1991), 109.

19. Eva Rathgeber, "Integrating Gender into Development: Research and Action Agendas for the 1990s," in J. Jabbra and N. Jabbra, eds., *Women and Development in the Middle East and North Africa* (Amsterdam, Neth.: Brill, Forthcoming), 10.

❧ 11 ❧

Women and the
International Political
Economy

Geeta Chowdhry

In the 1970s, experts on international relations bemoaned the "mutual neglect" accorded each other by the fields of international relations and international economics.[1] Since then, scholarship on international political economy has burgeoned. However, the relation between the international
political economy and women was ignored. Conventional literature on international political economy claims a gender-free discipline in which subjects, male or female, are subordinate to the world of state or nonstate
actors and issues of structures and regimes. "Yet in the theories which
depict this abstract system there seems to be a structuring-out of women
and their activities and a structuring-in of men and their activities."[2] In
the past decade, much Feminist writing has raised previously ignored gender issues. However, despite the existence of this Feminist scholarship, the
purdah of international political economy on issues of gender has yet to be
lifted: Gender remains veiled by the resistance of nonfeminist scholarship,
governments, and international agencies.

What is International Political Economy? There appears to be some basic
agreement among scholars about this. "It refers to a basic issue in social
theory: the relationship between politics and economics"[3] in the international arena and the effect of global politico-economic changes on state
capacity as well as on the life chances of individuals within the state. Beyond this basic agreement, there are diverse approaches to the study of
International Political Economy (or IPE). These approaches are: mercantil-
ist, liberal, interdependence, modernization, dependency, and world systems. None of these approaches has considered women or gender important
in IPE.

NONFEMINIST CONSERVATIVE APPROACHES TO IPE

The *mercantilist/neomercantilist* view in IPE is the economic counterpart to the Realist approach in international relations discussed in chapter 1. The assumptions of Realism are the assumptions of mercantilism/neomercantilism: The international arena is anarchical, and self-interest motivates nation-states to pursue power defined as "national interest." The issues of national interest, not private interests, are central to the decision-making process. States will use markets as well as other means to secure dominance and security for themselves.[4] However, if a conflict of interests between markets and the interest of the state emerges, states will not hesitate to regulate economic activity or to abandon the defense of corporations. The mercantilist/neomercantilists are skeptical about the benefits of free trade and have suggested that the careful manipulation of the international and domestic political economy has gone hand in hand with the pursuit of power and security. Thus, it is not only necessary but also prudent for states to pursue protectionist policies like subsidies for domestic production and high tariffs and regulations of imports.

Critics see neomercantilist arguments as self-defeating because the exclusive focus on the world of insecurity could well promote insecurity in the form of retaliation and diplomatic tensions, for example. These critics challenge the idea of an undivided, self-evolving, and obvious "national interest" to show that conflict about what constitutes national interest and appropriate policies is very much a part of international relations. They also argue that neomercantilists ignore the processes through which policies are made. Others fault the neomercantilists for failing to see that too much regulation may actually hurt rather than benefit the national and world economy. Still others see neomercantilists as friends of established business hiding behind the Realist rhetoric of power. All these critics fail to recognize that women are conspicuously (made?) absent from this discourse.

Liberal/neoclassical approaches to IPE have also been referred to as "laissez-faire" ("leave it alone") or "free-marketeer" perspectives.[5] These assume that market forces, when left alone by states, create efficient allocations of resources and benefits for all. International trade, particularly when conducted on the basis of comparative advantage, allows all societies to maximize their benefits—and, therefore, it should continue unhampered by regulations. The role of the state should be peripheral: "Governments should confine themselves to maintaining a framework within which free-enterprise and competition may flourish."[6]

The liberals/neoclassical economists have been criticized for not taking power into consideration, particularly on the subject of comparative advantage. Unhampered free markets in which freely choosing individuals or nations unhampered by class, monetary, or other social restrictions make rational decisions are "a series of heroic and unrealistic assumptions."[7]

However, none of these criticisms have extended their concern for power to incorporate either the impact of liberal assumptions on women or the gender biases in free markets. If free markets favor those who have power, then poor women who are often the most vulnerable members of their societies will rarely benefit from free markets.

The *interdependence* approach falls somewhere in between the neomercantilist and the liberal approaches to international political economy.[8] Challenging the assumptions of the mercantilists that states are the only guiding lights in the international political economy, interdependence theorists focus on the power of multinational corporations and other nongovernmental organizations. The interdependence approach in IPE is called Pluralist theory in the discussion of theories of world politics in chapter 4.

This view discredits the rather simplistic analysis of power that the neomercantilists use and rejects the liberal/neoclassical analysis that discounts power in the conduct of trade. The interdependence approach suggests that power is multidimensional and that its effect on states and other actors can be distinguished by the degree of "sensitivity" or "vulnerability," the issue area, the bargaining skills of the participants, and the flexibility of existing regimes.[9] The interdependence approach, although more complex in its conceptualization of power and international relations, has also ignored women as subjects as well as Feminist methods for reevaluating international relations.

Modernization theories include theories of political, economic, and psychological development.[10] Modernization theories are based on the tradition-modernity dichotomy, "the latest manifestation of a Great Dichotomy between more primitive and more advanced societies which has been a common feature of Western social thought for the past one hundred years."[11] According to the modernization theorists, the world is divided into two types of societies, traditional and modern, and the goal of all traditional societies is to become modern.

The process of modernization presumably will lead traditional societies to modernity if "traditional" and "primitive" (non-Western) values are replaced by "modern" (Western) ones. Attributes associated with modern/ Western societies are positively valued. Modern societies are seen as rational, egalitarian, achievement oriented, with a high degree of social mobility. If individuals in modern societies work hard and want to achieve, they are rewarded. Traditional societies are defined as fatalistic and hierarchical. Here kinship, not achievement, confers rewards, and citizens have little social mobility. Therefore, from this view, the culture of traditional societies is an obstacle to modernization. It is suggested that "outside influences"—that is, the West—will help bring about the economic, political, and psychosocial change necessary for modernization through aid, trade, and investment.

Modernization theory has little to say about women in the process of modernization. Modernization theorists recognize women as "tradition conservationists," the intermediaries through which tradition is preserved, recreated, and valorized.[12] Women's location within traditional societies that are nonegalitarian, hierarchical, and male dominated are responsible for creating women who are "backward" and "irrational." The process of modernization presumably will liberate women and set them free from tradition.

The modernization approach is too simplistic in its categorization of both the Western and the non-Western worlds. Relying on stereotyping, it creates derogatory caricatures of non-Western people. Modernization theory also does not recognize that modernization may be detrimental to the status of women.

NONFEMINIST RADICAL APPROACHES TO IPE

Two prominent radical approaches to IPE are dependency and world systems theories. These are discussed as "Critical theories" of world politics in chapter 4. The *radical* approaches share certain assumptions about the location and historical context of the debate: The debate occurs in the context of capitalism/imperialism and North-South relations. According to the radicals, the imperialist expansion of capitalist countries in Europe created the exploitation that characterizes the relations between the North (the developed nations) and the South (the less-developed countries). Although almost all the countries of the South have gained political independence from colonial rule, various processes that have been institutionalized in the IPE have maintained this unequal relationship—a condition called neocolonialism.

The *dependency* approaches share many of the assumptions of the "radicals" about North-South relations.[13] The more moderate form of dependency theory is often called the structuralist position. The structuralists suggest that historical continuities of colonialism in international economic arrangements place Third World countries at a structural disadvantage. The solution lies in changing the structure of the world economy so that it becomes more equal by promoting and protecting Third World products as well as by encouraging Third World leaders to adopt economic policies like import substitution that will make the South more self-reliant. This proposal calls for a New International Economic Order based on "fair trade" rather than "free trade."

The more radical of the *dependentistas* argue that the structuralists misinterpret the very root of the problem. The problem of the South does not lie in lack of funds or initiative. The radical *dependentistas* propose that the capitalist relationship of the North and South, developed through colonization and maintained through current neocolonial arrangements, keeps the South in poverty so that the North can remain rich. Multinational corporations, direct foreign investments, and unequal exchange mechanisms fostered through international class alliances are the means through which the exploitation of the South occurs.[14]

Many criticisms have been made of the dependency approaches. These range from accusations of economic determinism, conceptual obfuscation, and lack of empirical grounding, to being a metanarrative grounded in the modernist discourse. All the criticisms are silent on the treatment that dependency does not accord gender. Gender as a social construction is not discussed by the *dependentistas*.

World systems theory agrees with the basic premises of the *dependentistas* regarding the relation between the core (North/industrialized countries) and periphery (South/largely agricultural countries). It differs from them in suggesting that since the sixteenth century there has existed only one world system of capitalism. Feudalism or socialism or any other systems have not coexisted alongside capitalism; capitalism contorted those other systems into reflections of itself.[15]

World systems theory has been criticized for imposing the tyranny of the world system over its component parts, for an overemphasis on the power of core capitalist countries and not on the potential for class action, for ignoring intervening mechanisms that generate or mediate underdevelopment, and for being essentially Realist in its outlook. Women have been included in the system not because of any specific gender-related experiences but under the social category of class or under "households as an institution of the world economy."[16] However, this inclusion limits itself to the "add women and stir" variety. Moreover, this approach sees women's oppression as emerging from capitalism alone.

MISSING: WOMEN IN IPE

The study of IPE has been gendered. Specifically gender-related experiences have been made invisible, and women have been allowed to enter the world of IPE, along with men, only in a common category called "subjects" where women and their experiences are made to disappear under the universalizing wand of (hu)man knowledge. Feminist scholarship in IPE has worked to make women and gender visible by engaging in two, at times overlapping, tasks: deconstruction and reconstruction. The deconstructive task has systematically brought women's activities to the forefront to reveal the androcentric (male-as-norm) bias of knowledge in IPE. The reconstructive task has led to the development of gender-sensitive theories of IPE.

Deconstructive Feminist scholarship seeks to rectify the systematic exclusion of women from accounts of IPE and to expose its androcentric bias. Nonfeminist theories of IPE have relegated women to the *zenana,* the women's private quarters. Feminist scholarship, in critiquing these theories, tries to construct knowledge in which women's lives affected by and affecting IPE are brought center stage. Feminist scholarship has broadened the scope of international political economy, exposed and corrected its androcentric biases, and made it more akin to the real world by examining the presence of women in the global factory of multinational corporations, the agricultural sector, the informal sector, and the service sector.

We can see how women are brought center stage by examining the global corporation. The introduction of export-processing zones or free-trade zones in the Third World is on the increase. According to the liberal/ neoclassical model of international political economy, corporate investment attracted by the creation of free markets fosters development in the Third World. This model says that corporate investment is guided by an attempt to optimize profit and corporate employment by policies that seek a cheaper labor force. However, cheap labor is linked to the politics of race and gender, since Third World men provide cheaper labor than their Western counterparts and Third World women provide even cheaper labor than Third World men. Thus, the liberal/neoclassical model neglects the gender-based industrial politics of the real world.[17]

In my international relations classes, some students comment that while there has been a steady increase in the percentage of the female labor force, particularly in the export-oriented economies, they are not convinced that it warrants separate analysis. In other words, some believe that gender has nothing to do with women's employment in the global factory. Moreover, some students see Third World women as the beneficiaries of corporate-employment strategies: These strategies contribute to their liberation, not their exploitation.

Gender or the social construction of women and men, Feminist research suggests, has everything to do with the employment of women and is one of the main reasons that the employment of women is on the rise. Both factory managers and state government officials refer to socially constructed biological and emotional differences between men and women to explain the disproportionate hiring of women in electronics and textile industries. A Malaysian government brochure creates and uses "oriental female dexterity" to attract corporate investors: "The manual dexterity of the oriental female is famous the world over. Her hands are small and she works with extreme care. Who, therefore, could be better qualified by nature and inheritance to contribute to the efficiency of a bench assembly production line than the oriental girl?"[18] Managers of *maquiladoras* on the Mexican–U.S. border have also used similar social constructions of women to explain their employment:

Plant managers base their preference of women (particularly young women) over men for this kind of work upon presumed anatomical and inimical features that distinguish both sexes. It is consistently stated that women are more dexterous, patient and reliable than men. Their fine muscles, acute eyesight and nimble fingers make them particularly suitable for repetitive assembly work.[19]

Thus, the strategy of global corporations in favor of female employment is guided mostly by their need for cheap labor and a docile, nonunionized work force that can best be found in the most vulnerable and powerless population, that is, young women. Women are employed because of their "womanness" based on stereotypes about women and conceptions of gender as difference.

Does this lead to women's liberation or their exploitation? The answers are not found in the simple dualism of exploitation or liberation. The effects of corporate investment on women are complex and simultaneously liberating and exploitative. On the one hand, global corporations provide women with employment and wages that indigenous firms may not provide, thereby providing them with the necessary economic tools for liberation. However, certain costs are incurred. These costs include loss of family-support networks, loss of status and respect, and vulnerability to sexual attack. Also, such employment is often hazardous to the emotional and physical health of women. The health hazards of global factory women have ranged from "brown lung disease" found among textile workers to chronic eye problems in electronic factory workers. High anxiety and stress related to job insecurity, violation of safety codes, highly regimented work conditions, and violations of workers' rights have often been found. The practice of forced sterilization is an example of the control exerted by *maquiladora* managers on female factory workers. It is also economically exploitative since the wages received are extremely low when compared to international wages.

A Feminist perspective on IPE likewise brings women center stage in the *agricultural sector*. Although women have been dominant agriculturalists, especially but not exclusively in subsistence-crop farming, nonfeminist studies of agriculture do not list women as agriculturalists. Based largely on a traditional perception of Third World women as in the service of men, reinforced by gendered notions of men as farmers and women as farmers' wives, research as well as projects on agriculture and development have ignored women farmers with disastrous consequences for food production and hunger in the Third World. Nonrecognition of women as farmers limits women's access to land, credit, and other agricultural inputs, thereby drastically reducing the possibilities for increased food production in the Third World.

Ester Boserup's pathbreaking study entitled *Women's Role in Economic Development* (1970) was the first of its kind to challenge the misperception that women are not critically involved in agriculture.[20] Other researchers have supported Boserup's analysis for sub-Saharan Africa to show that women are crucial to agricultural production, particularly in the production

Table 11.1
Women's Work in the Food Systems
in Africa

Clearing Land	5%
Turning Soil	30%
Planting	50%
Weeding and Hoeing	70%
Harvesting	60%
Carrying Crops Home	80%
Storing	80%
Processing	90%
Marketing	60%
Carrying Water and Fuel	90%
Domestic Animal Care	50%
Hunting	10%
Cooking and Family Care	95%

Source: U.S. Department of Agriculture, "Extension Service Update," *International Newsletter* (July 1986).

of food in rural Africa.[21] In Africa women perform the lion's share of tasks relating to food systems, as Table 11.1 reveals.

Researchers have demonstrated that women in Latin America and Asia are active participants in the agricultural economy and that their invisibility is largely a function of nonfeminist methods for data collection. If data is based largely on the static and limiting category of the head of household, then women who are rarely listed as heads of households are rendered invisible like their work.

As stated by Nüket Kardam in chapter 10, women farmers have traditionally not been targeted by international development agencies like the World Bank and United States Agency for International Development (USAID). Consequently, extension agents, local lending agencies, and public suppliers of inputs have also ignored women farmers. However, as a result of the Feminist literature on agriculture, development agencies have recently started to recognize women as farmers and have also created Women in Development (WID) departments to fit programs to women's needs.

At least two criticisms have been made regarding these WID programs. First, the budget allocations for WID are minimal compared to the overall budget for development programs; and second, separating the women's component through the creation of WID seems to relegate women to a women's department, thereby freeing the "main" departments from implementing gender-sensitive programs.[22]

An example of this neglect can be seen in the gender and class effects of structural-adjustment strategies introduced by the International Monetary Fund (IMF) and the World Bank. These strategies typically include currency devaluation and reduction in public expenditures, which reduces health, education, and transportation services that poor families depend upon. As most of the Third World comes under structural-adjustment strategies, women farmers continue to be affected in dramatic ways, despite the presence of WID.[23]

Studies on the informal sector of household production in the Third World have performed the important task of linking "home production" to IPE, thereby moving women center stage again. For example, women working from their homes make lace in the small town of Naraspur in India and Persian carpets in villages in Iran for international firms in Washington, London, Paris, and Tokyo.

Women have been employed in the international service sector as "hostesses," "prostitutes," and "masseuses" providing services to tourists, corporate workers, and military personnel. Prostitution-tourism has become a part of the economic development plan for a number of Southeast Asian countries. The use of "Kisaeng" in South Korea and "hospitality girls" in Thailand and the Philippines are encouraged by the state governments to bring in foreign exchange. These are in fact euphemisms for prostitution. Because of poverty and hunger, women and girls are often coerced by family members to offer their sexual services for money. Government austerity programs also systematically and circumstantially coerce women into prostitution-tourism.

Poor women also provide "maid" services to middle- and upper-class households. In a patriarchal world in which domestic responsibilities and chores are still largely gender based, maids provide middle- and upper-class women the luxury of pursuing careers and/or some respite from the tedium of household chores. The internationalization of the maid industry was made visible during the Gulf War of 1991 as South Asian maids working for wealthy Kuwaiti households were left stranded in refugee camps. This issue was brought center stage once again during the search for an attorney general in the Clinton administration in the United States.

RECONSTRUCTION: FEMINIST THEORETICAL PERSPECTIVES ON IPE

In chapter 5, Sandra Whitworth examines three variants of Feminist theories: Liberal feminism, Marxist feminism, and Feminist Postmodernism. She then considers how each relates to the study of world politics. In chapter 6, Hamideh Sedghi considers how Third World women's perspectives may contribute to the development of alternative explanations of world politics. Here, we will see how these Feminist perspectives connect to and critique the theories of international political economy that we discussed at the beginning of this chapter.

Liberal feminists are both different from and similar to the liberal/neo-classical school of IPE. As Feminists, they are critical of the liberal/neoclassical belief in the efficiency, fairness, and integrity of free markets and technological development. They state that the results of market and modernization intrusions are not similar for men and women, since women are often marginalized by markets in the process of modernization. As liberals, they suggest the need to make sure that women are integrated in the development process. However, unlike the liberals, Liberal feminists are willing to encourage institutional intrusions to assure women's integration.

Ester Boserup's study was the first that called for the integration of women into development (WID). Boserup challenged the assumption that women in non-Western countries were obstacles to modernization. She "launched the first thoroughgoing feminist attack on conventional liberal assumptions, particularly on the view that technology liberates women."[24] Her work indicates that modernization affects women in negative ways, forcing them to abandon areas of kinship support, minimizing their autonomy and power to make bargains with patriarchy, and at the same time increasing their work loads. Modernization, according to Boserup, marginalized women and reserved the benefits of modernization for men. Her work has generated considerable research that has documented the marginalization of women in the process of modernization.

The contribution of Liberal feminists is remarkable, since their critiques have gotten the attention of international development agencies. The agencies responded by creating WID offices in development organizations to integrate women into development.[25] Liberal feminists have sought to achieve "transitional empowerment" for women in development by advocating their integration in modernization. They are also providing interesting challenges to mainstream research. By incorporating an analysis of gender, they are attempting to bring the "private" realm of households into the "public" realm of policy.

However, Liberal feminists neglect what "integration" of women into modernization really implies. As discussed earlier, women in most non-Western economies are participants in various ways in their economies. They also participate in the process of social change even though they are affected differently than men by this process. By emphasizing the need to "integrate" rather than to "recognize" the roles of women in the development process, the Liberal feminists "confirm the false notion that women are less central to major social processes than men."[26] This reinforces the liberal/neoclassical–economics premise that traditional economies, like women, need to be integrated in order to be modernized.

As much as the Liberal feminists have done for critiquing modernization theories for the theories' neglect of women, Liberal feminists themselves do not question the central assumptions of modernization. Instead, they present an internal critique of modernization. For them, modernization, based usually on the Western model, is the desired goal of traditional societies. Third World women will become like Western women, if cultural barriers to women's participation are removed in international, national, and local agencies. In seeking to make Third World women like Western women, Liberal feminists stay rooted in the parameters of liberalism. They fail to develop a Feminist economics that would center on the reproductive and productive capacities of women, recognize the structural impediments to women's participation, and advocate a woman-centered development.

Liberal feminism's suggestion of integration, adopted by WID, proposes a Band-Aid to "fix" the effects of modernization but not the process of modernization itself. WID has become for the non-Western women what welfare has been to poor women in the west. WID, like welfare, addresses only the symptoms of maldevelopment like poverty, not the reasons for its existence.

Marxist feminists see gender as an essential part of the strategy of global capitalization. Unlike the Liberal feminists, Marxist feminists have challenged the assumptions of modernization at the same time that they have challenged the nongendered critiques of other Marxists. For Marxist feminists, efforts at modernization have to be examined in the context of the global process of capital accumulation. In other words, the position of African and other non-Western women in the development process "is an outcome of structural and conceptual mechanisms by which African societies have continued to respond to and resist the global processes of economic exploitation and cultural domination."[27]

Marxist feminists suggest that the ability to control production and reproduction is crucial to the process of capital accumulation. The "backwardness" of the household is maintained so that capitalism can move forward. For example, this is done through direct recruitment of household labor and extraction of surplus value from the household, the maintenance of the household as the area of reproduction ensuring a cheap supply of labor force, maintenance of women as a reserve labor force to ease the state out of crisis, and the employment of female labor in the free-zone areas of Malaysia, Hong Kong, Taiwan, and more recently in the *maquiladoras*.

Marxist feminists argue that a real development process for women will only begin if a socialist, antipatriarchal revolution is fought on a world scale. Unfortunately, most revolutionary movements have shrugged feminism as an issue that will be addressed only after the socialist revolution is successful. This has led Marxist feminists to say that the "unhappy marriage of Marxism and feminism must either become a more progressive union or it must end in divorce."[28] To unite, the duality approach (Marxism, then Feminism) should be abandoned, say the Marxist feminists. The oppression of women is a core attribute of capitalism, and true socialism cannot be accomplished without a struggle against patriarchy.

Marxist feminists have been criticized from a variety of sources. Liberal feminists argue that socialist revolutions have shown that the suppression of women is not the sole preserve of capitalist relations of power. Third World ecofeminists and Feminist Postmodernists also criticize Marxist feminist positions because such positions do not differentiate among the peoples of the non-Western world; the answer lies in searching for differences within the categories of the non-Western world.

Feminist Postmodernism combines Feminist and Postmodern tools to provide a gendered analysis of difference and power. Postmodernism questions the assumptions of modernism. Modernism, based on nineteenth-century enlightenment, asserts that there are universal truths that can be studied and revealed through "objective" scholarship. Postmodernism questions the existence of universal truths as well as the existence of "objective" scholarship. Postmodernists tell us that there are only relative truths and that scholarship is always subjective. Therefore, they warn us against using grand theories to explain the reality of everyone. Postmodernists also examine the specificities and locations of power. According to Postmodernists, power is diffused. They agree with the liberals that it is present in the state. They also agree with the Marxists that it is present in the nationally and internationally dominant classes. However, they tell us that it is also present in symbols, language, and knowledge.

Feminist Postmodernists use Postmodernist tools to expose the ways in which society, and the knowledge produced by members of the society, is gendered. They also tell us how power in this gendered society is used to affect how we see or do not see gender. However, Feminist Postmodernists warn us against making any universalizing assumptions about women. They tell us that there are differences within the category "women." These differences stem from class, race, ethnicity, history, and the particular experiences of women. Until now, say Feminist Postmodernists, scholars other than women themselves have written about the experiences of women. Women have rarely been allowed to speak for themselves.

Feminist Postmodernism provides us with tools to critique the field of women in development. This field has been based on the notions of differences between non-Western/Western, tradition/modernity, unliberated/liberated. These categories have been used to deny subject status to people, particularly women. By focusing on the differences within these categories, Feminist Postmodernists can show the multiplicity of subjects that exist within "traditional" societies. For example, the stereotype of women from

Third World societies has always been that they are traditional, unliberated, and oppressed. Using Feminist Postmodernist tools, we can let Third World women speak for themselves. This will reveal the diversity of women in the Third World.

Feminist Postmodernism provides a theoretical strategy to deconstruct the basis of previous knowledge and power. It has exposed Feminist discourses that stereotype women and their "shared" oppressions, ignoring the particularities of race, class, history, and individual experiences.[29] At the same time, however, Feminist Postmodernism is problematic precisely because it makes any generalization—and, thus, any theorizing (moving from description to explanation)—difficult.

On the political level, Feminist Postmodernism can provide some of the answers to the problems facing the international women's movement. Women of color claim that the women's movement has represented the concerns of white middle-class women and has ignored issues central to the lives of women of color like imperialism and racism. Feminist Postmodernism's emphasis on difference can remedy that. At the same time, Feminist Postmodernism provides very little hope for political strategizing and action. Its focus on elevating differences and undermining commonalites hinders the organization of successful political movements.

A new and forceful critique of the intrusions of IPE in the lives of Third World women has come from what has been called "Third World Feminist perspectives," discussed by Hamideh Sedghi in chapter 6.[30] These perspectives have borrowed the best from Marxist feminists and Feminist Postmodernists. They borrow the Marxist feminist analysis of the effect of capitalism on women. They borrow the Feminist Postmodernist rejection of Western Marxism as a universal category, an alien model rooted in alien philosophies that have helped in the exploitation of the Third World. Third World Feminist perspectives help us focus on difference without sacrificing commonalities. They try to find answers in the experiences of poor Third World women who fight to survive the maldevelopment caused by Western models of development.

Third World Feminist perspectives see fundamental conflicts between modernization models constructed on the basis of Western patriarchy and the well-being of the women of the Third World. They argue that modernization models aim first at promoting the welfare of the West. Blind acceptance of these models of development has led non-Western countries to an impasse in development. This impasse can be overcome through the creation of a new model of development, a model based on the experiences of the new proletariat: impoverished women of the Third World. Third World Feminists suggest that these models are ecologically sound and are economically as well as culturally feasible.

Although Third World Feminist perspectives provide us with a non-Western alternative for development, this approach also creates an alternative "truth" that complements and contrasts the previous "truth" about Third World women. In their effort to valorize poor Third World women, these researchers have recreated Third World women as nurturers (as mothers). The role as nurturers is emphasized to show that Third World women are indeed different and may have knowledge and power that can pose a threat to Western patriarchal models. On the one hand, this argument undermines a claim about the diversity of Third World women and pushes them solely into the role of mothers. On the other hand, this reinforces Buchi Emecheta's insistence that the lives of Third World women cannot be compartmentalized; she is a writer because of, not in spite of, her children.[31]

CONCLUSION: RESISTANCE AND STRUGGLES

Although Feminist theorists agree that modernization as it exists marginalizes women, they disagree on how women in the Third World can overcome this marginalization. While these scholars debate the methods of these transformations, women in the Third World are organizing, struggling, and resisting these incursions into their lives. Women from the Third World refuse to become victims in this process as they seek ways through which they can get greater control of their lives.

Women have resisted the total control of women workers by multinational corporations collectively and individually. At the collective level, women have formed trade unions/organizations in the Free Trade Zones in Sri Lanka, Malaysia, the Philippines, Mexico and other countries to create structured avenues of struggles for women workers. However, the governments in these countries have often adopted harsh measures banning trade-union activity. As a consequence, women adopt individual-level strategies that can circumvent state legislation and at the same time provide avenues of resistance. In factories where women work numerous hours without a break, women have resorted to covert acts like damaging the components that they work on. Alternatively, women have resorted to having "fits" in the workplace. A woman having a fit is followed by others having fits and yet others leaving their work to watch or help them. Where multinational regimentation does not even provide women time for breaks, this is indeed a subversive way of acquiring breaks from the tedium of production.

In other areas, women have protested the harmful effects of modernization on the environment and on their lives. For example, in the foothills of the Himalayas, women of the Uttarkhand region asked the forest department to allot them a few ash trees on forest land so they could use it for producing agricultural implements. The forest officials not only scoffed at this idea but allotted the land to Simon Company, a sporting-goods manufacturer from Allahbad, India. The women knew the fate of their village was inextricably linked with the trees, so they formed the Chipko movement. *Chipko* is a Hindi word that means "to cling." The women of Chipko hugged the trees, in an example of Gandhian nonviolent protest, to prevent the logging. As a result of the persistent struggle of the women of Chipko, the government of India banned the felling of trees in that area.

There are also women's formal and informal credit organizations, such as the Grameen Bank in Bangladesh and SEWA in India, that provide loans to members to aid them in setting up businesses. These have been successful especially at countering the gendered practices of credits and loans facilitated by public and private lending institutions.

These are some examples of the efforts that women in the Third World are making to counter the effect of modernization and to make development sensitive to local needs. International institutions and governments must begin to follow the lead of these women in bringing about a localized, gender-sensitive, and people-based development. And theorists of IPE must recognize women's agency in development, environmental preservation, sustainable agriculture, and other areas, and acknowledge and correct the gendered basis of orthodox explanations of political economy.

NOTES

1. Susan Strange, "International Economics and International Relations," *International Affairs* 46 (April 1970): 304–15.

2. Christine Sylvester, "The Emperors' Theories and Transformations," in Dennis C. Pirages and Christine Sylvester, eds., *Transformations in the Global Political Economy* (New York: St. Martin's, 1990).

3. Martin Staniland, *What Is Political Economy* (New Haven: Yale, 1985), 1.

4. Peter Gourevitch, "The Second Image Reversed," *International Organization* 32 (Autumn 1978): 881–912; Stephen Krasner, *Defending the National Interest* (Princeton: Princeton University Press, 1978); Robert Gilpin, *U.S. Power and the Multinational Corporation* (New York: Basic, 1975).

5. See John Odell, *U.S. International Monetary Policy* (Princeton: Princeton University Press, 1982).

6. R. J. Barry Jones, "International Political Economy: Perspectives and Prospects. Part II," *Review of International Studies* 8 (January 1982): 40.

7. Charles Kindleberger, *Power and Money* (London: 1970), quoted in Jones, "International Political Economy," 46.

8. See Dennis Pirages, *Global Ecopolitics* (North Scituate, MA: Duxbury Press, 1978); see also Robert Keohane and Joseph Nye, *Power and Interdependence* (Boston: Little, Brown, 1977).

9. Keohane and Nye, *Power and Interdependence,* chaps. 1 and 2.

10. Samuel Huntington, "Change to Change," *Comparative Politics* 3 (1971): 283–322; Ronald Chilcote, *Theories of Comparative Politics* (Boulder, CO: Westview, 1981); Tariq Banuri, *Modernization and Its Discontent* (Helsinki: WIDER Working Papers, 1987).

11. Frank X. Sutton, "Social Theory and Comparative Politics," in Harry

Eckstein and David Apter, eds., *Comparative Politics* (New York: Free Press, 1963), 67.

12. Jane Jaquette, "Women and Modernization Theory," *World Politics* 34 (1982): 267–84.

13. See Ronald Chilcote, "Dependency," *Latin American Perspectives* 1 (Fall 1974); see also Anthony Brewer, *Marxist Theories of Imperialism* (London: Routledge & Kegan Paul, 1980).

14. See Andre Gunder Frank, *Capitalism and Underdevelopment* (New York: Monthly Review, 1967); see also Samir Amin, *Unequal Development* (New York: Monthly Review, 1976).

15. Immanuel Wallerstein, "The Rise and Future Demise of the World Capitalist System," in Immanuel Wallerstein, ed., *The Capitalist World Economy* (Cambridge: Cambridge University Press, 1979).

16. Immanuel Wallerstein and Joan Smith, "Households as an Institution of the World Economy," in Rae Lesser Blumberg, ed., *Gender, Family, and Economy* (Newbury Park, CA: Sage, 1991).

17. See, for example, Diane Elson and Ruth Pearson, " 'Nimble Fingers Make Cheap Workers,' " *Feminist Review* 7 (1980); June Nash and Maria P. Fernandez-Kelly, eds., *Women, Men, and the International Division of Labor* (Albany: SUNY Press, 1983); and Annette Fuentes and Barbara Ehrenreich, *Women in the Global Factory* (Boston: South End, 1983).

18. Linda Y. C. Lim, *Women Workers in Multinational Corporations* (East Lansing: Michigan State University Press, 1979), 7.

19. Maria P. Fernandez-Kelly, *For We Are Sold, I and My People* (Albany: SUNY Press, 1983), 42.

20. Ester Boserup, *Women's Role in Economic Development* (New York: St. Martin's, 1970).

21. See, among others, Jeanne K. Henn, "Women in the Rural Economy," in Margaret J. Hay and Sharon Stichter, eds., *African Women* (London: Longman, 1984); Anita Spring, "Women Farmers and Food in Africa," in Art Hansen and Della E. McMillan, eds., *Food in Sub-Saharan Africa* (Boulder, CO: Rienner, 1986); Carmen Diana Deere and Magdalena Leon, eds., *Rural Women and State Policy* (Boulder, CO: Westview, 1987); and Ben J. Wallace, Rosie Mujid Ahsan, Shahnaj Huq Hussain, and Ekramul Ahsan, *The Invisible Resource* (Boulder, CO: Westview, 1987).

22. Barbara Rogers, *The Domestication of Women* (London: Routledge, 1980).

23. See Geeta Chowdhry, *International Financial Institutions, the State, and Women Farmers in the Third World* (London: Macmillan, Forthcoming).

24. Jaquette, "Women and Modernization Theory," 270.

25. See Kathleen Staudt, *Women, Foreign Assistance, and Advocacy Administration* (New York: Praeger, 1985); and Nüket Kardam, *Bringing Women In* (Boulder, CO: Westview, 1990).

26. Hanna Papanek, "False Specialization and the Purdah of Scholarship," *Journal of Asian Studies* 34:1 (1984): 15.

27. Achola Pala, "Definitions of Women and Development," *Signs* 3:1 (1977): 12.

28. Heidi Hartmann, "The Unhappy Marriage of Marxism and Feminism," in Lydia Sargent, ed., *Women and Revolution* (Boston: South End, 1981), 1–43.

29. See Chandra Talpade Mohanty, "Under Feminist Eyes," in Chandra Mohanty, Ann Russo, and Lourdes Torres, eds., *Third World Women and the Politics of Feminism* (Bloomington: Indiana University Press, 1991); see also Anne Marie Goetz, "Feminism and the Limits to the Claim to Know," *Millennium* 17:3 (1988): 477–96.

30. See also Vandana Shiva, *Staying Alive* (London: Zed, 1989), and Gita Sen and Caren Grown, *Development Crisis and Alternative Visions* (New York: Monthly Review, 1987).

31. Referred to in Alice Walker's *In Search of My Mother's Garden* (New York: Harcourt, Brace, Jovanovich, 1983), 66–70.

Part III

PROSPECTS

Part III

❖ 12 ❖

Creating Change Through Adult Education: Suggestions for Two Priority Areas

Birgit Brock-Utne

Many of us who have chosen education as a profession tend to believe that education can make a difference in the lives of people. Some of us even think that *some* kinds of education are more likely to promote peaceful qualities in people than other types of education. As long as peace studies have existed as an academic field of study, peace education has been an essential part of it.

Through peace education children are supposed to learn to cooperate, to solve conflicts creatively and nonviolently, and to redirect aggressive and competitive behavior. Peace education is said to mean a socialization in empathy—in sharing, to the point of experiencing, the feelings of other living beings, their joy, their pain, and their grief. Peace education is said to mean a socialization in solidarity, in helping other people, in equalizing burdens and rewards. Through peace education youngsters, as well as grown-ups, are expected to get new knowledge, knowledge which will make them change their attitudes and behave in a different way. They are expected to learn to treat the environment and living beings with respect and justice.[1]

The field of peace education was for many years looked at as gender neutral, a field where sexism was a nonissue. It was only when Feminist scholars started to combine peace education with studies of gender-role socialization that certain gender-specific questions were asked.[2] We started asking questions like: Do we educate boys for war and girls for peace? Are girls more socialized in empathy than boys are? What are the consequences of having that sex which is less socialized in empathy and most in aggressive behavior rule the world? What is the relation between militarism and sexism? What will applying Feminist theories to the field of peace studies, including disarmament and human rights and development, mean for peace education?

Feminists also have asked what has happened to the women who have been peace educators. Some of the most vital works on global questions concerning peace in the wide definition of the word have been written by women. When we talk about peace in the wide definition of the word, we do not see peace solely as the absence of war. We see peace as an absence of all types of violence. This includes direct violence in everyday life, like incest and wife-battering, as well as direct violence on a larger scale, as in wars. It also includes the absence of what we call indirect or *structural violence.* This is a type of violence that may also kill but at a slower pace. When social structures or practices are built up so that some people become better off at a heavy cost to others, we have structural violence.[3]

One of the earliest critics of the way in which we destroy the environment of this planet was the Swedish author Elin Wägner in her book *Väckarklocka (Alarm Clock),* which appeared in 1941.[4] Later followed Rachel Carson's *Silent Spring* (1964), Carolyn Merchant's *Death of Nature* (1980), and Rosalie Bertell's *No Immediate Danger?* (1985).[5] When it comes to works on human rights, I find Katarina Tomasevski's book the most inclusive and thorough because she is able to see human rights in a wide perspective. By stressing economic and social rights as much as the more commonly mentioned civil and political rights, she focuses on the fate of the poor people of the world, especially women, since they are the poorest of the poor.[6] The structural violence committed by us in the so-called First World toward peoples of the Third World is dealt with brilliantly by Susan George in *How the Other Half Dies* (1976) and in *A Fate Worse than Debt* (1988).[7] The arms race and collective direct violence is dealt with intelligently and thoroughly by Helen Caldicott in *Missile Envy* (1986).[8]

While women have addressed important peace issues, they have not achieved as much public recognition or acceptance as male writers have. I have recently completed an evaluation of eight books on peace education in use in Swedish schools from preschool through high school. Because Sweden has emphasized the teaching of equality between women and men in all spheres of life, I expected the texts to reflect a gender consciousness. There is, however, hardly any mention in the texts and the manuals prepared for the lower grades of the way in which boys and girls are educated when it comes to using war toys or fighting to solve conflicts, or the way in which aggression in a boy is enhanced and in a girl suppressed. The high-school text is an anthology with excerpts from the works on peace from twenty-three authors. Among those are only *two* women, with one as a coauthor with a man!

There are strong mechanisms at work against women and their writings. The strongest of all the mechanisms is trying to silence the women and to make their works invisible.[9] If that attempt does not succeed, then the next mechanism that will be used is that of ridicule. The famous pacifist novel *Die Waffen Nieder! (Down With Arms!)* by the Austrian peace heroine Bertha Von Suttner, published in 1889, was such a work that the establishment at the time did not succeed in silencing.[10] Instead, Von Suttner was ridiculed by males as naive, impractical, and dangerous. Sybil Oldfield has described the similar fate of Jane Addams in the companion volume, *Women in World Politics.* After their deaths the mechanism of invisibility was used, making sure that they would be "forgotten" in the history books. The Swedish project has given me another example to add to my list of attempts at making the work of women invisible, to "forget" that women have written some of the most analytical and thorough works in the field. Not a single excerpt from any of the works that I have mentioned above has found its way into the anthology.

PEACE EDUCATION THROUGH ADULT EDUCATION

The first step for meaningful peace education is to ensure that gender receives prominent attention and that works by women are brought to the fore. But even when this is done, peace education faces another challenge.

Peace educators strongly favor a pedagogy that encourages and incorporates action, dialogue, involvement, cooperation, and participation. Such an approach is more congruent with the message of peace and nonviolence because it is, in itself, a way of teaching both about peace and *for* peace. Yet such an approach is difficult to use in the usual school setting where the teacher has the power over pupils by setting grades and sometimes even having to distribute them according to a normal distribution curve (a good example of structural inequality). The Norwegian peace researcher and educator Johan Galtung has for many years held the belief that the usual school system is not well suited for peace education.[11] It is difficult to teach peace in a setting where children are taught to compete against each other. It is difficult to teach about equality of states large and small when there is so little equality between teachers and pupils, or to teach about the equality of the sexes when the boys in the class are allowed to dominate the girls. Galtung asks, "Will it not merely sound hypocritical—or, even worse, remain empty words that are nullified through the much stronger message of verticality and dominance being normal and acceptable, conveyed through the structure itself?"[12]

Feminist teachers have to deal with this dilemma as well.[13] They and peace educators adhere to principles of developing the conscience; of promoting connectedness, cooperation, and dialogue; of conducting learning experiences together, starting with our daily experiences. Yet this pedagogy is often almost impossible to practice in schools.

I have been asked by students whether I find it totally impossible that peace education could occur within a formal university or college education.

I think this question needs to be debated. It is certainly more difficult to work with peace education in a setting where the work that students do is to be graded, where students are part of a competitive system, and where cognitive abilities count more than emotions and actions. To me a prerequisite when working with peace education in a formal setting like the university is an analysis by students and teachers of the system they are working in, of the structural inequalities and competition built into it.

A far greater potential for peace education occurs in settings where the genuine interest for learning guides both the student and the educator. Adult education is one such setting. By adult education I mean on-the-job training as well as community work, a type of education taking place outside of formal and competitive educational institutions like universities. The aim of the type of adult education that I describe here is to learn to perform the job that one is in better, or to understand more of the world that one is living in. The point is not to get a certificate or a degree but to be able to act in a better way. In the final document from the UNESCO World Conference in 1972, adult education is described as "an instrument of conscientization" and of "social transformation that wishes to create a society that is aware of the values of social solidarity."[14] The aim of adult education is here described as an education that regards a social being in a holistic manner.

These aims come close to the aims of transformative peace education from a Feminist perspective. In her book *Comprehensive Peace Education,* the noted American peace educator Betty Reardon says:

Most of the elements of what I now define as transformational peace education came into focus for me when I brought a feminist perspective to them. . . . It is through feminism that I have gained by insights into wholeness and integrity. Feminism is, I believe, the most fully current perspective on peace and peace education.[15]

I have often been invited as a discussant to local groups of the Nordic Women for Peace in Norway, Sweden, and Finland. The discussions going on in these groups impress me as the best application that one can find of the pedagogic principles that peace educators as well as Feminist educators and adult educators want to adhere to. The atmosphere is one of sharing, of learning from each other.

Adult educators may learn something from the way in which women work for peace. When I analyze the way in which women work for peace in this world, I find three main characteristics:[16]

1. Women working for peace make use of a varied set of nonviolent techniques, acts, and strategies, such as marches, building peace camps, writing letters, and making tea parties with women belonging to the "opposing" camp.

2. Women take as their point of departure the concern for the ultimate value of life, especially the life of children, but also the life of all human beings and of Nature.

3. Women's work for peace is transpolitical, often transnational, aimed at reaching women and sometimes also men and state leaders in the opposite camp.

Often women who are working for peace try to envision a new world, a "pragmatopia," where power is divided evenly between women and men, where everyone has satisfied the basic necessities of life, and where conflicts are solved nonviolently.[17] In a following chapter, Anne Sisson Runyan outlines several feminist utopias.

How can adult education seen from a Feminist perspective help to create change toward a more peaceful world? Are there specific topics that at this time seem to be so important that they ought to be priority areas for peace education among adults? As I shall discuss below, I find that there are two such areas: training in the use of nonviolent solutions to conflicts and ending the structural violence of death through starvation.

NONVIOLENT SOLUTIONS OF CONFLICTS

In the aftermath of the Gulf War there is a danger that the military establishments will gain self-confidence, stop questioning what they are doing, develop new military strategies and threats, and go on rearming the world. The end of the cold war may end up in a search for new enemies to justify a continued arms buildup. The military establishments may also point to the current civil wars going on in Bosnia, Somalia, and the former Soviet Georgia and Azerbaijan as justifications for a military buildup. We, who do not believe in violent solutions to conflicts, find that the above examples of continued direct violence, more than anything else, demonstrate a need for continued emphasis on peaceful conflict resolution.

One way to promote peace education is to acquaint ourselves with the thinking of the military strategists. The language of the strategic analysts can be learned. But there is a danger that the longer you are immersed in that language, the less you are able to think beyond that framework. The American peace researcher Carol Cohn spent a year of her adult life at the Strategic Defense Institute to learn the language of the defense intellectuals. In a penetrating article about that experience, she tells how she not only learned the language but almost became a part of the same thinking. "But as I learnt their language, as I became more and more engaged with their information and their arguments, I found that my own thinking was changing. Soon, I could no longer cling to the comfort of studying an external and objectified 'them.' I had to confront a new question. How can I think this way? How can any of us?"[18] In her concluding remarks about her experience, she warns against the dangers of total immersion in the world of the defense intellectuals: "The activity of trying to out-reason defense intellectuals in their own games gets you thinking inside their rules, tacitly accepting all the unspoken assumptions of their paradigms."[19]

The danger of thinking inside the rules of the defense intellectuals is an unfortunate outcome of the Gulf War. It seems to be forgotten that the likelihood of getting Iraq out of Kuwait through nonviolent means was great. It seems to be forgotten that the war in the Gulf could have been avoided altogether. In mid-December 1990, the Director of the CIA, William Webster, testified to Congress about sanctions. Iraqi exports, he said, had been slashed by 97 percent and the imports by 90 percent of the trade before Iraq annexed Kuwait. This was an unprecedentedly effective embargo.

But as a writer for the *Guardian Weekly* sighed, "Sanctions have—idiotically—become a code word for 'appeasement.' "[20] Why have those who have questioned the necessity of war fallen victim to the anachronistic label of "appeaser"? Does it have something to do with the fact that one of the main characteristics of women's work for peace has been the use of a varied set of *nonviolent* techniques, acts, and strategies? Could it be that men were afraid of being accused of being effeminate if they argued against the use of direct violence, against war? We know that many more women throughout the world were against the Gulf War than men were. In a Norwegian opinion poll published in the Norwegian newspaper *Aftenposten* on January 11, 1991 the Norwegian public had been asked if they would favor military action against Iraq if the occupation of Kuwait was not ended by the fifteenth of January. Only 34 percent of Norwegian women were in favor of military force as opposed to 72 percent of the men.

Such opinion polls should be followed up by more in-depth interviews. Why are men in favor of military force? Do such attitudes go together with other attitudes associated with the "typical" male? More research is needed into attitudes of adult people toward nonviolent solutions to conflicts. History books and curricula should be rewritten, and the now-hidden history of nonviolence and the lives of women should be illuminated. Adult learners who have been educated with history books filled with wars, men, and violent solutions to conflicts need to be reeducated. They need to learn that when both a violent and a nonviolent action have been used in a conflict, the violent one is the one that is described in history, even though it might have been the least successful of the two. For instance, in the case of the uprising against the dictatorship of Maximiliano Hernandez Martinez in El Salvador in 1944, the violent action of April 2 was not successful in obtaining the resignation of the dictator, whereas the nonviolent one of May 9 was. Yet it is April 2 that is celebrated, not May 9.[21]

When violent sanctions fall short of achieving their objectives, the conclusion is not drawn that violence has been tried and found wanting. Instead, military analysts ask what conditions favored the winner and where the loser went wrong. The assessment is not made that there is something wrong with the use of violence. However, when nonviolent struggles are not successful, it is easily concluded that nonviolence is not useful. Questions need to be asked about ways of improving nonviolent means of conflict resolution. Other questions that need to be asked have to do with the selection of "news" and the writing of history. Why is it that when nonviolent means would have achieved the end in a struggle in a much better way and in an even more efficient way, violent means are chosen instead? Why is it that history books give more attention to violent struggles that fail to achieve their objectives than to nonviolent struggles that succeed? Achievements through the use of nonviolence are suppressed in history books in the same way in which the achievements of women are. There was, for instance, a strong conflict of interest, great hostility, the planning for war, and weapons lined up on both sides of the frontier between Norway and Sweden in 1905. Most people expected a war and the military establishments had planned for it. But the war was avoided through diplomacy. Very little is written about the avoidance of this war in history books. Had the war been fought, it would most likely have taken up many pages in the school history books of the Nordic countries.

We need more studies of nonviolent solutions to conflicts. There has been little research and little publicity given to the way in which the United Nations helped peace come about, for instance, in Cambodia, Namibia, and Nicaragua. The number of people doing research on nonviolent solutions to conflicts is very small compared to all the strategic and military analysts doing research on violent "solutions" to conflicts. Such "solutions" are normally of a temporary kind.

What can *adult* education offer in this regard that other forms of education cannot? Many adults can draw on life experiences that include sustained cooperation and the successful resolution of issues through nonviolence. They may be more interested in applying that knowledge to world politics, to build creatively on their own experiences, and to communicate their insights to others. Others will have firsthand experience with violence; they are likely to sense the pain that others feel when world politics becomes violent and seek ways to prevent such pain. In addition to adults' being more receptive and sensitive learners, it is likely that teaching changes with adults as learners. Teachers are less likely to try to impose a hierarchical organization on the learning situation and more likely to engage in an honest discussion—one that listens for all ideas rather than the "right" answer. To be effective therefore, adult education must be continually conscious of its pedagogy, focus on the violence and injustice going on in the smallest of social units like the family, and pay explicit attention to the process of conflict resolution.

UNDERSTANDING STRUCTURAL VIOLENCE
THROUGH FEMINIST THEORY

A second area that I would like to see as a priority area for peace education falls within that part of the peace concept called the abolition of structural violence. It is hard to understand the problems of the Third World
unless a new theory of development is embraced. This theory has to take
account of Feminist insights showing that without an understanding of
what is happening at the microlevel, within the household unit, one will
have difficulties predicting the fertility rate of a country as well as eradicat-
ing hunger and starvation.

Development theories, both the neoclassical "modernization" approach
and the more radical alternative (embracing Marxist/dependency/world system variants), have hardly paid any attention to women at all. These standard theories tend to view the household as the "private, personal sphere,"
not a part of the political setup. In her chapter on women and development,
Nüket Kardam mentions that a more recent approach to the study of gender and development attempts to combine women's roles of reproduction
with their role in production. This approach analyzes the nature of women's
contribution within the context of work done both inside and outside the
household and rejects the public/private dichotomy that has commonly
been used as a mechanism to undervalue family and household-maintenance
work performed by women.

Development researchers with a Feminist perspective have now started
asking who does the work in the family, who makes *the more influential
decisions,* and who gets the rewards. An interesting Indian study, reported
in the Indian Feminist magazine *Manushi,* makes it clear that the traditional male-constructed economic indicators such as average household income, per capita income, and per capita food consumption fail to tell us
who actually gets how much of what.[22] Those indicators do not get at such
fundamental questions as, How are economic resources distributed within
the family and with what consequences? Which family members have acquired greater decision-making powers over others? Who within the family
makes how much contribution to family income? What is the labor contribution of each family member? When the researchers examined internal
distribution of money, of food, and of decision-making power within land-
holding as well as landless Indian families, they found a steady pattern of
discrimination against women that varied little from one class to another.
Men, often the husband, sometimes sons or a father-in-law, usually decided
whether the woman would work outside the home, what her earnings
would be spent on, and to what extent the woman would be able to participate in decision making. The lives of women were hedged by crippling
restrictions.

Such patterns of discrimination are common, though often hidden behind the so-called gender-neutral economic indicators often used in discussing development. The findings, for instance, of the UN High Commissioner for Refugees in 1980 are not mysterious: Even after adequate supplies of basic food and supplements (earmarked for vulnerable groups) were available in refugee camps, women and children continued to suffer from malnutrition.[23]

When people are educated to a Feminist perspective, they can begin to have a real understanding of such things as food crises, development, and justice. Rae Lesser Blumberg, for instance, has found that the greater a woman's relative economic power within the household, the greater the likelihood that her fertility pattern will reflect her own perceived utilities and preferences—rather than those of her mate, family, state, and so on.[24] Generally, women use their greater economic leverage to achieve lower fertility. Lower fertility, in turn, can enhance economic growth and diminish the demand for relatively scarce food resources.

A Feminist perspective would help development planners overcome their blindness to the well-documented role of women as producers of some 80 percent of the locally consumed and marketed food in Africa, accounting for 60 to 80 percent of all labor hours in agriculture.[25] It would help development planners think about expressions such as "the farmer and his wife" or abstractions such as "farmers" and realize that the food-growing farmers of Africa are mostly women. And such a perspective would call into question why 97 percent of all African agricultural extension agents are male.[26] Many studies from Third World countries show that the male extension agents transmit the agricultural information to the husband when the wives are the full-time farmers. Often the information is not transmitted by the husband to the wife. Sometimes it is incorrectly transmitted.[27]

Another fact, to which development planners seem blind, is the practice of "separate purses" in most agrarian households in Africa. Women have control over what they locally produce. Blumberg points to several studies showing that incentives directed toward "the household" do not elicit as much response from women farmers as incentives directed to them.[28] She points to the Cameroon SEMRY Irrigated Rice Project in which cultivating the irrigated fields is a joint conjugal activity, but the husband gets all the income. Researchers found that wives were very reluctant to work in the rice fields because the work there competed with women's sorghum production and other income-generating activities. Although a married woman uses her sorghum primarily for feeding her family, it is her own sorghum.

Insufficient attention to women producers and their incentives seems to be a crucial but little recognized factor in the African food crises. Blumberg claims that "ironically, if given appropriate technical/credit aid and incentives, African women farmers may be the single most cost-effective available resource to alleviate the food crisis."[29] Without a Feminist analysis using gender as a central theoretical concept and looking at the internal economy of the household, planners may actually worsen the food crisis. For instance, since Tanzania introduced its International Monetary Fund– and World Bank–sponsored Economic Recovery Program in 1986, the country has shifted from being a net importer to a surplus producer of food. This may appear to be a big achievement, but health statistics show that half of the children of Tanzania are malnourished and 5 to 7 percent severely malnourished. Rural malnourishment of women and children has increased, claims Valerie Leach, head of the Analysis and Evaluation section of UNICEF. *Urban* malnutrition is less, she suggests, because women in towns are more at home and frequently give the children the snacks that they make and sell outside the home. As most of the agricultural work is done by rural women, the push to become a surplus food producer has meant that women must work harder and do not get the time to feed their children.[30]

It would seem clear that those individuals most in need of adult education in this priority area are the Third World government officials and the decision makers from international aid agencies. I suggest seminars in peace education for such officials on a worldwide scale. For some days these officials should try to learn from Feminist insights about development and try to start discussing what looking at gender as a central theoretical concept would mean for the way in which they think about development.

CONCLUSION

Peace education and adult education are intertwined. They are both necessary. I have tried to suggest how adult education can help create change toward a more peaceful world. I have emphasized two priority areas for peace education among adults: helping individuals find nonviolent solutions to conflicts and creating a more positive, just understanding of development. I would hope that as adults become more educated in these areas, they would help revise the education that their children receive.

As a reader of this chapter, you may feel uncomfortable. You are in a period of transition, from a competitive, hierarchical educational environment, toward an independent adulthood where the kind of education that I am talking about becomes more meaningful. Is my vision of the future something that you must await "until you're older"? Not at all. I think there are two pressing things that you can do *now.* The first is to try to formulate some answers to the following questions about implementation.

1. How can we encourage or persuade government officials and development planners to learn about gender?
2. How can we encourage adults to think about and explore nonviolent conflict resolution? How do we encourage them to think about creative applications of their own personal experiences to the arena of world politics?

3. How can we devise effective ways of teaching peace education in the typical school setting that sends so many messages that undercut the hopes for peace?

4. How can we encourage men and women to give heed to the experiences of women who have thought carefully about world politics and who have, against great obstacles, put themselves into world politics?

The second pressing thing that you can do *now* is suggested by the questions that I have just posed. The "we" of those sentences include *you*, if you choose to include yourself. How can you become involved in adult education?

NOTES

1. Birgit Brock-Utne, "Formal Education as a Force in Shaping Cultural Norms Relating to War and the Environment," in Arthur Westing, ed., *Cultural Norms, War and the Environment* (Oxford: Oxford University Press, 1989), 83–101.

2. See Birgit Brock-Utne, *Educating for Peace: A Feminist Perspective* (New York: Pergamon, 1985); Birgit Brock-Utne, *Feminist Perspectives on Peace and Peace Education* (New York: Pergamon, 1989); Betty Reardon, *Militarism and Sexism* (New York: Teachers College Press, 1985); and Betty Reardon, *Comprehensive Peace Education: Educating for Global Responsibility* (New York: Teachers College Press, 1988).

3. Brock-Utne, *Feminist Perspectives,* 39–73.

4. Elin Wägner, *Väckarklocka* (Stockholm: Delfin, 1978).

5. Rachel Carson, *The Silent Spring* (London: Penguin, 1964); Carolyn Merchant, *The Death of Nature* (San Francisco: Harper & Row, 1980); Rosalie Bertell, *No Immediate Danger? Prognosis for a Radioactive Earth* (London: Women's Press, 1985).

6. Katarina Tomasevski, *Development Aid and Human Rights* (London: Pinter, 1989).

7. Susan George, *How the Other Half Dies* (Harmondsworth, Eng.: Penguin, 1976), and Susan George, *A Fate Worse Than Debt* (Harmondsworth, Eng.: Penguin, 1988).

8. Helen Caldicott, *Missile Envy: The Arms Race and Nuclear War* (Toronto: Bantam, 1986).

9. See Brock-Utne, *Educating for Peace,* 63–70.

10. Bertha Von Suttner, *Die Waffen Nieder!* (Dresden: E. Pierson, 1889).

11. Johan Galtung, "Peace Education: Problems and Conflicts," in Magnus Haavelsrud, ed., *Education for Peace: Reflection and Action* (Guilford, England: IPC Science and Technology Press, 1976), 80–87.

12. Ibid., 81.

13. Kathleen Weiler, *Women Teaching for Change* (Amherst, MA: Bergin & Garvey, 1988).

14. The Third UNESCO World Conference on Adult Education, *Adult Education in the Context of Continued Education* (Tokyo: UNESCO, 1972).

15. Reardon, *Comprehensive Peace Education,* 10.

16. Brock-Utne, *Educating for Peace,* 37–70.

17. Birgit Brock-Utne, "The Feminist Experience and Social Change in Europe and Africa," in Elise Boulding, ed., *New Agendas for Peace Research* (Boulder, CO: Lynne Rienner, 1992), 33–43.

18. Carol Cohn, "Sex and Death in the Rational World of Defense Intellectuals," in Diana Russell, ed., *Exposing Nuclear Phallacies* (New York: Pergamon, 1989), 128.

19. Ibid., 155.

20. *Guardian Weekly* 143 (December 1990), 1.

21. Christopher Kruegler and Patricia Parkman, "Identifying Alternatives to Political Violence," *Harvard Educational Review* 55 (February 1985): 109–117.

22. B. Horowitz and Madhu Kishwar, "Family Life: The Unequal Deal," *Manushi* 11 (1982).

23. UN High Commissioner for Refugees, "The Situation of Women Refugees the World Over," Document No. A/CONF. 94/24, 1980.

24. Rae Lesser Blumberg, "Toward a Feminist Theory of Development," in Ruth A. Wallace, ed., *Feminism and Sociological Theory* (Newbury Park, CA: Sage, 1989), 161–200.

25. Ruth Sivard, *Women . . . A World Survey* (Washington, DC: World Priorities, 1985), 5, 17; United Nations Secretary General, "Effective Mobilisation of Women in Development," UN/A/33/238, 1987, 5.

26. Burton Swanson and Bassi Jaffe, *International Directory of National Extension Systems* (Champaign: University of Illinois, Bureau of Educational Research, 1981).

27. Alice Stewart Carloni, *Women in Development: AID's Experience, 1973–1985* (Washington, DC: Agency for International Development, 1987), 1:16.

28. Blumberg, "Feminist Theory of Development," 176–77.

29. Ibid., 182.

30. Interview reported by Colleen Lowe Morna, "Tanzania: Overworked Mothers, Underfed Babies," *Women's Feature Service,* Special Issue (July–October 1990): 4.

✣13✣

"If Men Are the Problem . . ."

Ralph Pettman

Why have a chapter with the title, "If men are the problem . . ."? Why ask "if" at all? Is the answer not obvious? Men are the majority of policy makers. The efforts of women in world politics that were discussed earlier in this anthology are always and everywhere mediated by male administrators. Men own and manage most of the world's production and finance. They promulgate all the big systems of human belief. The question would hardly seem to merit more than the briefest reply.

All the more reason to find out how and why such a distorted state of world affairs came about. All the more reason to wonder why it has not notably changed despite the growing awareness of it.

I shall begin by asking whether, in the relations among nations, women are as subordinate as male preponderance makes them appear. "If men are the problem" becomes "What is the problem?" I then turn to who is to blame for the world's ills. "If men are the problem," does it also mean that men are to blame? Finally, I shall consider whether a female-dominated world would be better than the one we have today. "If men are the problem" thus leads to the question, "Are women the solution?"

In discussing the issue in these three ways I shall be using—albeit briefly—most of the main approaches to contemporary Feminism. These include the postmodernist, Marxist/socialist, biological, psychoanalytic, liberal, and radical approaches.

WHAT IS THE PROBLEM?

As a sex, men are highly visible in world politics. Every strategic forum, every diplomatic summit, every department of foreign affairs, every military force features males almost exclusively. Do men, as a consequence, dominate world affairs?

Women would certainly not appear to have an equal say in the forums where world affairs are determined. Any meeting of the United Nations General Assembly, for example, is notably a male meeting. Women are conspicuous by their absence. Some women do participate directly in such forums and in the ones that feed in to them. Most women, however, get little chance to say in any direct way how the patterns of human practice in world affairs should be shaped.

Since the institutions that enact world affairs are mostly male, they also reflect male concerns. Men rule in such a way as to preserve their preponderance. It is no accident that "all democratic experiments, all revolutions, all demands for equality have so far, in every instance, stopped short of sexual equality." [1]

Women do participate in world affairs. In countries where women can vote they help choose the men who represent them at home and abroad. They are the wives and lovers of most male policy makers, and as such they can wield considerable influence. They are one-third of the world's paid work force, and they do two-thirds of the world's work (paid and unpaid). This makes them an intrinsic part of the world political economy. [2] They are also leaders and members of social movements for peace, sustainable development, and cultural integrity. The women of Greenham Common, for example, set a global example for grassroots commitment, as do groups of female villagers in Bangladesh. Their ideas are clearly part of the mental context in which the patterns of global political practice are made.

Women remain, nonetheless, more marginal than men in world affairs. It is still notably more difficult for women than men to get a hearing on global issues. This prompts one to ask why it is that men continue to dominate in this way and why women overall continue to remain subordinate? To answer this I will turn to two schools of Feminist thought. The first, Postmodernist feminism, argues that how we think is man-made. Only deconstruction of our current modes and categories of thought will make us free. The second, Marxist-socialist feminism, highlights male exploitation of female labor.

Postmodernist feminists draw close attention to the socioeconomic and political practices that make female subordination appear normal and natural. They highlight the problems posed by the basic modes of thought that define our contemporary sense of identity. The "modern" way of thought, they argue, is male centered. They wish to go beyond this to a "postmodernist" mode that is more dynamic and complex and less dominated by men.

What is the "modern" way of thinking that Postmodernist feminists would have us transcend? It is the contemporary tendency to objectify everything so that everything (and everyone) can be pictured as an object.

This mental ploy is highly productive. By reasoning this way, we are seemingly freer to generalize and experiment. We are less inhibited in our research by the personal and social contexts in which all thought occurs. We can create ordered thought systems of great technical utility. We can, in other words, "do science" in the pursuit of universal "truth." We can also imagine "states" that are "sovereign" abroad and unified "nations" at home. We can create a world politics out of states-as-things that is seemingly "objective" and "real."

Postmodernists see this mental ploy as a kind of trick. To them knowledge is contingent. It is conditioned by the contexts in which it has been acquired. The thing-world of "states" is an example of such contingent knowledge. Because contexts differ, knowledge is always partial. The pursuit of universal "truths" of any kind is therefore a conceit, a false goal in whose pursuit we do harm to humans.

Postmodernist feminists (as far as they venture any general statement at all) see objectivism and the pursuit of a universal truth as a male conceit. Thinking like this, they say, not only unduly exalts rationality and emotional detachment, but also leads to a malecentric science that categorizes and dichotomizes "men" and "women," as well as "strong states" and "weak states," "First World" and "Third World," and "war" and "peace." It stereotypes "the observer" as active, rational, and masculine and "the observed" as passive, irrational, and feminine. Who would want passive, irrational people running the world? Who would not want it run by rational, active, masculine people—namely, men?

Objectifying thinking also makes for a particular kind of individualism, one that values autonomy and interpersonal distance. Objectifying thinkers typically depict such autonomy as masculine as well. Values like relatedness and a sense of interpersonal connectedness (values that are far from intrinsically feminine, but that thinking of this sort depicts as feminine) are devalued. It does not take much to imagine the influence that objectivist thinking of this sort can have on world affairs. Difference and division between autonomous "states" come to seem natural and inevitable. Collaboration and compromise must always be contrived. They must always take an effort of a seemingly unnatural kind.

Postmodernist feminists want us to change the mental context in which we see world politics—indeed, in which we think of all aspects of life. If, in other words, "the history of Western thought is the history of thought by members of a group with a distinctive social experience—namely, men—then we are led to a new set of questions about the social nature of that thought" and a new set of questions about how justified and reliable such thinking, including scientific thinking, might be.[3] Postmodernist feminists wonder whether our current conceptualizations represent what men and women "actually" are as opposed to how they are usually made out to be. They question whether the categories "men" and "women" or "masculine" and "feminine" open up our thinking or close it down. Similarly, they ask if concepts such as "state" and "national security" inhibit thought. How are such categories constructed, they ask, and for whom?

Marxist/socialist feminists, on the other hand, turn from the realm of ideas to the realm of the material. From this perspective the problem is not a matter of thinking about how to think but a question of how we organize matter. In part because of the scientific thinking described above, we live now in the middle of the most productive age in all human history. We live in a time of industrial revolution, transforming matter in myriad ways to serve our wants and needs.

Our age is capitalist in that people produce and exchange goods and services for profit. It is also capitalist in the more specialized sense that while some own or manage the means to make such profits (capitalists), others must sell their work for wages to provide the labor power that makes profits possible in the first place. This more specialized sense of the concept of capitalism is the classical Marxist one, and it sees the capitalist way of producing and distributing wealth as determining all social relationships. Capitalism fosters intense productivity but it does so, in this view, at great cost to communal integrity and at great cost to the sense that workers have of their own self-worth. Those in work are part of production chains that allow (so the argument runs) little life satisfaction.

Marxist/socialist feminists subscribe to various versions of this sort of analysis. To them, however, "workers" are not only found in the waged sector of the economy. Many workers are in the unwaged sector, and most of these unwaged workers are women. Capitalists derive great benefits from the unpaid labor of those who work at home doing the communal and domestic caring tasks—the child bearing and the child rearing and the looking after of the aged, as well as the moral support of the wage-earning breadwinners—services that classical Marxist theory neglects.

Given the lack of material rewards for homemaking and its distance from public power, most men make sure that they do little of it. This is generally one job that they are happy to give to women. To reinforce their position, men find it useful to separate the public realm of male production from a private realm of female reproduction. Marxist/socialist feminists are concerned, therefore, not only about the class divisions in capitalist society between owners (and managers) of the means of production and those in paid labor. They are also concerned with the "housewifization" or privatization of the world's women.

Because unpaid homemaking creates more profits for capitalists (they do not have to pay anyone to make it possible for workers to come to work), capitalists encourage it. And because (mostly male) capitalists see it as women's traditional nurturing role to work unpaid at home, it is mostly women who get "housewifized."

Women do, of course, work as wage laborers. The productive dynamism of industrial capitalism promises largesse for all. In reality, however, Marxists see such largesse accruing to some. Most get little. This unevenness in the capitalist mode of development is manifest at all levels. It is particularly manifest, however, between men and women. Women in paid work invariably earn less than their male counterparts do. Even in work, in other words, capitalism exploits women more than men.

In 1985, for example, at the end of the United Nations's Decade for the Advancement of Women, it was found that "with few exceptions . . . women's relative access to economic resources, income, and employment ha[d] worsened, their burdens of work ha[d] increased, and their relative and even absolute health, nutritional, and education status ha[d] declined."[4] After ten key years, despite a specific attempt by the world community to focus on and reduce gender inequity, more, not less, women in the world were worse off, and they were worse off compared to men. The feminization of world poverty is particularly apparent in developing countries where the economic progress of women has "virtually stopped."[5]

To Marxist/socialist feminists this is an appalling waste of human potential. It also means structural violence on a massive scale, since uneven development means the starvation and degradation of women across the globe. The add-on consequences are clear. Since it is women who bear the main responsibility for subsistence agriculture, for food preparation, and for family health care, their impoverishment means more general impoverishment. In some cases this now means the loss of an entire generation.

The problem, as such Feminists see it, is the patriarchal character of contemporary industrial capitalism. The exploitative consequences of this system can be seen in the poverty-ridden slums of any Third, former Second, or First World country. They can also, however, be seen in the declining material status of the world's women. "On the most fundamental level," as Leghorn and Parker argue, "men have structured their economies on the foundation of women's slavery."[6]

Marxist/socialist feminists would characterize the problem as primarily that of male imperialism. Women are the world's "last colony"[7] and in Marxist/socialist terms their colonial status is a key consequence of how capitalism works to not only exploit labor in general but female labor in particular.

ARE MEN ALSO TO BLAME?

If the problem is industrial capitalism, the problem is social and institutional. This suggests that more enlightened social practices—genuinely egalitarian ones, for example—would make a difference. In principle more enlightened social practices should put an end to patriarchy.

In practice, however, male dominance persists regardless of the mode of production of the day. Even where an effort has been made to replace capitalism with socialism, patriarchy has persisted. Why is this? Is there something "natural" about it that will never go away?

The whole question of "natural" differences is highly contentious. Is there "scientific" evidence that might demonstrate a biological difference between the sexes of a sort that might determine in turn a male and a female way of behaving? Are gender traits "innate"—like the supposed male penchant for aggressiveness or the supposed female penchant for nurturing? Does every society develop institutions and socialization practices that express these stereotypic gender traits in sex-specific ways? Do they do so (if they do) because they must and because only in this way can they operate most efficiently?[8]

To answer these questions, I shall now turn to two other ways in which gender differences are discussed. In the first, I shall contrast the arguments of biological determinists, who see an essential biological difference between men and women, with those of environmental voluntarists, who see "nurture" as more important than "nature." In the second, I shall look at the psychoanalytic argument that biological differences between males and females are manifested most importantly as psychological ones.

What do biological determinists say? S. Goldberg, for one, argues that aggression is the "only sexual difference that we can explain with direct . . . biological evidence."[9] In this author's view, this "fact" is nonetheless sufficient to account for the inevitability of patriarchy, for male dominance, and for males' attaining most of any society's high-status positions. It is the larger amount of the hormone testosterone that most men have, in other words, that gives them their "insuperable 'head start.' "[10] The hormonal difference creates behavioral outcomes like greater aggressivity in most males and less aggressivity in most females. Goldberg sees men as literally programmed to prevail.

Environmental voluntarists, like R. Bleier, disagree. Bleier notes the brain's "enormous capacity to learn, invent, remember, symbolize, make choices; to have self-awareness, beliefs, convictions, intent and motivation; and to create and transmit cultures."[11] As far as this author is concerned it is the amount of external input that the brain requires as part of its normal development that matters most. As a consequence, one can conclude that it is "not possible to separate biological from cultural factors in any adequate explanation of the development of human behaviors and characteristics nor to defend the notion of an immutable core of instinct or nature beneath and outside of culture and learning."[12] We cannot ever know, in other words, what is "nature" as opposed to what is "nurture."

We cannot escape the fact that male control of political power is universal. The exceptional female leaders like Margaret Thatcher are precisely that—exceptional. The emphasis placed upon power as control—that is, upon dominance and subordinance rather than competence—is also universal. It is also male specific. Does this indicate fundamental predispositioning of the sort that Goldberg describes? Does it suggest a male and a masculinist bias to human society of the "natural" sort that Goldberg sees there? Is it more than a convention that a masculinist construction of politics (in terms of dominance and subordinance) should be preferred to a feminist construction of politics as competence? Does human biology really prescribe dominance and subordinance rather than compassion and competence as our inescapable lot in world affairs?

The debate goes on, not only because it is difficult to establish empirically what role "nature" and "nurture" play, but because "science" as the way of answering this question is suspect. If one accepts, as Postmodernist feminists do, that science itself has a male bias, then surely the status of science as a court of appeal is debatable. Most scientists are male. No matter how objective they may be, their gender—that is, their masculine ways of being (as they learned them growing up)—is likely to affect what they think is important.

The debate continues as well because of a desire to establish who or what is to blame. To the Goldberg school, male dominance is the result of a surfeit of male hormones. Men cannot help themselves. It is therefore harder to hold them accountable for what they do, and it is harder to see what can be done to bring about more equality. In Goldberg's terms it would be undesirable even to try.

Even if we accept Goldberg's argument, however, the "fact" of greater male aggressivity does not negate the need for and our capacity to achieve equality of opportunity for all. How acutely we feel this need depends on the value that we place upon individual self-realization. The cultural creativity of humankind is sufficiently extensive, Bleier believes, to allow in principle for the conscious limitation of any biological "determinants" or "predispositions." Slavery has largely been abolished. There is no reason that patriarchy should not be as well. It depends on how much we want to emancipate women and men.

And, of course, we do not have to grant Goldberg's case at all. The evidence that links sex and aggressivity or passivity is very inconclusive. There is no biologically compelling reason why the diverse talents of the female half of our species should be underutilized in any way. It is thoroughgoing female liberation that would seem to provide for the most reasonable use of our evolutionary advantages as a species. Indeed, the longer the subject is studied, the more arbitrary and the less "natural" female subservience of any sort appears to be.

If we do not grant a case like Goldberg's, then male dominance looks more and more like a culturally perpetuated conspiracy. For this, the men who know better can indeed be held to blame, as to a lesser extent can the women who know better and who collude in perpetuating their plight.

It is conceivable that all this might be happening unconsciously. Men and women might not know any better because the "knowing" involved is precognitive. There is certainly a large psychoanalytic literature that suggests as much. Is this literature able to establish, however, direct causal links between sociocultural concepts of gender and the fact of biological sex in the context of the human unconscious?

Psychoanalytic determinists think so. According to S. Freud, for instance, "children go through distinct psychological development states, and the temperament of any given adult is the product of how he/she deals with these states. Gender, in other words, is the product of sexual maturation. Because they experience their sexuality differently (as a result of biology), girls and boys ultimately end up with contrasting gender roles." [13]

The deterministic nature of this account was readily apparent to early critics. K. Horney, for example, argued that "patriarchal culture creates women as feminine (passive, masochistic, narcissistic), and then convinces them that 'femininity'—actually a defensive adaptation to male domination—characterizes their true selves. . . . Women do not [however] want to be men because [as Freud argued] they are enamored of the penis; they want to be men because men are in control of society." [14]

Freudian theory survives mainly because it serves an important political purpose. If male dominance can be ascribed to men's love of their mothers, as Freud said it could (a love that men are supposed to transcend only out of fear that their jealous fathers will castrate them—and a love that, once transcended, ostensibly creates greater strength of character), men cannot escape their destiny—which is biologically assigned. This is very convenient. It lets men off the hook. How can they be to blame if their biology determines their psychology in this direct and unconscious way?

The same conclusion could be used to advocate doing away with (most) men altogether. Then again, we could bring culture back in. We could acknowledge the enormous part that experience plays in shaping gender behavior and the learned nature of every human psychological response. This would allow at least for the possibility of change.

And so it goes. In the end, it remains difficult to know who to "blame" for the willingness of many women to "forgive and . . . forget male abuse and/or neglect" [15] or who to blame for the domineering behavior and truculence of many men. In the end, it is not clear who or what to change.

ARE WOMEN THE SOLUTION?

It is "natural" for human beings to inherit male or female chromosome counts. It is equally "natural" to complete the genetic "hard wiring" that we inherit by going on to acquire gendered cultural characteristics of great diversity and complexity. Determining human gender is always a process, and it is never historically complete. It is also a political process, one that apportions power at every level, including the global level.

The fact that men have public power in world politics and that they use it not only against each other but also to dominate women does not explain how they got it in the first place. Which is why, despite the attempt by cultural voluntarists to find nothing but social conditioning at work as far back as they can go, the issue of biological determinism continues to resurface.

The trouble with determinism is the sense it fosters that change is not likely to achieve much or that only the most radical of changes will achieve anything of lasting value. Determinism either sees change as doomed to failure and the only sensible course as one that works within the limits that "nature" provides. Or it sees change as only meaningful if what "nature" ostensibly "recommends" is subverted root and branch.

Many are attracted to neither extreme. They seek other alternatives. Not everyone, as noted already, accepts that biological sex determines (or even predisposes) the gender roles that people are assigned by their cultures. Many would say that what we are we learn to be. And if this is so, then we may, to some extent at least, be able to do some unlearning too. We may, for example, learn new gender roles and new gender behavior patterns of a more egalitarian sort. That may be the start toward the solution.

To develop this debate further, I shall turn to another two schools of Feminist thought. The first, Liberal feminism, argues the importance of individual self-realization and equality of opportunity. The second, Radical feminism, argues for separation of a sort that will make women free by asserting their dominance over men.

Liberal feminists argue that "we" are all fundamentally human beings. Our humanity is most commonly defined as our capacity to reason, a characteristic that in liberal parlance we all share. It is our most important quality. Our skin color, our age, our disabilities, our sexual preferences, our class or caste status, and our biological sex are seen to be secondary qualities that do not determine our status as human beings.

Historically, of course, women have been depicted (mostly by male depicters) as "essentially" emotional, intuitive, nonrational creatures—and, thus, less capable than men, especially in handling something as complex and dangerous as world politics. Liberal feminists would argue that it is no longer possible to deny women their essential humanity like this. Women are entitled to all the fundamental rights that liberals claim as necessary for any individual to lead a humane life—a life of civil and political freedom, material security, and spiritual well-being. Political freedom means full and unfettered access to all policy-making positions. Regarding policy, it means a concern for human rights in world politics and foreign policy.

Rights claims are fundamental moral claims. They articulate a number of basic values—freedom, justice, equity, and aversion to pain—that specifically express our empathy with others. They assume that such values are universal. The attempt to realize these values, however, can lead to many conflicts and contradictions. It is not easy to maximize the freedom that an individual enjoys and to make sure that there is parity of access to life's opportunities for all. Nor is it easy to decide whether to emphasize economic rights over political rights.

Reconciling the policy outcomes of values like freedom and equity—and this includes foreign policy outcomes—is never achieved outright and forever. This is particularly so, given the different emphases that different cultures place upon each value and the different meanings that they give them as well. The endeavor can be creative nonetheless. Many see the Liberal project kept alive by the attempt to maximize such values, to reconcile the differences between them, and to make common ground between incommensurable cultures. In this view, women are a solution. Their presence in politics and their perspective foster this endeavor.

Because of the stress that they place on individual self-realization, Liberals of all sorts are criticized by those who believe in the integrity of the community more than the self-realization of the individual. Marxist/socialists also criticize Liberals for espousing a doctrine that they believe to be a sham. Liberalism, as they see it, is used by industrial capitalists to help conceal the exploitative and inhumane nature of the social relationships on which contemporary capitalism is based.

Because of its stress on self-realization, Liberal feminism also sees women's liberation as something of a bootstrap operation. Women are supposed to liberate themselves by cutting the ties of patriarchal conditioning and by standing up, as separate persons, in all their actual, rather than potential, glory. Each woman is supposed to solve the problem of her own subordinance by finding the will to reject the age-old assumption that a male or female biology means a life bound by (culturally defined) masculine or feminine ways.

Finding such a will and choosing to exercise it is not simple, however. If practically every society is dominated by men—who, in the main, make it hard for women to find the requisite will to cut the ties of patriarchy— then it is not surprising that so many women, so far at least, have largely failed to do so.

Liberal social practices, in short, have their limits. Equality of economic opportunity, for example, is meant to benefit all women, but in practice it benefits only a few. Socialist revolutions that likewise subscribe to the same principle, as well as that of equality of outcomes, still end up with men mostly in charge. It is not surprising, therefore, that most Radical feminists see the solution for women not as female self-realization but as female dominance or female separatism.

Radical feminists depict female dominance as the destruction of gender hierarchies or the inversion of all the male structures of personal and social privilege and power. The route to change is some form of separatism. This begins with the definition of women as beings in their own right rather than as beings defined with reference to what male or masculine might be. Women traditionally have been depicted—to their detriment—either as a lesser version of men (less strong, less intelligent), as the opposite of men (weak, stupid), or as another part of the species (where strength and intelligence, e.g., are no longer relevant). In every case, the dominant referent is male.[16]

Reasonably enough, Radical feminists want to know why it is that women cannot be the dominant human referent—that is, why men cannot be depicted as inferior to women, as the antithesis of women, or as beyond the female pale. That redefinition would make women's characteristics and values most important in—and, therefore, more likely to be the predominant motivations and patterns of—contemporary world politics. In the following chapter, A. S. Runyan examines how Radical feminists offer new visions about world politics. The suggestion is that visualizing the Radical feminist alternatives of a more just, equal, and peaceful world is an important step toward creating these alternatives. Women could be the solution.

One problem with this approach, as Runyan notes, is the way in which it leads to biological essentialism and a heightened sense of the particularity of women's bodies. Liberal feminists and Marxist/socialist feminists find this heightened sense most frustrating, since they want to be able to bring about reforms by changing society, not biology.

Despite such frustrations, however, "were it not for radical feminists, we would have been even slower to understand the connections among . . . pornography, prostitution, sexual harassment, rape, and women battering," among a host of other issues involving women's control of their bodies and their reproductive processes.[17] As R. Tong argues, "What feminists owe to radical feminism is the conviction that what women share is their sexuality," that female sexuality embodies its own power, and that "even if there is no such thing as an essential female nature . . . it is good—indeed extremely good—to be a woman."[18]

CONCLUSION

Men do dominate world politics and male dominance is promoted and protected by a host of hegemonic strategies that vary across the world and that have changed over time. Though the strategies differ, the end result remains the same: men in power, and using that power to police the mental paradigms, the social practices, the sort of manual and professional labor (both paid and unpaid), and the political institutions that perpetuate male dominance worldwide.

Patriarchy is the most pervasive of human constructions. It is no accident, therefore, that world politics should be first and foremost about patriarchy. State making, wealth making, and the making of contemporary minds is fundamentally about defining and furthering a system that perpetuates the preponderance of men.

This would not be a problem if we lived in the best of all possible worlds. But we do not. The world that men make is arguably a poorer version of what it could be. Making the world better means making a new kind of world politics. And that cannot be done, all Feminists argue, without confronting its most fundamental feature—namely, male dominance.

Men are not likely to share their power readily. So what is to be done? The six approaches described above provide for a wide range of prescriptions in this regard. The kind of Feminism that you find most appropriate will determine in turn what kind of action you think best in dealing with the man problem in world affairs.

What do I think? In my view, politics is not intrinsically sex specific—and that includes world politics. This is not to deny the masculinist nature of the contemporary state, for example, or of the world market, or of the dominant global ideology of modernism. It is to say that political thoughts and institutions are not inevitably gendered. I do not accept, in other words, the determinism of either biological, psychoanalytic, or radical approaches.

What about liberalism? Liberal feminism promotes many worthy ideals, especially those of self-realization and equality of opportunity, but it does not, to my mind, adequately counter the Marxist/socialist argument that liberal ideals act as a smoke screen for the inequities of industrial capitalism.

So I would argue the case for both the liberal ideal of self-realization and the socialist notion of the need for radical socioeconomic changes that have communitarian outcomes. I would argue for both one and the other.[19] What about you?

NOTES

1. R. Miles, *The Women's History of the World* (London: Michael Joseph, 1988), 239.

2. Cited in J. Langmore and D. Peetz, eds., *Wealth, Poverty, and Survival* (Sydney: George Allen & Unwin, 1983), 67. For this work, they get one-tenth of the world's income. They own less than one-hundredth of the world's property.

3. S. Harding, "Is Gender a Variable in Conceptions of Rationality? A Survey of Issues," in C. Gould, ed., *Beyond Domination* (Totowa, NJ: Rowman & Allanheld, 1983), 44.

4. G. Sen and C. Grown, *Development, Crises, and Alternative Visions: Third World Women's Perspectives* (New York: Monthly Review, 1987), 16.

5. United Nations, *1989 World Survey on the Role of Women in Development* (New York: United Nations, 1989), 6.

6. L. Leghorn and K. Parker, *Women's Worth: Sexual Economics and the World of Women* (London: Routledge & Kegan Paul, 1981), 281.

7. M. Mies, V. Bennholdt–Thomsen, and C. von Werlhof, *Women: The Last Colony* (London: Zed Books, 1988), and Leghorn and Parker, *Women's Worth,* 283–84.

8. S. Goldberg, *The Inevitability of Patriarchy* (New York: Morrow, 1973).

9. Ibid., 118.

10. Ibid., 119.

11. R. Bleier, *Science and Gender: A Critique of Biology and Its Theories on Women* (Elsmford, NY: Pergamon, 1984), viii.

12. Ibid.

13. R. Tong, *Feminist Thought: A Comprehensive Introduction* (London: Unwin Hyman, 1989), 139.

14. Ibid., 148.

15. Ibid., 172.

16. N. Jay, "Gender and Dichotomy," *Feminist Studies* 7 (Spring 1981): 38–56.

17. Tong, *Feminist Thought,* 138.

18. Ibid.

19. At the same time, I am very aware of the masculine nature of the analytic discourse in which these arguments are made.

❖ 14 ❖

Radical Feminism: Alternative Futures

Anne Sisson Runyan

Radical feminism is a form of Feminism that argues that women's oppression around the world is rooted in patriarchy, generally defined by Radical feminists as a worldwide system of male dominance over all aspects of life, ranging from the family and the economy to the state and the international system. According to a Radical feminist perspective, patriarchy, as the source and cause of women's oppression, arises from differences between male and female sexual and reproductive roles. Radical feminists claim that men's aggressive sexuality and women's lack of reproductive freedom have kept men in power over women.

Radical feminists associate men's aggressive sexuality with men's desire to have power over others. This desire has translated into a variety of what Radical feminists call "power-over" systems. Under patriarchy, which values the masculine trait of aggression over the feminine trait of compassion, power is equated with sufficient physical, military, and economic strength to control the behavior of others. Thus, Radical feminists argue that the exercise of power over others that is so common in families and societies and among states is the result of patriarchal assumptions that equate masculine aggression with strength and feminine compassion with weakness. From a Radical feminist perspective, these patriarchal assumptions about what constitutes strength and weakness create the kinds of hierarchies that justify men's power over women, adults' power over children, humans' power over nature as well as white people's power over people of color, wealthy people's power over poor people, and developed states' power over developing states.

RADICAL FEMINISTS' CRITIQUES OF WORLD POLITICS

At the center of Radical feminists' critique of world politics as "power politics" is their particular concern about the connection between male violence and militarism.[1] They have been especially critical of the nuclear arms race, seeing it as the most extreme expression of patriarchy. Penny Strange, a member of the British organization Women Opposed to Nuclear Technology (WONT), argues that underlying the war system of patriarchal societies is a "male cult of toughness" that ties men's sexual identity to violence. On the other hand, women in patriarchal societies are held to be passive and helpless, and the work that they are traditionally assigned to do is devalued and even despised. As Strange notes: "Among these despised feminine qualities are survival skills—cooperating, admitting dependence, subsistence farming, preparing food, bringing up children. A boy learns not to show emotion, not to admit dependence: to compete, to try to get the better of others; he learns to value work for money over domestic work, the tending of machines more than the tending of children."[2] Moreover, boys and, later, men must continue to prove their manhood by engaging in acts and/or threats of violence against women to purge themselves of any feminine qualities that would make them appear weak. Exercising violence against women, Strange argues, is the earliest form of power-over that men learn, uniquely preparing them for military service.

Many Radical feminists have revealed the ways in which the military, and especially the U.S. military, infuses sexual imagery into military training. Male recruits are taunted with such epithets as "sissy" and "faggot" when they fail to act aggressively enough to kill. Military drill songs are replete with phrases that associate men's penises with guns (the power to kill) and with rape (the power to humiliate the "enemy," usually described in racist ways, by violating the "enemy's" women). The irony of this training is that at the same time that male recruits are told that the military "will make men out of them," they are, in fact, made to be "men" by being subordinated and coerced by their male superiors. As a result, male recruits must "prove" their manhood while remaining obedient to the pecking order of the military. This ensures that male recruits will embrace the ideology of war, which requires that they not only be willing to kill the "enemy" on command, but also be willing to be killed on behalf of the military hierarchy and in support of maintaining the international hierarchy.

These hierarchies of men over women and officers over recruits, Radical feminists insist, lay the basis for hierarchies in the international system. For example, Strange argues that "international politics closely resembles gang fights in the playground. The leader is the one acknowledged to have superior force: his power is then augmented by his position—in effect, the power of his underlings is added to his own. They give this power to him and get certain benefits—protection, enhanced prestige from the relationship to the leader."[3] Thus, from the Radical feminist view, the international system of unequal and competitive states can be seen as one big male-protection racket wherein the strong extort the weak to enter into various military and economic alliances or relationships that mostly benefit the strong.

Radical feminists argue that this male-protection racket has its origins in patriarchal thinking that assumes that "man" should have dominion over natural resources. In particular, Western patriarchal thinking, which Radical feminists claim is reflective of the worldview of largely white men in power in the West, considers not only the natural world but also white women and Third World peoples as raw materials that can be exploited for political and economic gain. This constant extraction of resources—which increasingly impoverishes women, Third World peoples and states dependent on "aid" from elite men and First World states—is what makes the male-protection racket possible. This racket undermines any attempts to develop self-reliance that might release dominated peoples and states from the contemporary international hierarchy. Thus, for Radical feminists, the struggles of "weak" states against "strong" are related to the struggles of women against patriarchal domination. "The aim of self-reliance is paralleled by the struggle of many women who refuse to be victims any longer, yet also refuse to become oppressors. What is being struggled against is at root the same thing—a hierarchy grounded in and perpetuated by sexual dominance."[4]

Since Radical feminists believe that sexual dominance underlies other forms of domination, their primary prescription for change in world politics involves change in sexual identities and relations. Women's nurturing capacities need to be expanded beyond the private realm of the home where they tend to service largely the needs of men who will take no responsibility for providing the emotional support and child care necessary for the survival and reproduction of healthy human beings. Women should be valued for the survival skills that they can foster not only in the family but also in the polity. Men, in turn, must learn caring values and practices that will enable them to struggle with women to bring about an end to social and political hierarchies. As Strange puts it: "Our vision is of each person a whole person; of women reclaiming their autonomy and self-assertion: no longer seeking 'femininity' in submission and helplessness: of men learning to care, to nurture, to show emotion, to admit weakness, no longer having to prove their manhood in acts of domination and violence, instead seeking positive peace through cooperation and confidence-building."[5]

In order for this vision to become reality, Radical feminists argue that the links between violence against women and violence among states must be taken seriously. Moreover, there must be concerted efforts to ensure that women and men should participate equally in all social, economic, and political institutions and movements and at all levels of decision making.

Finally, Radical feminists maintain, we must create both "an alternative sexuality which is not based on dominance but relies on respect for other people, equality of power, sensitivity, and an ability to receive and give generously"[6] and "alternatives to reliance on increasingly menacing weapons and a highly trained professional group for our defense."[7] Thus, the Radical feminist agenda is firmly based upon the notion that the "personal is political" and propounds that the only way out of contemporary, patriarchal world politics is nothing short of a revolution in sexual roles, identities, and relations. Reformist, top-down strategies, such as current attempts to replace cold war power politics with UN–sponsored collective security efforts, will not produce a new world order, for it will leave intact many systems of power-over among states and peoples and between the sexes that will continue to rely on violence or the threat of violence to maintain the "peace" under conditions of continued hierarchies and gross inequalities.

Perhaps the most interesting contribution that Radical feminism can make is in the debate about a "new world order" in the post–cold war period. Radical feminists have been particularly active in envisioning alternative societies, often in the future, that do not rest upon "power-over" systems. In place of "power-over" systems, some Radical feminists posit "empowerment" or "power-to" systems based on women's nurturing capacities as mothers. These Radical feminists argue that maternal practices give rise to a care ethic that constitutes "power" as a process of sharing and enablement, not some military or economic attribute to be wielded against others.[8]

Alternative futures posited by Radical feminists are often presented in the form of feminist utopian novels written largely by Western (mainly U.S.) feminists during the first wave of feminism in the nineteenth and early twentieth centuries and the second wave of feminism in the 1970s and 1980s. These feminist utopian novels (sometimes referred to as feminist speculative or science fiction) give us images of more equal, just, and peaceful societies that few of us living under systems of domination can imagine. In doing so, they provide an implicit critique of our current world order and the dominant structures and practices that maintain it.

Radical feminist utopias roughly take two forms: integrated feminist futures that envision societies that are genderless and separatist feminist futures in which women create their own societies. Integrated feminist futures rest on the premise that men can learn to be nurturers and share power with women to produce healthier relationships among people, while separatist feminist futures rest upon the notion that men will always be the problem and women will always be the solution. While representing two variants of Radical feminist thought, these two forms of Radical feminist utopias do suggest that when gender roles change, so do the political, economic, and social structures of whole societies and, possibly, whole worlds.

INTEGRATED FEMINIST FUTURES

In contrast to most utopian or science fiction literature written by men—which devotes considerable attention to futuristic reorganizations of the "public" sphere of politics, economics, and technology—Feminist utopian literature is more concerned with possible reorganizations of the "private" sphere of family, kinship, and sexuality. Feminist utopias are less about constructing "top-down" blueprints for some future new world order, and more about positing how human beings and relations might be different (that is, more egalitarian, consensual, democratic, cooperative, and decentralized) in worlds where social stratification and exploitation are eliminated. In doing so, Feminist utopian writers offer us descriptions of different economic, political, and technological structures and practices that arise from changed social arrangements. However, in most cases, the complex restructuring of more egalitarian "private" relations creates less of a need for complex "public" structures, which all too often maintain social hierarchies.

For example, in her brief sketches of five utopian novels which she believed represented the most "desirable" Feminist scenarios, Magrit Eichler identified three that have very simplified, yet highly participatory, governmental and economic structures.[9] In Dorothy Bryant's *The Kin of Ata Are Waiting for You*,[10] the approximately 150 residents of Ata, a small island located in the center of the world and from which all humanity originated, have no need for a governmental structure beyond nightly assemblies in which the residents share their dreams to keep hope alive that those who have left the island and lost their dreams will return to fulfill the collective dreams of Ata. The Atans maintain a subsistence economy, which is neither plentiful nor technologically "advanced" but which, nonetheless, feeds all. People work according to their own rhythms and abilities, and "bad dreaming" is the only consequence for not doing one's share or failing to share with others.

These minimal formal economic and governmental structures are made possible by egalitarian and nonpossessive family and sexual relations. Women and men may have multiple, consensual partners of either sex and can choose to form egalitarian monogamous relations. Women choose if and when to become pregnant, and birthing takes place in the assembly hall with all the "fathers" with whom the woman has shared sexual relations. Children dream their own names and are cared for by the community. These nonpossessive relations are, in turn, made possible by the refusal to gender human beings. The terms "man" and "woman" and "he" and "she" do not exist in the Atan vocabulary. Names have no gender connotations, and all are spoken of and to as "kin."

Ursula Le Guin's *The Dispossessed*[11] begins on a moon (Anarres), which has been settled by anarchists who left their "advanced," but repressive home planet (Urras) to create a more nonhierarchical society. As anarchists, these people resist any kind of overarching governmental structure; however, these anarchists are products of an "advanced" society and, thus, enlist the aid of computers to set up a system of Production and Distribution Coordination (PDC). This system ensures that work assignments are meted out fairly, as consonant with people's interests as possible, in order to produce and distribute sufficient things to meet people's basic needs. There is no exchange of money as people eat communally and pick up what they need for their households from various product centers. While the centralized PDC runs against the grain of the generally decentralized world of Anarres, PDC meetings are open to all members of the society who may debate and vote, and volunteers run the PDC for only four years, after which they are replaced by new volunteers.

Although a more technologically complex and "productive" society than Ata (but more resource poor than Urras), Anarres rests upon similar egalitarian and highly varied familial and sexual relations. Anarres was founded by a woman named Odo, who was both an anarchist and a feminist; thus, a fundamental principle of Anarres is the total equality of women and men. This means that women and men can engage in the same productive work, share equally in the reproductive work of parenting, and have the same sexual rights. There is no formal marriage, although monogamous heterosexual or homosexual partnerships can be formed. Children are named by computer and may sleep in children's houses or with their parents with whom they maintain close emotional ties. However, there are no possessive pronouns in the language of Anarres—no "mine," "ours," "yours," or "theirs." Similarly, there is no concept of status; however, people are respected for the work that they do in their chosen fields, which are quite varied on Anarres, despite its poor resource base, and can be pursued in the context of meeting societal needs.

Mattapoisett is the utopian society that Marge Piercy takes us to in her novel, *Woman on the Edge of Time.*[12] We are never sure if Mattapoisett is the fantasy of Connie Ramos, a Latina welfare mother struggling to survive incarceration and shock therapy in an inner-city mental hospital, or a place in the future of the United States that Connie has access to because of her marginalized status that makes her more receptive to communications from "other-world" inhabitants. Mattapoisett not only has eliminated gender, but also has made biological sex quite ambiguous. All babies are created in test tubes, but each child is parented by three comothers, males as well as females. Aided by hormones, male and female comothers breastfeed. These comothers and others provide "family" for children, who nonetheless live in children's houses. Adults all live alone, but eat together and can enter into a variety of relationships with either sex. "Per" for person is used instead of the gender pronouns "he" and "she."

Like Anarres, Mattapoisett is essentially a decentralized society with limited resources (although it appears to be in a climate more hospitable than a moonscape and is kinder to the environment than Anarres is). Unlike Ata, where there is no concept of the individual, Mattapoisett puts a premium on giving each person the space to live as s/he pleases. However, there are no claims to private property, and there is a strong cooperative ethic to ensure that each village is self-sufficient. Bartering among villages is common, people's basic needs are met, and ecologically sound and shareable luxuries are available.

Mattapoisett's governmental structure is highly representative and very grassroots or "bottom up" in orientation. Both men and women of all ages are chosen by lot to sit on planning councils, which include an "Earth Advocate" and an "Animal Advocate." In both village and regional planning councils (the latter is composed of representatives from village councils), consensual decisions are made in regard to dividing up scarce resources equitably and ecologically.

According to Lucienta, Connie's guide in Mattapoisett, the key to breaking down all social, economic, and political hierarchies was the rearrangement of parenting roles.

It was part of women's long revolution. When we were breaking all the old hierarchies. Finally, there was one thing we had to give up too, the only power we ever had, in return for no more power for anyone. The original production: the power of birth. Cause as long as we were biologically enchained we'd never been equal. And males never would be humanized to be loving and tender. So we all became mothers. Every child has three. To break the nuclear bonding.[13]

This Radical feminist theme—that mothering can be repressive when it is women's sole responsibility but can be liberating when women, men, and the community share it—resonates throughout these three utopias. Although only in Mattapoisett are men and women altered biologically to induce shared "mothering," implicit in all of these stories is the idea that men must learn to adopt a more caring ethic in relation to children and the environment to make more nonhierarchical, peaceful, and just societies possible. Not all Radical feminist utopian writers, however, believe that men can be "reformed"—and, thus, some of these writers envision more separatist societies based on the premise that if there is to be a future that supports life, it must be female.

Before, however, we turn to separatist feminist futures, it is important to ask what integrated feminist futures offer us as far as changing contemporary world politics is concerned. In some ways, we could argue, not a great deal because the societies presented assume that all deep oppositions among people, at least within the utopian society, have disappeared. Thus, politics becomes largely a matter of negotiating differences of opinion among largely homogeneous, similarly endowed, and generally like-thinking individuals in relatively small societies. There are various inferences in these novels about the difficult struggles that generated this outcome, but there are no real details as to how it was accomplished politically. Indeed, in most cases, these societies developed by separating themselves, somehow nonviolently, from larger and far more heterogenous and conflictual worlds. Thus, Feminist utopias of these types tend to render world politics as we know it irrelevant, for they posit that we can and must exit our current conditions to create new ones, rather than attempt to grapple with existing, seemingly no-win conditions.

It is important to note, however, that world politics does occasionally intervene in these stories. Anarres is sometimes surveilled or sabotaged by Urras, and Mattapoisett is ultimately faced with a war on its frontier against beings from a future that is the logical conclusion of hierarchical world politics-as-usual. These experiences do begin to distort the societies—and, thus, they serve as cautionary tales about how we must change our ways in all societies for any to survive.

In this sense, these utopias can be seen as not so much reducing politics as allowing it to flourish. In worlds where there is no war to resolve conflicts and no hierarchies to keep different voices from being heard, *all* people must negotiate their differences of opinion in the spirit of equality and openness. In short, these utopias offer us glimpses of what real democratic world politics might look like, allowing us to question claims about the democratization of world politics as it is currently organized.

SEPARATIST FEMINIST FUTURES

Frances Bartkowski identifies two categories that are most characteristic of separatist feminist futures writing: the "mother-text" and the "amazon-text."[14] "Mother-texts" have their origins in nineteenth-century, first-wave feminism, which was strongly influenced by utopian socialists of the time who criticized the rise of industrial capitalism. The most representative and enduring "mother-text" from this period was Charlotte Perkins Gilman's *Herland,* first published in 1910.[15] "Amazon-texts" were primarily the product of the second wave of feminism and proliferated during the height of Radical feminism in the 1960s and 1970s. Representative examples of "amazon-texts" include Monique Wittig's *Les Guerilleres,*[16] Suzy McKee Charnas' *Motherlines,*[17] and Sally Miller Gearhart's *The Wanderground.*[18]

Herland, a remote women-only society thought to be only legend until a small group of adventurous men stumble upon it, is not a world of armed amazons (as men's legends would have it), but a world of mothers. For 2,000 years, since a devastating war in which men killed each other and women killed off the few remaining male victors, these women have organized their society around the collective birthing, care, and education of children, producing a country (about the size of Holland) without want, ecological destruction, or danger. As one of the male visitors to Herland put it: "As I learned more and more to appreciate what these women had accomplished, the less proud I was of what we, with all our manhood, had done. You see, they had no wars. They had no kings, and no priests, and no aristocracies. They were sisters, and as they grew, they grew together— not by competition, but by united action." [19] The women of Herland also had no sex, since they believed that this gave rise to jealousies and posses- sive feelings. They reproduced (only) female children by "parthenogenesis" or "virgin birth," a capacity that they somewhat miraculously developed after the war. Writing out of a period awash with the Victorian ideals of motherhood and domesticity and before "a period surrounding World War I emphasizing 'sexual liberation' and 'romanticizing the importance of sex- ual pleasure,' " [20] Gilman could see no way to combine sexuality, which she defined as aggressive male sexuality, with the generative qualities of mother love. Indeed, when one of the male visitors attempts a rape, men are again banished from Herland, since they endanger its future.

The theme of men and male sexuality as inherently violent and war producing is continued in contemporary separatist feminist utopias. How- ever, the amazonian heroes of these texts are allowed " 'some' violence— specifically that necessary for self-defense and the expression of anger, both of which are rare luxuries for women today." [21] The need for self-defense is very present in the stories of Wittig, Charnas, and Gearhart. Wittig's women actually wage a "primitive," yet inventive, war against their male oppressors in the pages of *Les Guerilleres,* a war which does not end by the end of the book but results in some nascent new communities where women and a few men are trying to forge nonpatriarchal language, tradi- tions, and practices. According to Bartkowski: "Where Gilman offers a uto- pian image of what she believes to be innately feminine functions and tasks in a world women 'might' create, Wittig represents women performing functions which have not historically been theirs. The guerilleres remake war, language, body, and history in the formations of new collectivities." [22]

In *Motherlines,* too, women are constantly endangered by the existence of the men of Holdfast, a society in which men are bonded through war and the rigors of preparing for it. The virulently patriarchal society of Holdfast arose out of the ruins of the Wasting, an environmental catastrophe. How- ever, there were women who set up a society of their own after the Wast- ing—the Riding Women of the Grasslands. In addition to these "women," there were "free fems" who were the escaped sexual slaves of Holdfast. Initially, the "women" were suspicious of the "free fems" who were tainted by patriarchy, while the "free fems" were wary of these powerful and self- assured "women." Eventually, however, the "free fems" learned the survival skills of the "women." While the "free fems" wanted to go back to Holdfast to fight against the men and reclaim their homes with their new-found warrior skills, the "women" feared that this might lead to the destruction of all women. We do not know what is ultimately chosen by the end of the book, but the "women" and "free fems," once divided, have forged a new, albeit still fragile, alliance with each other.

In *The Wanderground*, Sally Miller Gearhart tells a chilling story of the rise of the New Witch Trials (presumably in contemporary America) designed to repress the growing independence of women. The only escape for women, who are rounded up Nazi-style to serve as sexual and reproductive slaves, is to flee to the Hills, away from the City, where men live.

The women of the Hills, of the Wanderground, find new relationships with each other and the environment, developing the capacity to communicate telepathically with each other and nature. However, they must always be on guard on the perimeter of the Hills since marauding men from the City are always trying to recapture them. Ultimately, they forge some fragile bonds with gay men who have also escaped from the City, in preparation for a possible full-scale attack by the men of the City in the not too distant future.

All of these separatist feminist stories depict women who resist, and even fight against, patriarchal worlds lurking just beyond their communities' borders—worlds from which they have freed themselves by living in isolated, "primitive" gathering (and sometimes hunting) societies. In all the stories, lesbian sexuality is celebrated as nonaggressive and loving, while birthing (of female children) is seen as a sacred and communal act. In this way, contemporary Radical feminist utopian writers, distinct from writers like Gilman with their Victorian sensibilities, were able to reconcile sexuality with mother love, seeing lesbian sexuality as more consonant with birthing and raising (female) children to be full human beings, expressing care and anger without doing violence to the community that cares for them. Thus, although seen primarily as "amazon-texts," these stories do meld women-warrior themes with mothering themes, leaving the women space to act aggressively against patriarchy and, at the same time, to create more caring, peaceful, and just societies.

According to some Radical feminist thought, however, such societies may have to exclude men in order to develop and survive, which is a quite simplistic, problematic, unrealistic, escapist, and, perhaps, ultimately undesirable prescription for social and political change. Moreover, almost all the separatist feminist utopian novels envision women's societies emerging from horrible holocausts of one kind or another. As a result, women can build new communities from scratch without having to deal with old structures. But the prospect that only destruction can bring about change is not a very hopeful one.

Moreover, as with some integrated feminist futures, these stories suggest that while new societies can be built, they are always in danger of being dismantled by power politics wielded by those outside their borders. Because men in separatist stories are deemed to have violent natures, there is, in fact, no escape from world politics as power politics. The threat of warfare with men is constant; as a result, these societies of women are extremely tenuous and, in various ways, increasingly "contaminated" by the need to be militarized to guard against this threat.

In this sense, separatist feminist futures offer us no real alternatives to "world" politics as it is currently practiced, even as they provide us with images of women as the most capable of producing more egalitarian and just societies.

PROBLEMS WITH RADICAL FEMINIST FUTURES AND ANALYSIS

Radical feminist interpretations of contemporary world politics and the futuristic visions offered in Feminist utopias have been criticized by other Feminists who argue that women's oppression, as well as all other systems of domination are far more complicated than Radical feminist analysis would lead us to believe. In particular, Feminist critiques of Radical feminism take issue with Radical feminism's (1) biological determinism, (2) notion that women's experiences of oppression are the same, (3) faith in maternal values, and (4) tendency to reduce the problems of world politics to men's aggressive sexuality.

First, these critics have argued that male supremacy is not the result of male biology or female biology, although rape and forced motherhood are forms of social domination. One's biological sex is not necessarily the determinant of one's gender identity (i.e., masculine or feminine). Instead, gender identity is a social construction that varies over time and across cultures. While the general subordination of women by men appears to be a fairly cross-cultural phenomenon, individual women and men do not necessarily conform to the gender stereotypes of masculine and feminine, which, in their Western forms, translate into aggression and passivity. These patriarchal stereotypes do operate to sustain inequalities between men and women, but there are many other forms of domination, such as classism, racism, imperialism, and militarism that have been linked to women's subordination. Although these systems of domination have also been linked to the maintenance of male supremacy, or patriarchy, they have not necessarily been caused by it.[23]

Second, women are not all oppressed in the same ways. Women have different experiences of oppression depending upon their class, race, nationality, and sexuality. These differences often separate women, pitting them, consciously or unconsciously, against each other, as was the case initially with the "free fems" and "women" in *Motherlines*. Sometimes men are allies in women's struggles against various types of oppression, and sometimes they are not. Moreover, because men are also separated and stratified according to class, race, nationality, and sexuality, only a few men who are on the top of all social hierarchies actually benefit from male supremacy. In addition, while some men within all classes, races, and nationalities have engaged in rape, some Feminists are now arguing that rape is not an expression of "power-over" but is really the result of men's sense of powerlessness to control their lives.[24]

Third, tying caring values to maternal practices is very problematic. It denies men the opportunity to learn caring values through more equal parenting and other forms of stewardship (of, e.g., the environment). It also ties women solely to mothering, which remains a very undervalued practice and oppressive institution for women who continue to be denied reproductive freedom to choose whether, as well as how, to have and raise children. Some of the utopias that we looked at tried to resolve this dilemma by making mothering a community responsibility or by biologically altering males to become mothers. However, mothering, as a socially constructed institution and set of practices that vary across cultures and time, does not always translate into care, since some mothers do abuse their children and have certainly been known to send their children to kill and to be killed in war. It is likely, though, that as long as women's (and men's potential) reproductive work is undervalued, most women will continue to be poorly paid, second-class citizens in the public realm of work and political leadership. As well, those men at the top of public-realm hierarchies, who are the major beneficiaries of women's undervalued reproductive and productive labor, will not be held responsible for caring for others.[25]

Finally, critics of Radical feminism argue that the nature of world politics cannot be reduced solely to women's and men's sexuality. There is growing evidence that world politics, as it is currently practiced and studied, is "gendered." Briefly, this means that the high politics of aggression and violence among unequal states and those men (and a few women) who rule them dominate the agenda of world politics observers and practitioners.[26] However, this does not mean that states are aggressive because men, as a result of their sexual nature, must be aggressive. While there appear to be links between patriarchal thinking and the creation and maintenance of the current international hierarchy, it is just as likely that the structure of this hierarchy produces and sustains sexual aggression and gender inequality. In other words, male aggression may be the *result* of unequal and competitive relations that arise from militarism and capitalism, not necessarily the *cause* of them. Changing sexual and gender relations would significantly affect this hierarchy, but changing these relations, while necessary, would not be sufficient for bringing about an end to related, but also different problems of racism, classism, militarism, and imperialism. Like sexism, these problems have arisen from very complex social, cultural, economic, and political histories, structures, and processes.

In short, other Feminist perspectives argue that while sexist oppression exists and is bound up with other forms of oppression, it is not the result of a simple polarity between men and women. Neither controlling men's purported aggressive sexuality nor encouraging values supposedly arising from maternal care are sufficient for ending sexist oppression and other forms of social domination.

Many of the problems with Radical feminist analyses of world politics are present in feminist utopian novels and the alternative world orders that they offer. The places to which they take us are too often isolated enclaves to which none of us can really escape. Indeed, few of us may want to go to these "no-places" because, too often, they are represented as homogeneous (largely white) communities where there is little diversity among women and among men (where they are present). Such homogeneous communities bear little resemblance to "our" world, a world of differences, created by gender, race, class, and nationality divisions that oppress and separate but that also create solidarities among peoples.

Unfortunately, the solidarities of the women in the separatist feminist utopias grew out of oppression by men; thus, Radical feminist utopias do not really get us out of the modern-day polarities of men versus women and war versus peace. As a result, these stories of wars between women and men reproduce the "us"-and-"them" thinking so prevalent in contemporary world politics. Thus, these stories offer little regarding alternatives to traditional ways of dealing with difference and resolving conflict. Because the women's and men's worlds are viewed as so incommensurable, cooperation lies largely beyond the pale. The only "choices" left are coerced integration back into hierarchical worlds or war to remove the "threats" that the different worlds constitute to each other. There are tentative "rapprochements" at the end of some of these stories, but the profound pessimism of these stories (not surprising in the face of the profound and widespread sexism to which these writers were responding) leaves us little hope for reorganizing intersocietal (and, thus, international) relations.

Moreover, to the degree that these stories continue to associate men with aggressive sexuality and rapacious technology and women with pacifism, primitivism, and nature, there seems to be no way in our own world for men to participate in creating alternative societies or for women to gain the skills and empowerment necessary to struggle for alternative societies as men's equals. Finally, these stories assume too much loving sisterhood among women and too much brutish brotherhood among men. Women are deeply divided by race, class, sexuality, nationality, and ideology—but this means that so, too, are men. All women are not feminists nor do all feminists share the same visions of better worlds. But patriarchy, too, is not monolithic since a variety of men do not necessarily benefit from it. Thus, diverse women and men of conscience, who refuse the dominant and oppressive gender roles of feminine and masculine, can choose to work together for better futures. As Lynne Segal points out:

The dangers are that focusing on sexual differences as "the" project for feminism denies what was most important about the political project of feminism: all the new issues feminism placed on the "political" agenda. This was not just a question of the dependent, relatively impoverished and sometimes brutalised and sexually abused situation of women compared to men. It raised more general questions: the nature of human "needs" and how they are met (how we live, relate to and care for each other); the nature of "work" and how it is recognised and rewarded; and the nature of "politics" and how we organise for change and to what end.[27]

Radical feminist utopias allow us to imagine, however partially and imperfectly, ways in which we might rethink personal, societal, and intersocietal relations. Although flawed regarding their premises and analyses of the myriad of oppressions that are present in and sustained by contemporary world politics, the value of these and other Feminist utopian writings lies in the way in which they "look closely at how those who inhabit the future are made, or how they are reinscribed in culture, however real or imaginary, where social, intellectual, and economic possibilities are not arranged by gender but by capacity."[28] They reveal the socially constructed nature of both the "public" and "private" spheres as well as self-identity. Change in any of these dimensions—which are not separate, but interlocking—can bring about changes in the other dimensions. This suggests that all seemingly fixed boundaries can be crossed and that new connections can be made in place of old divides.

Contrary to much Radical feminist utopian writing, however, the future is not female. Women as well as men are complicit in creating the current world politics-as-usual. None of us are innocent since we all act in ways that sustain unequal relations among people and societies. There is no "pure" place to escape to like an Ata, Anarres, Mattapoisett, Herland, or Wanderground. Even if there were, we know that many of these "no-places" were fragile and susceptible to being overrun by another, more hostile future, offering only temporary escape with few alternatives for cooperative transformation. Thus, rather than defend tenuous borders against "enemies," we would be wise to find connections with "others" of different genders, sexualities, races, classes, and nationalities in order to reshape our personal, societal, and international identities and relations—and, thus, create future "world orders" worth living in.

NOTES

1. See Susan Brownmiller, *Against Our Will: Men, Women, and Rape* (New York: Simon & Schuster, 1975); Susan Griffin, *Pornography and Silence: Culture's Revenge against Nature* (New York: Harper & Row, 1981); Pam McAllister, ed., *Reweaving the Web of Life: Feminism and Non-Violence* (Philadelphia: New Society, 1982); Judith Hicks Stiehm, ed., *Women and Men's Wars* (Oxford: Pergamon, 1983); Betty Reardon, *Sexism and the War System* (New York: Teachers College

Press, 1985); Diana E. H. Russell, ed., *Exposing Nuclear Phallacies* (Oxford: Pergamon, 1989); and Robin Morgan, *The Demon Lover: On the Sexuality of Terrorism* (New York: Norton, 1989).

2. Penny Strange, "It'll Make a Man of You: A Feminist View of the Arms Race," in Diana E. H. Russell, ed., *Exposing Nuclear Phallacies* (Oxford: Pergamon, 1989), 113.

3. Ibid., 118.

4. Ibid., 119.

5. Ibid., 125.

6. Ibid.

7. Ibid.

8. See Sara Ruddick, "Maternal Thinking," in Joyce Trebilcot, ed., *Mothering: Essays in Feminist Theory* (Totowa, NJ: Rowman & Allanheld, 1984), 231–62.

9. See Magrit Eichler, "Science Fiction as Desirable Feminist Scenarios," in Magrit Eichler and Hilda Scott, eds., *Women in Futures Research* (Oxford: Pergamon, 1982), 51–64.

10. Dorothy Bryant, *The Kin of Ata Are Waiting for You* (New York: Random House, 1971).

11. Ursula Le Guin, *The Dispossessed* (New York: Avon, 1974).

12. Marge Piercy, *Woman on the Edge of Time* (New York: Fawcett Crest, 1976).

13. Ibid., 105.

14. Frances Bartkowski, *Feminist Utopias* (Lincoln: University of Nebraska Press, 1989), 23.

15. Charlotte Perkins Gilman, *Herland,* with an Introduction by Ann J. Lane (New York: Pantheon, 1979).

16. Monique Wittig, *Les Guerilleres* (New York: Avon, 1969).

17. Suzy McKee Charnas, *Motherlines* (New York: Berkeley, 1976).

18. Sally Miller Gearhart, *The Wanderground* (Watertown, MA: Persephone Press, 1979).

19. Gilman, *Herland,* 60.

20. Bartkowski, *Feminist Utopias,* 30.

21. Joanna Russ, "Recent Feminist Utopias," in Marlene S. Barr, ed., *Future Females* (Bowling Green, OH: Bowling Green State University Popular Press, 1981), 82.

22. Bartkowski, *Feminist Utopias,* 44.

23. See Maria Mies, *Patriarchy and Accumulation on a World Scale* (London: Zed, 1986); Lynne Segal, *Is the Future Female? Troubled Thoughts on Contemporary Feminism* (London: Virago, 1987); and Chandra Talpade Mohanty, Ann Russo, and Lourdes Torres, *Third World Women and the Politics of Feminism* (Bloomington: Indiana University Press, 1990).

24. See bell hooks, *Feminist Theory: From Margin to Center* (Boston: South End, 1984).

25. See Segal, *Is the Future Female?* See also Jean Bethke Elshtain, *Women and War* (New York: Basic Books, 1987).

26. See Cynthia Enloe, *Bananas, Beaches, & Bases: Making Feminist Sense of International Politics* (Berkeley: University of California Press, 1990).

27. Segal, *Is the Future Female?,* 217–18.

28. Bartkowski, *Feminist Utopias,* 163.

Conclusion

Peter R. Beckman and Francine D'Amico

From what you have read and from your discussions with others, we hope that you are asking, along with us, "What next?" That question is an open invitation to begin your *own* inquiries into the relations between women, gender, and world politics.

Because we are members of an academic community, our instinctive response to the "What next?" question is to pose a fresh set of questions and search for answers. The first step into the future that you might take, therefore, is to explore some of the questions that you have found interesting. Only as we push our thinking outward and encourage others to do the same will we come to a clearer understanding of whether and how gender matters when it comes to world politics.

Our reading of the preceding chapters has suggested a number of questions that we present below. You might see them as projects that you might wish to undertake along with us.

PERSPECTIVES

What might you as a student do regarding theory, those intellectual devices that give us a particular perspective on world politics? Is that not really the province of the trained scholar? Possibly, but this area of study is so new that fresh questions as well as fresh insights are not only possible, but they are also necessary if the perspectives are to continue to evolve in useful ways.

Following the example of all the contributors to this volume, you should feel comfortable asking two central questions of any theory or perspective on world politics: (1) How does it deal with women and gender? (2) If it doesn't deal with women and gender (and most will not explicitly), what happens if we bring a gender consciousness to the theory?

Furthermore, you now have a basic perspective of your own to consider:

gender → world politics → gender

This is but a shorthand way to remember a diverse set of claims and hypotheses. For instance, this word picture hypothesizes that gender helps shape world politics. "Gender" here might refer to gender-as-difference: Either through biology or socialization practices, men and women seem to differ in their attitudes, perceptions, and behaviors, and those differences have meaningful consequences for world politics. Alternatively, "gender" might refer to gender-as-power and the claim that the power hierarchy expressed in gender relations plays itself out in world politics.

Furthermore, the word picture hypothesizes that world politics, in turn, shapes gender. Recall Rebecca Grant's argument that the cold war created particular feminine and masculine stereotypes in the United States and that, in turn, those stereotypes allowed a remilitarization of U.S. foreign policy. The word picture also suggests that events in world politics might affect women in particular ways. Margaret Galey's discussion of specialized UN institutions such as UNIFEM suggests that women in various countries might be mobilized by the international community's putting "women's issues" on the international agenda.

The chapters also suggested that the linkages between gender and world politics can be complex. The Postmodern feminists that Sandra Whitworth and Ralph Pettman have discussed emphasize the distinctness of individuals and their experiences—a point that Hamideh Sedghi has made as well in examining Third World Feminist perspectives. Even if we see more commonality than these perspectives might allow, we can still recognize the complexity. Geeta Chowdhry has illustrated this point when she noted that global corporate investment in the Third World both liberated women and exploited them. Finally, while being alert to the complexity, we can still accept the possibility of meaningful generalizations, such as Nüket Kardam's observation that developmental aid initially had a negative effect on most women in the Third World.

Equipped with our two basic questions and our own general perspective, and alert to complexity, you are prepared to explore the theories or models that others have offered regarding world politics. Where are such theories? One prime location is world politics textbooks. Do the theories or models presented there deal with gender? Marilyn Myerson and Susan Stoudinger Northcutt have examined six commonly used introductory-level international relations textbooks.[1] By looking at the index listings of subjects and names of individuals, they found that the *experiences* of women in world politics were "largely bypassed or ignored" in the texts, since less than 6 percent of the index references were to women. By looking at the bibliographies of the texts, they found that the *scholarship* of women researchers—

who do most gender analysis in the discipline—was underrepresented, since works by women scholars constituted less than 7 percent of the works cited. Women are, it is true, outnumbered by men in the field, but women constitute a growing proportion of researchers in the field: for example, 25 percent of the members of the International Studies Association are women.

Myerson and Stoudinger Northcutt have also examined how each of the texts addressed gender and women's issues—or did not. For example, they looked for gender-neutral language, analysis of contributions of women to the global economy, and frames of reference emphasizing cooperative rather than confrontational approaches to international affairs. They concluded that women are invisible in these texts. "Women's experiences, concerns, and lives are excluded from textbooks, thus omitting a significant slice of humankind and their contributions." Furthermore, while a few of the texts that they examined have attempted to become gender neutral in their use of language, each remained *gender blind.*

That is, gender is not an explicit category of analysis. Gender relations are not discussed; gender-oriented assumptions which underlie such basic concepts as war, the state, development, and power are not examined. Particularly disturbing is the omission of any discussion of women and development . . . and the persistence of the view that violence, including war, is legitimate.[2]

You might follow up on Myerson and Stoudinger Northcutt's study by examining your own textbooks or those in the library or bookstore for their recognition of and response to gender. You might compare new editions with earlier editions of the same work. Recall that all books that claim to speak about *human* behavior may have a very strong but unconscious gender component. It is logically possible for gender and women to be unimportant, of course, but as Karen Feste has suggested, that is a matter for thought and discussion and evidence, rather than unreflective presumption. Certainly texts that refer consistently to "statesmen" or male leaders can reinforce a rigidity in our thinking about who participates in world politics and with what effect.

In addition to textbooks, you might look for gender in the theories that appear in the scholarly literature. This literature consists of the books and articles that academics write principally for themselves, although some may hope to reach a wider audience to have some influence on public policy debates. You might examine copies of the prominent periodicals in the field, such as *International Studies Quarterly, World Politics, Foreign Affairs, Foreign Policy,* and *International Security,* or the more general scholarly publications in political science, such as *American Political Science Review* and *Journal of Politics.* When the authors talk about world politics, do they seem aware of the issues of gender? What might happen to their perspectives on world politics and foreign policy if a gender consciousness is introduced?

There is, as well, a growing body of scholarly literature devoted to the analysis of gender and world politics. Several recent books would make especially good follow-ups to questions raised in this text regarding perspectives. Rebecca Grant and Kathleen Newland's anthology, *Gender and International Relations,* examines gender bias in international relations theory, women's role in the League of Nations and in contemporary international affairs, and gender planning and women in development issues.[3] Another recent anthology, *Gendered States,* edited by V. Spike Peterson, chronicles the work of participants in the "Gender and International Relations" conference held at the Wellesley College Center for Research on Women in October 1990.[4] Conference participants offered Feminist critiques and reformulations of such concepts as "the state," "sovereignty," and "security" in their examination of international relations theories.

In *Global Gender Issues,* V. Spike Peterson and Anne Sisson Runyan have explored "how world politics looks when viewed through a gender-sensitive lens." They have examined global gender inequality "as a central, not peripheral, dimension of world politics."[5] In looking at gendered divisions of power, violence, labor, and resources in the world, they have described the politics of women's resistance to these inequalities and offer strategies for "ungendering" world politics. In *The Morning After,* Cynthia Enloe has examined the gendered politics of national security and identity constructed during the cold war years and has asked how these are being reconstructed during the current era of demobilization and demilitarization.[6] In thinking about "the morning after" the cold war, Enloe has suggested that as we look forward to what the "New World Order" has in store, we remember that what comes next depends to a great extent on what went before.

The women and men whose thinking appears in these books are representative of a trend in the field to make gender one's academic specialty. Christine Sylvester has recently identified three types of research efforts currently underway to make women visible and to take gender seriously.[7] The first effort tries to enlarge the scope of the international relations field beyond the narrow construction of international relations as "what states do" and issues of war and security. Researchers examine what International Relations is as a field, and how people theorize about it—as we have done in the first part of this book and are now encouraging you to consider doing yourself.

The second research area that Sylvester has identified considers "who owns, is constituted by, accepts, challenges, and rejects IR's [international relation's] wars and peaces" by supplying evidence and analysis of women's experiences through the use of narratives and empirical research (something we did in all parts of this book). The third research strand explores the "intersections of gender and development issues"[8] in international relations, which Kardam, Chowdhry, and Birgit Brock-Utne did in their chapters.

Her article, like the anthologies identified above and the endnotes in this text, can point you to additional sources.

Indeed, one of the hallmarks of an emerging area of academic investigation and discussion is the appearance of specialized journals. Gender has long been a subject for psychology and sociology, as reflected in the journal *Sex Roles.* More recent additions include *Gender and Society, Women and Politics, Women's Studies Quarterly, Signs,* and *Feminist Studies.* Browsing an issue of each may suggest a number of questions about women and world politics. For a more systematic approach, you might consult *Women Studies Abstracts,* which provides an indexing of relevant articles from a variety of publications.

There is another general approach to theory that you might consider as well. Instead of beginning with theory, you might begin with events or evidence and try to formulate questions that would lead to theorylike generalizations. One way to do this—and to become acquainted with additional sources of information regarding women—would be to examine various statistical compendiums. These include *Women in the World: An International Atlas,* edited by Michael Kidron; *Women of the World: A Chartbook for Developing Regions,* compiled by Ellen Jamison; and *Women . . . A World Survey,* compiled by Ruth Leger Sivard.[9] The United Nations has also compiled a set of statistics about women—including unwaged labor by women—as a part of its Decade for Women commitment. *The World's Women: Trends and Statistics 1970–1990* includes data on women, families, and households; education and training; health and childbearing; housing, settlements, and environment; women's work and the economy; and public life and leadership.

There are also compendiums of national data that you might examine in order to build theory. For instance, *The Statistical Abstract of the United States* shows that in the 1981–1983 U.S. House of Representatives, nineteen women served; in 1993–1994, forty-seven served. Can we imagine differences that this might make for world politics? Is forty-seven enough "mass" to have a critical voice in shaping U.S. foreign policy? Does the fact that these women are divided into two political parties change our hypotheses? You might try exploring some of these questions by looking at standard textbooks on comparative governments and political systems. Do certain types of political systems (such as parliamentary systems) give women a greater opportunity to occupy leadership positions or to form coalitions across parties to influence governmental policy?

Compilations of statistical data can also help us to identify trends over time and to think about what the trends might mean. For instance, drawing on the annual editions of *The Statistical Abstract of the United States,* we have this picture about women's education in the United States (see p. 222).

What might these changes mean? You might suspect that the number

	Enrolled in Higher Education (millions)			
	1960	1970	1980	1990
Males	2.3	4.4	5.4	6.5
Females	1.2	3.0	6.0	7.5

	Percent of Profession Who Are Women	
	1983	1991
lawyers	15	19
professors	36	41
economists	38	46

of women in policy-making positions is partially a function of the number of women in the pool of individuals from which policy makers and foreign policy bureaucrats are drawn. Higher education and certain professions create that pool. In addition, this is also the recruitment pool for journalists, commentators, academics, and other shapers of public opinion. The change over time suggests that women should now constitute roughly half of all the new entrants into the U.S. foreign policy bureaucracies, and that in twenty-five years' time that proportion will be found across the entire range of U.S. foreign policy–making positions. (Does the evidence support these assertions?) What might be some of the consequences for world politics as women in the United States reach positions of parity within the foreign policy establishment?

QUESTIONS AND HYPOTHESES REGARDING PERSPECTIVES AND POLICIES

Such specific questions regarding the effect of changing numbers of women in the U.S. House of Representatives may be the most interesting route to theory for you. The chapters of this book are an important beginning place for such questions as well. Here are some of the questions that intrigued us. We have categorized them by the type of question that they pose so that if the questions that interested us are not your cup of tea, you still have a general method of formulating your own questions. You'll note that the categories overlap. There is no problem in that; we are looking for different paths to the same goal—namely, to find interesting questions.

We should also point out explicitly something that you may have observed as you read the chapters: In one way or another, each contributor was concerned with perspectives, policies, and prospects. We divided this book into three sections according to the emphasis that the contributors gave to a particular topic, but each contributor dealt with all three. In the following discussion, we will draw freely from the various contributors' observations.

1. The "making-connections" question. This kind of question places two concepts together and asks if they might be connected in an interesting way. Consider Karen Feste's linking together of women leaders and the initiation of war between nations. With that possible connection in mind, we might ask, Why would we expect women leaders to initiate war with greater (or lesser, or similar) frequency compared to men leaders? What theory or perception might provide a rationale for our statement?

Making this hypothesized connection between women leaders and war allows us to think of other "connection" questions as well. For instance, if women leaders opt for war—we can point to Margaret Thatcher and the Falklands and Indira Gandhi and Bangladesh as examples—how did such women overcome the socialization experiences that told them that women should avoid conflict rather than make a calculated use of force? Feste suggests that the position women leaders occupy may override socialization experiences. What kinds of positions can overcome socialization experiences? How might positions also override *men's* socialization experiences?

Attempting to formulate connections between concepts is a part of theory construction and is something you should now feel empowered to do. The general pattern of questioning is to ask if two concepts might be related and why we might expect that to be the case.

2. The "under-what-conditions" questions. Most theories strive for some level of generalization—as Peter Beckman has reported of Realist theory, which claimed that all states generally seek power. J. Ann Tickner, in challenging Realist theory, has argued that "a Feminist perspective on international relations would assume that the potential for international community" existed as well. Most social science generalizations, however, will be incorrect to some degree. We can exploit that complexity by asking, Under what conditions might states (or the men who generally have governed them) *not* seek power? Or to illustrate the point from a Feminist theory perspective, we may ask, Under what conditions might women, even those attempting to uphold Feminist ideals, think of power in world politics more in terms of "power over" (the Realist perspective) rather than "power to"? The general pattern of questioning is to ask, Under what conditions would I expect a particular pattern to hold true or not to hold true?

3. The "change-across-time" question. We can push our theoretical thinking by asking how the passage of time might change things. Consider Hamideh Sedghi's point that women in the Third World have faced a two-edged sword in times of international crisis: Do they subordinate their gender interests to those of male elites when there is a foreign threat, or

do they defend their gender interests and create disunity, thereby weakening the chances for national survival? Either way they decide, they run the risk of losing what they value. This has been a dilemma for women in the Western world as well. What should a militant suffragette in Britain have done when Britain declared war on Germany in August 1914: Drop her demands for the vote until the war was won, or insist that the vote be granted in order to gain her support for the war?

In the past, women have tended to subordinate their gender interests to state or survival interests. *And* they may have subordinated their attitudes about *how* world politics should be conducted, giving up a preference for cooperation and problem solving for a more traditional approach of conflict and power politics. We can now ask, are women in the First or Third Worlds *still* called on to make these debilitating choices? Or has the passage of time meant that women in some countries have become more influential and, thus, more able to avoid sacrificing their gender interests *or* their vision of what world politics should be?

Rebecca Grant's study of the effect of cold war world politics on gender in the United States suggests another type of change-across-time question: With the end of the cold war, is there a new world politics, and if so, what effect might it have on gender? The post-1991 world, after all, is not polarized into great rivalries between very powerful states, a condition generally unknown in the twentieth century. Should not that change affect gender? How? One of the important things about being gender-conscious is that we can begin to look for gender effects as they *take place.* Similarly, we can address the change-across-time question to Jean Bethke Elshtain's point that our understanding of gender depends upon the war stories that we tell. What kind of war stories (or peace stories) will be told in the post–cold war epoch? How might those stories influence gender conceptions? Have we, for the first time, reached the point where there can be an end to the gendered vision of the "just warrior" and "beautiful soul," to be replaced by a genderless "chastened patriot"? Will we have what Tickner called a "citizen defender"?

4. The "unintended consequences" question. Policies and programs have *intended* consequences—the goals that the implementors sought to achieve. It is always useful to ask what *un*intended effects might occur as well, not only in things seemingly unrelated to the policy at hand, but also in consequences that might undermine the program itself. Nüket Kardam's point about the negative effect of development programs on women is illustrative. Policy makers presumably did not intend to sabotage their efforts to promote Third World development; but in not having a gender consciousness, their policies did sabotage their efforts.

What unintended consequences might we hypothesize regarding gender and world politics? Margaret Galey's analysis of how international organizations have taken up and institutionalized "women's issues" has raised the question of whether the consequence of this has been to *decrease* gender as a part of world politics. Creating a separate category implies that world politics itself is not a woman's issue and that world politics is not heavily related to gender. She has also asked if the actions taken by such international organizations had an effect on governments and international diplomacy. Perhaps an unintended consequence is that governments have tucked "women's issues" into parts of their bureaucracies in order to keep such issues under their control. Asking what some of the unintended consequences of this policy might be can lead to fruitful theorizing.

5. The "context" question. J. Ann Tickner and Francine D'Amico have pointed out that the kind of theory that we create may be a response to the conditions in the world that seemed to call forth that theory. Violent times seemed, for instance, to make Realist theory a plausible way to understand how the world operated. You might try to imagine the context in which we are now living. For instance, what kind of theoretical claims might be most natural for a context in which the threat of a large-scale war of catastrophic proportions seems to have receded greatly?

Of course, a sensitivity to context and complexity leads us to ask *whose* context we are considering. If Feminist and Pluralist theorists are correct, there has always existed a cooperative context. Recall that during the height of the cold war, cooperative relations between NATO members were significant features of world politics, including the decision by Britain, France, and Germany, deadly enemies in World Wars I and II, to redefine their fundamental relations. Asking what the world looks like to a number of different actors such as women, Britons, Japanese manufacturers, Third World farmers, or U.S. students can expand the range of our thinking and the insight of perspectives.

Add the contextual fact that women are appearing in more positions of power and participating in formal politics in greater numbers than ever before. And also add—we dare hope—a greater sensitivity to the issue of gender as an important factor in life. Does that context suggest particular arguments that might be made to explain why a potentially new world operates as it does?

6. The "what else" question. If gender influences world politics, might other characteristics of humans have an effect as well? What about race, class, ethnicity, and nationality? How do these factors come into play? How might their *combination* have particularly important consequences? And since we suggested that world politics might have particular gender consequences, our "what else" question encourages us to consider how world politics affects these factors. Hamideh Sedghi's discussion of Saudi women, for instance, has noted the interplay of gender and class.

ANSWERS?

After a while, it becomes tiresome to be confronted with an endless series of questions. What might you do for answers? We can only make some preliminary suggestions—ones that emphasize what you might be able to do almost immediately to begin to respond to the questions or hypotheses that you are interested in. Your instructor will be a very helpful source in this regard as well.

You are looking for information to make women and gender visible in world politics. It might come in a variety of forms. Karen Feste, for instance, has described studies of aggregated data, such as the number of wars that were initiated in a particular year. You might construct such data by examining newspapers or yearly records such as *The World Almanac.* Some compendiums, such as those we mentioned earlier in this chapter, have already collected the data for you. Hamideh Sedghi's chapter, on the other hand, drew on memoirs and accounts of Third World women. Reading biographies and autobiographies of particular women, or reading women's accounts of their political participation in revolutionary movements or in anti–nuclear weapons protests, can be important sources of information.

In general, look for information on the *experiences* of women. Books will provide that, and we would call your attention to the companion volume, *Women in World Politics*, as an excellent place to start. But you should consider three other possibilities. The first is to ask women about their experiences. In a college community, you have a number of groups that you might begin with. You might interview women and men in your classes, or in the faculty and administration. You might be looking to see if there are gender differences. For instance, can you devise a number of questions that would determine if men and women responded differently to questions regarding "power to" as opposed to "power over"? Or, you might try to interview women who are currently in, or have been in, positions in which world politics is part of their lives. Some of these opportunities may come with visiting speakers on your campus.

It would be important to formulate in advance some of the questions that you wish to ask. That gives a focus to your interview and helps ensure that when the conversation ends you can apply the results to the research questions that you are working on.

The second alternative is to observe women who are participating in or responding to world politics. You might attend meetings of women's groups, and of organizations with both men and women that have an interest in world politics. Or you might observe women in world politics. For instance, you might examine the words used by women policy makers who are giving speeches or responding in news conferences to questions regarding world politics.

A third alternative is to create a laboratory-type environment where you can develop information through experimentation. For example, Doreen Kimura has reported that as "men's and women's brains are organized along different lines from very early in life," men and women tend to have different abilities when it comes to certain kinds of perceptual and reasoning tasks.[10] Experimental exercises indicate that men tend to have a greater spatial sense, understanding connections between geographic points, while women tend to be better with recognizing and working with distinct landmarks. That suggests to us that perhaps men "see" maps differently than women do. Men might read maps with political boundaries with an eye to the spatial distribution of power: where power is, who threatens it, and who benefits from it. Women may see political boundaries more as an indication of location: for example, France is west of Germany. We are not claiming that there is such a difference; rather, we are saying that here is a possible connection between gender and world politics that *you* might think of exploring in an experimental setting.

PROSPECTS

Developing information of the kind that we have been talking about would allow us to say something about *existing* conditions. But what about tomorrow and the more distant tomorrows? It is important for you to think about prospects, because you will be the one to experience what the future brings.

As Sandra Whitworth has pointed out in chapter 5, Feminist theory argues that we create our future, be it in the way in which we give genders to our children or in the types of politics that we bequeath them. We would like you to think for a moment in these terms as well: You have an opportunity to shape our collective future. If that is the case, you would want to think about the future that you would like to live and compare it as best you can with other futures—futures that may be in creation at this moment. How would you change what you do not like, or maintain what you do like? What would happen if others adopted your perspective and prescription? How can you persuade others to give serious attention to the future that you see as most attractive?

Birgit Brock-Utne has pointed out that critics of peace proposals have often denigrated such proposals as "naive" or as "appeasement." Visions of the future and pathways to reach those futures might attract such labels as well. She has reminded us that underlying those labels, however, may be powerful gendered images. Women are stereotyped as unrealistic and foolish, especially when it comes to "power," and males who contemplate such proposals are effeminate "Nervous Nellies." Her proposal to educate adults to have a gender consciousness may be exactly what you have to begin doing in order to prevent the glib use of such pejorative labels and to force us all to think more carefully about whether certain actions will indeed help build the kind of future that we want.

Ralph Pettman has invited us to become Feminists, to see what kinds of different futures might be possible from a variety of Feminist perspectives. But no matter the perspective, he believes that in order to create the future, we need to confront a pervasive condition: male dominance. You need to ask if a continuation of this global patriarchy supports, disrupts, or has no effect on the kind of future that you would like to build. As he implies, if some current condition of life makes the desirable future less likely, we are impelled to ask, What should we do to change that condition?

Anne Sisson Runyan's description and critique of alternative societies shows how various novelists have dealt with male dominance in those imagined societies. She has noted that both separatist and integrated visions describe a future that had already arrived. The novelists provide brief explanations for why that future had emerged—for instance, an environmental catastrophe called "the Wasting" in *Motherlines*. But what is often missing in these works is the description and explanation of how today rearranged itself to create tomorrow. There may, in fact, be some cataclysmic event that does bring about change in our coming future, but other paths to the future may be more likely. Indeed, we probably do not want to wait for such an event—let alone desire its occurrence.

Novelists, of course, do not owe their readers complete descriptions or explanations. Their craft is to provide partial images so that we may see and understand ourselves better. Rather, it is up to *us* to fill in the gaps. *How do* we get from today to the desired tomorrow?

You have a part to play here. It comes in framing your own answers to two questions: What future would you recommend to others? How would you recommend that we bring it about? It is a tall order to ask you to come up with such answers. The following are some partial steps in that direction that you might take today.

Examine the futures that other writers have presented. George Orwell's *1984* and H. G. Wells' *The Shape of Things to Come* are two classic examples. What does world politics look like in their vision? What happens if a gender consciousness is introduced? Does a gender consciousness suggest new paths that we might take if we wish to avoid unattractive futures or if we wish to increase the likelihood of securing the attractive ones?

Examine the past and make a speculative statement about what might have been if certain features were different—especially features regarding women and gender. For instance, suppose that in 1914, women in Europe had the vote and had been organized to promote women's issues. Would the history of World War I have been different? Why? Or suppose that there had been a gender consciousness among the delegates negotiating the charter creating the United Nations in 1945. Would that organization be fundamentally different? Why?

Consider how world politics is a part of your everyday life, and how you are a participant in world politics. Sandra Whitworth has concluded her chapter by urging you to take a Feminist perspective in order to make such a consideration. "Rather than the mainstream vision of despair that depicts world politics as both inaccessible and unchangeable, this vision sees international relations as both accessible and subject to change . . . . World politics is both personal and possible." When you think in these terms, you are capable of describing the future of world politics in very personal but very meaningful terms.

THE BEGINNING

We said in our preface that the future began when you opened this book. That wasn't exactly true. Every day, the future begins, no matter what you do. The point of the book is to encourage us all to mold a future in which all humans can have hope and confidence. We suspect that a concern with gender will have to be part of the endeavor. In your look to the future, you might ask what kind of world politics might help foster and support a genderless society, and, conversely, how might the creation of genderless societies transform world politics?

We have spun off reams of questions. That is important. But so too is groping toward conclusions, no matter how tentative they may be. That is where you come in. The future begins today, not only as you ask Why? and Why not? but also as you begin the search for satisfying answers.

NOTES

1. Marilyn Myerson and Susan Stoudinger Northcutt, "The Question of Gender" (Paper presented at the International Studies Association annual conference, Atlanta, Georgia, April 4, 1992). The six texts are: K. J. Holsti, *International Politics,* 5th ed. (Englewood Cliffs, NJ: Prentice-Hall, 1988); Charles Kegley and Eugene Wittkopf, *World Politics,* 3d ed. (New York: St. Martin's, 1989); James Ray, *Global Politics,* 5th ed. (Boston: Houghton Mifflin, 1992); John Rourke, *International Politics on the World Stage,* 3d ed. (Guilford, CT: Dushkin, 1990); Bruce Russett and Harvey Starr, *World Politics,* 3d ed. (San Francisco: Freeman, 1989); and John Spanier, *Games Nations Play,* 7th ed. (Washington, DC: CQ Press, 1990).

2. Myerson and Stoudinger Northcutt, "Question of Gender," 14–15.

3. Rebecca Grant and Kathleen Newland, eds., *Gender and International Relations* (Bloomington: Indiana University Press, 1991).

4. V. Spike Peterson, ed., *Gendered States: Feminist (Re)Visions of International Relations Theory* (Boulder, CO: Lynne Rienner, 1992).

5. V. Spike Peterson and Anne Sisson Runyan, *Global Gender Issues* (Boulder, CO: Westview, 1993), 1, 10.

6. Cynthia Enloe, *The Morning After: Sexual Politics at the End of the Cold War* (Berkeley: University of California Press, 1993).

7. Christine Sylvester, "Feminist Theory and Gender Studies in International Relations," *International Studies Notes* 16:3–17:1 (Fall 1991–Winter 1992): 32–38.

8. Ibid., 34; see also ibid., 32–35.

9. Michael Kidron, ed., *Women in the World* (New York: Simon & Schuster, 1986); Ellen Jamison, *Women of the World* (Washington, DC: U.S. Department of Commerce/USAID, 1985); Ruth Leger Sivard, *Women . . . A World Survey* (Washington, DC: World Priorities, 1985).

10. Doreen Kimura, "Sex-Differences in the Brain," *Scientific American* 267 (September 1992): 118–25.

Selected Bibliography

Adamson, Nancy, Linda Briskin, and Margaret McPhail. *Feminist Organizing for Change: The Contemporary Women's Movement in Canada.* Toronto: Oxford University Press, 1988.

Agarwal, Bina. "Who Sows? Who Reaps? Women and Land Rights in India." *Journal of Peasant Studies* 15:4 (July 1986): 531–81.

————. *Agricultural Modernization and Third World Women.* Geneva: ILO, 1981.

Ahmed, Leila. *Gender in Islam.* New Haven: Yale University Press, 1992.

Alturki, Soraya. *Women in Saudi Arabia: Ideology and Behavior Among the Elite.* New York: Columbia University Press, 1986.

Amnesty International. *Women in the Front Line: Human Rights Violations against Women.* New York: Amnesty International, 1990.

Azari, Farah, ed. *Women of Iran.* London: Ithaca, 1983.

Bandarage, Asoka. "Women in Development: Liberalism, Marxism, and Marxism-Feminism." *Development and Change* 15:4 (1984): 495–515.

Barr, Marlene S., ed. *Future Females: A Critical Anthology.* Bowling Green, OH: Bowling Green State University Popular Press, 1981.

Barrios de Chungara, Domitila. *Let Me Speak!* New York: Monthly Review, 1978.

Barry, Kathleen, Charlotte Bunch, and Shirley Castley, eds. *International Feminism: Networking against Female Sexual Slavery.* New York: International Women's Tribune Centre, 1984.

Bartkowski, Frances. *Feminist Utopias.* Lincoln: University of Nebraska Press, 1989.

Baxter, Sandra, and Marjorie Lansing. *Women and Politics: The Invisible Majority.* Ann Arbor: University of Michigan Press, 1980.

Beck, Lois, and Nikki Keddie, eds. *Women in the Muslim World.* Cambridge: Harvard University Press, 1978.

Beneria, Lourdes, ed. *Women and Development: The Sexual Division of Labor in Rural Economies.* New York: Praeger, 1982.

Beneria, Lourdes, and Gita Sen. "Accumulation, Reproduction, and Women's Role in Economic Development." *Signs* 7:3 (1981): 279–98.

Benhabib, Seyla, and Drucilla Cornell, eds. *Feminism as Critique.* Minneapolis: University of Minnesota Press, 1987.

Bernard, Jessie. *The Female World from a Global Perspective.* Bloomington: Indiana University Press, 1987.

Boserup, Ester. *Women's Role in Economic Development.* New York: St. Martin's, 1970.

Boulding, Elise. *Women: The Fifth World.* New York: Foreign Policy Association, 1980.

Bridenthal, Renate, and Claudia Koontz, eds. *Becoming Visible: Women in European History.* New York: Houghton Mifflin, 1977.

Brock-Utne, Birgit. *Feminist Perspectives on Peace and Peace Education.* New York: Columbia Teachers College, 1989.

———. *Educating for Peace: A Feminist Perspective.* New York: Columbia Teachers College, 1985.

Brown, Wendy. *Manhood and Politics: A Feminist Reading in Political Theory.* Totowa, NJ: Rowman & Littlefield, 1988.

Brownmiller, Susan. *Against Our Will: Men, Women, and Rape.* New York: Simon & Schuster, 1975.

Bulbeck, Chilla. *One World Women's Movement.* London: Pluto, 1988.

Bunch, Charlotte, and Shirley Castley. *Developing Strategies for the Future: Feminist Perspectives.* New York: International Women's Tribune Centre, 1980.

Buvinic, Mayra. "Projects for Women in the Third World: Explaining their Misbehavior." *World Development* 14:5 (1986): 653–64.

Buvinic, Mayra, and Sally Yudelman. *Women, Poverty, and Progress in the Third World.* Washington, DC: Foreign Policy Association, 1989.

Charlton, Sue Ellen. *Women in Third World Development.* Boulder, CO: Westview, 1984.

Charlton, Sue Ellen, Jana Everett, and Kathleen Staudt, eds. *Women, the State, and Development.* Albany: SUNY Press, 1989.

Chowdhry, Geeta. *International Financial Institutions, the State and Women Farmers in the Third World.* London: Macmillan, forthcoming.

Cohn, Carol. "Sex and Death in the Rational World of Defense Intellectuals." *Signs* 12:4 (1987): 687–718.

Confronting the Crisis in Latin America: Women Organizing for Change. Santiago: ISIS International and DAWN, 1988.

Conover, Pamela Johnston. "Feminists and the Gender Gap." *Journal of Politics* 50 (1988): 985–1010.

Cooke, Miriam, and Angela Woollacott, eds. *Gendering War Talk.* Princeton: Princeton University Press, 1993.

Deere, Carmen Diana, and Magdalena Leon, eds. *Rural Women and State Policy in Latin America.* Boulder, CO: Westview, 1987.

De Lauretis, Teresa. *Feminist Studies/Critical Studies.* Bloomington: Indiana University Press, 1986.

Diamond, Irene, and Gloria Feman Orenstein, eds. *Reweaving the World: The Emergence of Ecofeminism.* San Francisco: Sierra Club Books, 1990.

Duberman, Martin, Martha Vicinius, and George Chauncey, Jr., eds. *Hidden from History: Reclaiming the Gay and Lesbian Past.* New York: New American Library, 1989.

Eichler, Magrit, and Hilda Scott, eds. *Women in Futures Research*. Oxford: Pergamon, 1982.

Elshtain, Jean Bethke. *Women and War*. New York: Basic Books, 1987.

Elshtain, Jean Bethke, and Sheila Tobias, eds. *Women, Militarism, and War*. Savage, MD: Rowman & Littlefield, 1990.

Enloe, Cynthia. *The Morning After: Sexual Politics at the End of the Cold War*. Berkeley: University of California Press, 1993.

————. "Tie a Yellow Ribbon 'Round the New World Order." *The Village Voice*, February 19, 1991, 37.

————. *Bananas, Beaches, & Bases: Making Feminist Sense of International Politics*. Berkeley: University of California Press, 1990.

————. *Does Khaki Become You? The Militarization of Women's Lives*. London: Pluto, 1983.

Epstein, Cynthia Fuchs, and Rose Laub Coser, eds. *Access to Power: Cross-National Studies of Women and Elites*. London: George Allen & Unwin, 1981.

Ferguson, Kathy. *The Feminist Case Against Bureaucracy*. Philadelphia: Temple University Press, 1984.

Fernandez-Kelly, Maria P. *For We Are Sold, I and My People: Women and Industry in Mexico's Frontiers*. Albany: SUNY Press, 1983.

Fernea, Elizabeth Warnock, and Basima Qattan Bezirgan, eds. *Middle Eastern Women Speak*. Austin: University of Texas Press, 1977.

Fraser, Arvonne. *The UN Decade for Women: Documents and Dialogue*. Boulder, CO. Westview, 1987.

Friedan, Betty. *The Feminine Mystique*. New York: Norton, 1963.

Fuentes, Annette, and Barbara Ehrenreich. *Women in the Global Factory*. Boston: South End, 1983.

Galey, Margaret E. "Gender Roles and UN Reform." *PS: Politics and Political Science* 22:4 (December 1989): 813–20.

————. "The Nairobi Conference: The Powerless Majority." *PS: Politics and Political Science* 19:2 (June 1986): 255–65.

————. "International Enforcement of Women's Rights." *Human Rights Quarterly* 6 (November 1984): 463–90.

————. "Promoting Non-Discrimination against Women: The UN Commission on the Status of Women." *International Studies Quarterly* 23 (June 1979): 273–302.

Genovese, Michael A., ed. *Women as National Leaders*. Newbury Park, CA: Sage, 1993.

Gilligan, Carol. *In a Different Voice*. Cambridge: Harvard University Press, 1982.

Gladwin, Christina, ed. *Structural Adjustment and African Women Farmers*. Gainesville: Florida University Press, 1991.

Grant, Judith. "I Feel Therefore I Am: A Critique of Female Experience as the Basis for Feminist Epistemology." *Women and Politics* 7:3 (1987): 99–114.

Grant, Rebecca, and Kathleen Newland, eds. *Gender and International Relations*. Bloomington: Indiana University Press, 1991.

Griffin, Susan. *Pornography and Silence: Culture's Revenge against Nature*. New York: Harper & Row, 1981.

Harding, Sandra. *Whose Science? Whose Knowledge?* Ithaca: Cornell University Press, 1991.

Harding, Sandra, ed. *Feminism and Methodology.* Milton Keynes, England: Open University Press, 1987.

Harstock, Nancy C. M. *Money, Sex, and Power: Toward a Feminist Historical Materialism.* New York: Longman, 1983.

Hatem, Mervat. "The Politics of Sexuality and Gender in Segregated Patriarchal Systems: The Case of Eighteenth and Nineteenth Century Egypt." *Feminist Studies* 12 (Summer 1986): 250–74.

Hess, Beth B., and Myra Marx Ferree, eds. *Analyzing Gender: A Handbook of Social Science.* Newbury Park, CA: Sage, 1987.

Higonnet, Margaret Randolph, Jane Jenson, Sonya Michel, and Margaret Collins Weitz, eds. *Behind the Lines: Gender and the Two World Wars.* New Haven: Yale University Press, 1987.

hooks, bell. *Feminist Theory: From Margin to Center.* Boston: South End, 1984.

Hornaday, Ann. "The Worst Places to Work." *Ms. Magazine* 1 (May 1990): 81–82.

Howes, Ruth H., and Michael R. Stevenson, eds. *Women and the Use of Military Force.* Boulder, CO: Lynne Rienner, 1993.

Jaggar, Alison. *Feminist Politics and Human Nature.* Sussex, Eng.: The Harvester, 1983.

Jaquette, Jane, ed. *The Women's Movement in Latin America.* Boulder, CO: Westview, 1991.

Jayawardena, Kumari. *Feminism and Nationalism in the Third World.* London: Zed, 1986.

Jones, Kathleen B., and Anna G. Jonasdottir, eds. *The Political Interests of Gender.* London: Sage, 1988.

Kamel, Rachel. *The Global Factory: Analysis and Action for a New Economic Era.* Philadelphia: American Friends Service Committee, 1990.

Kandiyoti, Deniz, ed. *Women, Islam, and the State.* Philadelphia: Temple University Press, 1991.

Kardam, Nüket. *Bringing Women In: Women's Issues in International Development Programs.* Boulder, CO: Lynne Rienner, 1991.

———. *International Norms, the Turkish State and Women.* Working Paper No. 5. Los Angeles: Center for Near Eastern Studies, UCLA, 1991.

———. "Social Theory and Women in Development Policy." *Women and Politics* 7:4 (Winter 1987): 75–76.

Karl, Marilee, and X. Charnes, eds. *Women, Struggles, and Strategies: Third World Perspectives.* Rome: ISIS International, 1986.

Keiffer, Miriam G., and Dallas M. Cullen. "Women Who Discriminate against Other Women: The Process of Denial." In *Sage Contemporary Social Science Issues,* vol. 15, edited by Florence Denmark. Beverly Hills, CA: Sage, 1974.

Kelly, Rita Mae, and Mary Boutilier. *The Making of Political Women: A Study of Socialization and Role Conflict.* Chicago: Nelson-Hall, 1978.

Keohane, Robert O. "International Relations Theory: Contributions of a Feminist Standpoint." *Millennium: Journal of International Studies* 18:2 (1989): 245–53.

Keohane, Robert, ed. *Neorealism and Its Critics.* New York: Columbia University Press, 1986.

Klein, Ethel. *Gender Politics.* Cambridge: Harvard University Press, 1984.

Lim, Linda Y. C. *Women Workers in Multinational Corporations: The Case of the Elec-*

tronics Industry in Singapore and Malaysia. Michigan Occasional Papers. East Lansing: Michigan State University Press, 1979.

Maguire, Patricia. *Women in Development: An Alternative Analysis.* Amherst: Center for International Education, University of Massachusetts Press, 1984.

Marks, Elaine, and Isabelle de Courtivron, eds. *New French Feminisms.* New York: Schocken, 1981.

McAllister, Pam, ed. *Reweaving the Web of Life: Feminism and Non-Violence.* Philadelphia: New Society Publishers, 1982.

McGlen, Nancy E., and Meredith Reid Sarkees. *Women in Foreign Policy: The Insiders.* New York: Routledge, 1993.

Mies, Maria. *Patriarchy and Accumulation on a World Scale: Women in the International Division of Labor.* London: Zed, 1986.

———. *The Lacemakers of Naraspur: Indian Housewives Produce for the World Market.* London: Zed, 1982.

Mies, Maria, Veronika Bennholdt-Thomsen, and Claudia von Werlhof. *Women: The Last Colony.* London: Zed, 1988.

Mitter, Swasti. *Common Fate, Common Bond: Women in the Global Economy.* London: Pluto, 1989.

Mohanty, Chandra Talpade, Anne Russo, and Lourdes Torres, eds. *Third World Women and the Politics of Feminism.* Bloomington: Indiana University Press, 1991.

Molyneaux, Maxine. "Socialist Societies: Progress toward Women's Emancipation?" *Monthly Review* 34 (July–August 1982): 56–100.

Morgan, Robin. *The Demon Lover: On the Sexuality of Terrorism.* New York: Norton, 1989.

———. *Sisterhood Is Global: The International Women's Movement Anthology.* Garden City, NY: Anchor, 1984.

Morgenthau, Hans. *Politics among Nations.* 3d ed. New York: Knopf, 1964.

Nash, June, and Maria Fernandez-Kelly, eds. *Women, Men, and the International Division of Labor.* Albany: SUNY Press, 1983.

Nicholson, Linda J., ed. *Feminism/Postmodernism.* New York: Chapman & Hall, 1990.

Ong, Aihwa. *Spirits of Resistance and Capitalist Discipline: Factory Women in Malaysia.* Albany: SUNY Press, 1987.

Peteet, Julie M. *Gender in Crisis: Women and the Palestinian Resistance Movement.* New York: Columbia University Press, 1991.

Peterson, V. Spike, ed. *Gendered States: Feminist (Re)Visions of International Relations Theory.* Boulder, CO: Lynne Rienner, 1992.

Peterson, V. Spike, and Anne Sisson Runyan. *Global Gender Issues.* Boulder, CO: Westview, 1993.

Pettman, Ralph. *International Politics: Balance of Power, Balance of Productivity, Balance of Ideologies.* Melbourne: Longman Cheshire, 1991.

Pirages, Dennis C., and Christine Sylvester, eds. *Transformations in the Global Political Economy.* London: Macmillan, 1990.

Randall, Vicky. *Women and Politics: An International Perspective.* 2d ed. Chicago: University of Chicago Press, 1987.

Rathgeber, Eva. "WID, WAD, GAD: Trends in Research and Practice." *Journal of Developing Areas* 24 (July 1990): 489–502.

Reardon, Betty. *Sexism and the War System.* New York: Teachers College Press, 1985.

Riley, Denise. *"Am I That Name?": Feminism and the Category of "Women" in History.* Minneapolis: University of Minnesota Press, 1988.

Robbins, Pauline Frederick. "People in Glass Houses." *Ms. Magazine* 3 (January 1975): 46–49.

Ruddick, Sara. *Maternal Thinking.* Boston: Beacon, 1989.

Runyan, Anne Sisson, and V. Spike Peterson. "The Radical Future of Realism: Feminist Subversions of IR Theory." *Alternatives* 16 (1991): 67–106.

Rush, Ramona, and Donna Allen, eds. *Communications at the Crossroads: The Gender Gap Connection.* Norwood, NJ: Ablex, 1989.

Russell, Diana. *Lives of Courage.* New York: Basic Books, 1989.

Russell, Diana E. H., ed. *Exposing Nuclear Phallacies.* Oxford: Pergamon, 1989.

Sassoon, Anne Showstack, ed. *Women and the State: The Shifting Boundaries of Public and Private.* London: Hutchinson, 1987.

Scott, Joan Wallach. *Gender and the Politics of History.* New York: Columbia University Press, 1988.

Segal, Lynne. *Is the Future Female? Troubled Thoughts on Contemporary Feminism.* London: Virago, 1987.

Sen, Gita, and Caren Grown. *Development, Crises, and Alternative Visions: Third World Women's Perspectives.* New York: Monthly Review, 1987.

Shapiro, Robert Y., and Harpeet Mahajan. "Gender Differences in Policy Preferences." *Public Opinion Quarterly* 50 (1986): 42–61.

Sherrick, Rebecca L. "Toward Universal Sisterhood." *Women's Studies International Forum* 5:6 (1982): 655–61.

Shiva, Vandana. *Staying Alive: Women, Ecology, and Development.* London: Zed, 1989.

Sivard, Ruth Leger. *Women . . . A World Survey.* Washington, DC: World Priorities, 1985.

Spender, Dale, ed. *Men's Studies Modified: The Impact of Feminism on the Academic Disciplines.* Oxford: Pergamon, 1981.

Staudt, Kathleen, ed. *Women, International Development, and Politics.* Philadelphia: Temple University Press, 1990.

———. *Women, Foreign Assistance and Advocacy Administration.* New York: Praeger, 1985.

Stiehm, Judith Hicks, ed. *Women and Men's Wars.* Oxford: Pergamon, 1983.

Stienstra, Deborah. "Gender Relations and International Organizations: The Role of International Women's Movements in the League of Nations and the United Nations System." Ph.D. diss., York University, North York, Ontario, Canada, 1992.

Sylvester, Christine. *Feminist Theory and International Relations in a Postmodern Era.* Cambridge: Cambridge University Press, 1994.

———. "Feminist Theory and Gender Studies in International Relations." *International Studies Notes* 16:3–17:1 (Fall 1991–Winter 1992): 32–38.

———. "Some Dangers in Merging Feminist and Peace Projects." *Alternatives* 12 (October 1987): 493–510.

Tannen, Deborah. *You Just Don't Understand: Men and Women in Conversation.* New York: Ballantine, 1990.

Tavris, Carol, and Carole Wade. *The Longest War: Sex Differences in Perspective*. San Diego: Harcourt Brace Jovanovich, 1984.

Terborg, Rosalyn, Sharon Harley, and Andrea Benton Rushing, eds. *Women in Africa and the African Diaspora*. Washington, DC: Howard, 1987.

Tickner, J. Ann. *Gender in International Relations: Feminist Perspectives on Achieving Global Security*. New York: Columbia University Press, 1992.

————. "Hans Morgenthau's Principles of Political Realism: A Feminist Reformulation." *Millennium: Journal of International Studies* 17:3 (Winter 1988): 429–40.

Tinker, Irene, ed. *Persistent Inequalities: Women and World Development*. New York: Oxford University Press, 1990.

Tinker, Irene, and Michele B. Bramsen, eds. *Women and World Development*. Washington, DC: Overseas Development Council, 1976.

Tong, Rosemarie. *Feminist Thought: A Comprehensive Introduction*. Boulder, CO: Westview, 1989.

United Nations. *The World's Women, 1970–1990: Trends and Statistics*. New York: United Nations, 1991. ST/ESA/STAT/SER.K/8

————. *Nairobi Forward-Looking Strategies for the Advancement of Women*. New York: UN Division for Economic and Social Information, 1986.

Urdang, Stephanie. *Fighting Two Colonialisms: Women in Guinea Bissau*. New York: Monthly Review, 1979.

Waltz, Kenneth. *Theory of International Politics*. New York: Random House, 1979.

Weed, Elizabeth. *Coming to Terms: Feminism, Theory, Politics*. New York: Routledge, 1989.

Whitworth, Sandra. *Feminism and International Relations*. London: Macmillan, forthcoming.

————. "Gender in the Inter-Paradigm Debate." *Millennium: Journal of International Studies* 18:2 (1989): 265–72.

Index

About the Editors and Contributors

PETER R. BECKMAN is Professor of Political Science at Hobart and William Smith Colleges, Geneva, New York.

BIRGIT BROCK-UTNE is Associate Professor at the Institute for Educational Research at the University of Oslo, Norway, and Professor of Education at the University of Dar es Salaam, Tanzania.

GEETA CHOWDHRY is Assistant Professor of Political Science at Northern Arizona University, Flagstaff, Arizona.

FRANCINE D'AMICO is Visiting Research Fellow for the "Women and the Military" project of the Peace Studies Program, Center for International Studies, Cornell University, Ithaca, New York.

JEAN BETHKE ELSHTAIN is Centennial Professor of Political Science and Professor of Philosophy at Vanderbilt University, Nashville, Tennessee.

KAREN A. FESTE is Associate Dean at the Graduate School of International Studies, University of Denver, Colorado.

MARGARET E. GALEY is an independent scholar and has been an educator and a congressional consultant on U.S.–UN relations.

REBECCA GRANT is an analyst with the Department of the Air Force, Chief of Staff Operations Group, Washington, D.C.

NÜKET KARDAM is Assistant Professor of International Policy Studies and Public Administration at the Monterey Institute of International Studies, Monterey, California.

RALPH PETTMAN is Professor of Politics at Victoria University, Wellington, New Zealand.

ANNE SISSON RUNYAN is Associate Professor and Chair of Political Science and Director of Women's Studies at Potsdam College of the State University of New York, Potsdam, New York.

HAMIDEH SEDGHI is Assistant Professor of Political Science at Hobart and William Smith Colleges, Geneva, New York.

J. ANN TICKNER is Associate Professor of Political Science at the College of the Holy Cross, Worcester, Massachusetts.

SANDRA WHITWORTH is Assistant Professor of Political Science and Research Fellow in the Centre for International and Strategic Studies at York University, North York, Ontario, Canada.

ISBN 0-89789-305-0

9 780897 893053

90000>

HARDCOVER BAR CODE